To Sam,
with memories of
Malibu and The SEJ
conference —

[signature]
September '99

WARNING

Restricted Area

It is unlawful to enter this area without permission of the Installation Commander.

Sec. 21, Internal Security Act of 1950; 50 U.S.C.797

While on this Installation all personnel and the property under their control are subject to search.

Use of deadly force authorized.

Also by David Darlington

The Mojave
In Condor Country
Angels' Visits

Area 51

An Owl Book   Henry Holt and Company   New York

David Darlington

Area 51
The Dreamland Chronicles

Henry Holt and Company, Inc.
Publishers since 1866
115 West 18th Street
New York, New York 10011

Henry Holt® is a registered trademark
of Henry Holt and Company, Inc.

Grateful acknowledgment is made to the following for permission to
reprint previously published material: Presidio Press for *Dark Eagles:
A History of Top-Secret U.S. Aircraft Programs* by Curtis Peebles;
Las Vegas Sun for "TV Crew's Guide to Secret Site Is Arrested,"
July 21, 1994; and Associated Press.

Library of Congress Cataloging-in-Publication Data
Darlington, David.
Area 51: the dreamland chronicles / David Darlington.
p.   cm.
Includes index.
ISBN 0-8050-6040-5
1. Unidentified flying objects—Sightings and encounters—Nevada—
Rachel Region. 2. Area 51 Region (Nev.)—Description and travel.
3. Government information—United States. 4. United States Dept.
of Defense—Appropriations and expenditures.   I. Title.
TL789.5.N3D37   1997   97-23507
001.942'09793'14—dc21   CIP

Warning sign photograph courtesy of Mark Farmer

Area 51 map inset material courtesy of Peter Merlin

Henry Holt books are available for special promotions and
premiums. For details contact: Director, Special Markets.

First published in hardcover in 1997 by
Henry Holt and Company, Inc.

First Owl Books Edition 1998

Designed by Kate Nichols

Printed in the United States of America
All first editions are printed on acid-free paper. ∞

3   5   7   9   10   8   6   4

With love and gratitude, this book is dedicated to two people
who lived through and raised me
during the hysterical historical period that it describes:
My parents,
David A. and Patricia Houser Darlington

To the extent that the figures of myth are characteristically depicted as quarreling, cheating, vulnerable, seeking revenge, tearing apart and being torn apart, we find evidence of "mythic patterns" among competing UFO researchers as they contend to fashion for the UFO phenomenon a consistent mythos, or plot. . . . An epic drama of individuals seeking to make meaning of epic events and experiences in which (to borrow an apt phrase from the psychologist James Hillman) "the supposed surety of fact and illusion of fiction exchange their clothes" . . .

"We have here a golden opportunity of seeing how a legend is formed," wrote the great philosopher-psychologist Carl Jung about flying saucers. . . . For over forty years, the curiously compelling acronym "UFO"—*as an idea at work in the world soul*—has shaped human belief and imagination in complicated ways. A robust contemporary prodigy has emerged in our midst, enticing us with the vivid ambivalence of its images, systematically resisting definitive explanation, fostering rancorous debate, comprising a provocative enigma of global proportions.

—Keith Thompson, *Angels and Aliens*

Contents

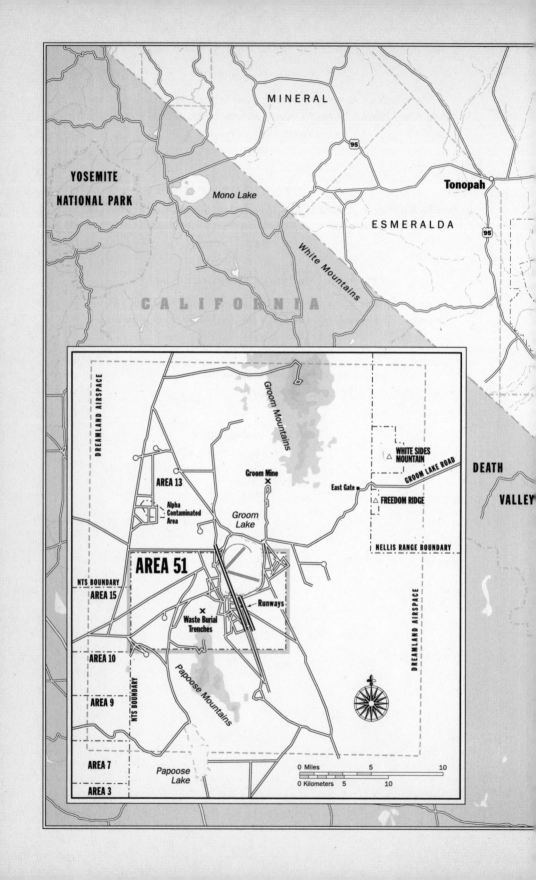

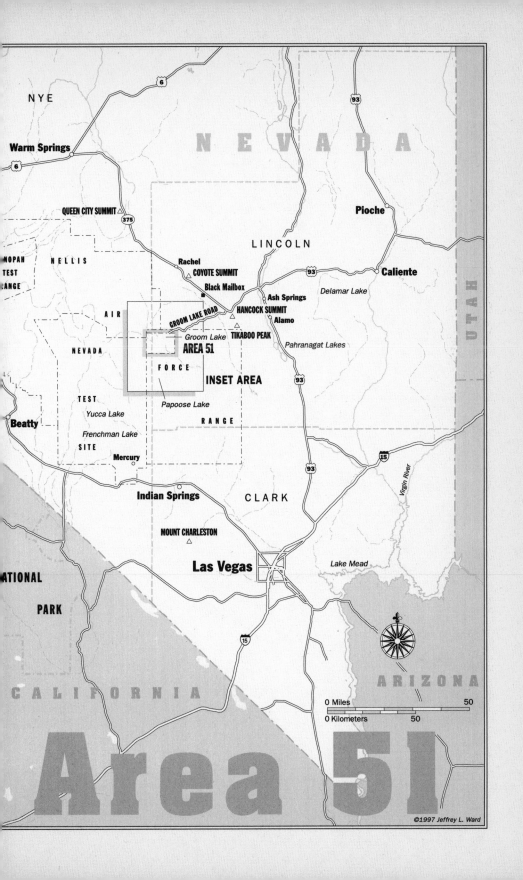

NYE

6

Warm Springs

6

N E V A D A

QUEEN CITY SUMMIT △

375

Pioche

LINCOLN

MOPAH
TEST
RANGE

N E L L I S

Rachel
COYOTE SUMMIT △

Black Mailbox

Ash Springs

93

Caliente

Delamar Lake

A I R

GROOM LAKE ROAD

HANCOCK SUMMIT △

Alamo

N E V A D A

Groom Lake

AREA 51

F O R C E

INSET AREA

TIKABOO PEAK △

Pahranagat Lakes

93

T E S T

Yucca Lake

Papoose Lake

R A N G E

Beatty

Frenchman Lake

S I T E

Mercury

15

Virgin River

Indian Springs

C L A R K

93

MOUNT CHARLESTON
△

Las Vegas

Lake Mead

ATIONAL

PARK

15

C A L I F O R N I A

A R I Z O N A

0 Miles   50
0 Kilometers   50

Area 51

©1997 Jeffrey L. Ward

Area 51

PROLOGUE

Millennial Nightmares

It started with the Cold War. Not only Area 51, the Black Budget, and the CIA, but all the business about flying saucers. When an Idaho pilot named Kenneth Arnold saw nine objects in the sky near Mount Rainier, Washington, on June 24, 1947, and a mysterious craft came down on a ranch near Roswell, New Mexico, one week later, it marked the opening of an era—one ushered in, through channels both scientific and psychological, by the atomic bomb.

I'm not referring to the mere fact of the sightings themselves. As any UFO book will eagerly tell you, records of unexplained airborne objects can be traced back to ancient times, popping up throughout the history of art and religion. Nor do I mean the recent rash of alien-abduction stories, which have plenty of predecessors in folktales about fairies and goblins. I'm talking about the modern relationship between these things and technology—specifically a type of technology that can destroy the world, and the culture of secrecy that it created.

The Cold War justified the dangerous urge of a democratic government to hide its workings from the public. In the process, it convinced American citizens that the government was hiding its workings from them. This destruction of mutual trust was intrinsic to the way in which the flood of UFO sightings that followed World War II was handled, both by the government and by the citizens—though whether the Bomb (and the specter of communism) actually made people see flying saucers is not a question I am prepared to answer. Could the phenomenon itself have been physically triggered by atomic explosions? Was some kind of metaphysical intelligence disturbed by the path that *Homo sapiens* was taking? Might actual extraterrestrial beings have been attracted to Earth by sudden flashes appearing over interstellar distances? Or was the collective *terrestrial* imagination simply so traumatized by the technopolitics of the time that it responded hysterically, conjuring visions of alien intruders?

Much psychological analysis has been applied to the science-fiction films of the 1950s—*Invasion of the Body Snatchers*, *It Came from Outer Space*, et al.—which, we are told, served as a pressure valve for Cold War tensions, portraying an incomprehensible enemy that threatened everything Americans held dear. But what about the parallel fact that the "real-life" human witnesses of the time—George Adamski, Truman Bethurum, Orfeo Angelucci, and George Van Tassel, people who claimed to have had actual contact with extraterrestrials—described the visitors as a kind of cross between Mahatma Gandhi and Marilyn Monroe: kind, wise, beautiful, and blonde? Or the subsequent reversal that, as time went on, the cinematic aliens became friendly (if still ugly—*E.T.* and his ilk) while the real-world tales turned terrifying, with bizarre sexual experiments being conducted in antiseptic laboratories? Or that now, with the likes of Saddam Hussein playing the bogeyman role vacated by the Soviets and a CIA veteran ceding the presidency to a ravenous baby boomer (united across their generations by Yale degrees), our most popular onscreen entertainments are the sinister conspiracies of *The X-Files* and a Fourth of July showdown between all-consuming extraterrestrials and a spineless young chief executive who is nevertheless a veteran combat pilot, calling shots from the most top-secret research site of the Cold War era? With this as our celluloid sublimation, are the real-life stories about to resume an aspect of reassurance?

The answer depends on who you talk to. I am in contact with certain authorities who insist there is no cause for consolation. Some believe that extraterrestrials "on the downside of an evolutionary curve" are here for our DNA. Others deny that the creatures in question come from outer space at all; rather, they are being manufactured in "Frankenstein factories" at Area 51, the secret (though celebrated) government installation at Groom Dry Lake in southern Nevada, as part of an elaborate hoax designed to enslave the world population before a bogus "extraterrestrial" threat. Still others straddle the fence between these anxious positions, combining them with the conviction that mass mental slavery is indeed the aim of an evil "Illuminati."

The validity of these viewpoints is, in my opinion, undercut by the fact that the people who hold them are deeply disturbed. With the help of ostensibly more levelheaded researchers, however, I have assembled a less sensational—if equally incredible—story.

The popular intelligence, as advanced by the movie *Independence Day*, holds that alien corpses and technology from Roswell are being housed at Area 51. According to my sources, this claim is false. The discs came not from Roswell but from a crash near Kingman, Arizona, and they've been housed not at Groom but Papoose Lake, also known as Area "S-4," south of Area 51. (Actually, there is little likelihood that the material is even at S-4 anymore, now that so much attention has been directed to that region.) Since 1953, a satellite government outside the control of Washington, D.C., has pursued this matter in a secret program (which may or may not be descended from the fabled "Majestic 12" committee, allegedly mandated by President Truman) headquartered at Los Alamos, New Mexico, directed in part by Dr. Edward Teller, and created by then–Vice President Richard Nixon. Moreover, this program has been conducted not by our species alone, but with the limited cooperation of extraterrestrial biological entities ("EBEs") from the Zeta Reticuli star system—who, incidentally, are not slimy and reptilian, but answer to the classic description of the "typical" gray alien: hairless and roughly four feet tall, with big, dark, wraparound eyes. For reasons not yet fully explained, these beings have a pressing need for the element boron, which is found throughout the American Southwest; this fact, together with the concentration of top-secret military facilities in that part of the country, partly explains why so much UFO activity has been reported there. There is some speculation that a deal was struck between the visitors and the U.S.

government, allowing the extraction of boron in exchange for advanced technology, but this allegation extends beyond the knowledge of my sources. Neither can they confirm or deny the existence of underground installations linked by an extensive tunnel system, much less stories of subterranean vats containing human body parts—which, in light of the alien-abduction trend, have arisen from the charge (also unconfirmed by my informants) that the bargain involves human research specimens.

This is a basic outline of the scenario that my contacts have been scrutinizing. Some of it is based on the testimony of a disreputable young technician who claims to have been employed in the secret program. More of it comes from a conservative elderly engineer who says he worked for thirty years in the satellite organization and purportedly has the permission of his supervisors to begin discussing details of the experience. This man's background is itself somewhat murky—as might be expected, one must acknowledge, of someone who has spent half his life in such a covert endeavor. His name, however, is not a secret. He is a frequent speaker at UFO conventions and symposia, where he usually ranks as the most down-to-earth participant among a fraternity of fantastic theorists, radical researchers, and out-and-out charlatans. These gatherings, which tend to celebrate the elopement of stridency and gullibility, provide forums for people with big answers to confront people with big questions; invariably, they anticipate that some very big news is going to be revealed in the very near future.

My colleagues are disposed to distance themselves from this sort of thing. They don't consider themselves "ufologists" so much as amateur detectives with eccentric interests. Wary of obsession or conversion, they try not to identify too much with the mystery that they're pursuing, making it a constant exercise, for example, to employ the term "folklore." Like the reality of flying saucers themselves, which despite widespread testimony remains unaccompanied by physical proof, the question of whether this tale is "true" or has been somehow summoned up from a labyrinth of psychosocial forces is not one that my sources are prepared to answer. Everybody seems to agree, however, that it's a heck of a yarn. As the team leader himself has said, "All we're looking for is a good story, which is something so rare in this life that, when one finally comes along, we wouldn't want to mess it up with evidence."

One of the field's less reliable researchers recently announced that the next eighteen months will be pivotal to execution of the hidden agenda.

He predicts a "paradigm shift" for the year 1998, which, when divided by the number of the Trinity, equals the Satanic figure 666. In other words, the cat's about to get out of the bag; it's time to surround ourselves with "gold, guns, groceries, and God." With the approach of the year 2000, we can expect such revelations to rise like a lakeful of hungry trout, rippling the surface of popular consciousness with expanding portents and prophecies. The Cold War might be over, but the millennium is about to arrive. And even if the culture of secrecy is under fire, paranoia is alive and well, holed up in the desert north of Las Vegas under an assumed name: Dreamland.

The Dreamland Chronicles

By a route obscure and lonely,
Haunted by ill angels only,
Where an Eidolon, named NIGHT,
On a black throne reigns upright,
I have reached these lands but newly
From an ultimate dim Thule—
From a weird clime that lieth, sublime,
Out of SPACE—out of TIME. . . .

For the heart whose woes are legion
'T is a peaceful, soothing region—
For the spirit that walks in shadow
'T is—oh 't is an Eldorado!
But the traveller, travelling through it,
May not—dare not openly view it;
Never its mysteries are exposed
To the weak human eye unclosed;
So wills its King, who hath forbid
The uplifting of the fringèd lid;
And thus the sad Soul that here passes
Beholds it but through darkened glasses.

—From "Dreamland"
by Edgar Allan Poe

ONE

Freedom Ridge

One day in October 1993, I left my home in northern California and drove east through the Great Central Valley, through the burnished Gold Rush foothills, past the polished granite of Yosemite, over the vertiginous Sierra Nevada crest, past the blue expanse of Mono Lake and streaked cinder slopes of its adjoining craters, through the forests that give way to sagebrush west of Benton Hot Springs, below cloud-capped Boundary Peak in the bristlecone-dotted White Mountains, and into that vast and vacant territory, that wide-open alternation of elevation and depression, that enormous interior drainage bowl of dry-lake-dotted desert—that congenitally uncontrolled kingdom which despite being composed almost wholly of federal land and a vociferously patriotic American populace hardly seems part of the United States, realm of the piñon pine and juniper, scourge of gamblers and forty-niners, home to untamed mustangs, unreined brothels, and unbridled atomic bombs: the fastest-growing state in the Union, the Silver State, that sovereign state of mind called Nevada.

The welcome sign to Tonopah High School said HOME OF THE MUCKERS. East of town along U.S. Highway 6 was the missile-flanked entrance to the Tonopah Test Range, from which squadrons of stealth fighters embarked for the Persian Gulf in 1990. The most common road sign contained the black silhouette of a prancing bull within the customary yellow diamond, underscored by the words OPEN RANGE. Wild horses gamboled on the plains; fighter jets carved the sky with contrails; mountains sucked streaks out of the clouds to pummel the darkened earth with storms. In places where rain had recently fallen, the surface of the two-lane blacktop steamed in the sun. Rainbows shimmered above shining mesas. The air was redolent of sage.

As I turned south on Nevada 375 at Warm Springs—an unpeopled intersection with a collection of cottonwoods and an abandoned pool of hot water—I entered the fallout zone: the swath of the West that took the brunt of atmospheric testing in the 1950s, when nuclear bombs were detonated only if the wind was blowing this way. As I topped plutonium-tinged Queen City Summit and crossed the line between Nye and Lincoln counties, ahead and below in the gathering dusk, adjacent to an unnamed playa, I could see the scattered trailer homes that comprise the town of Rachel: population 100, elevation 4970 feet, established approximately 1978. Within the enormity of Sand Springs Valley, it looked like some research compound on a distant planet.

Luckily, the red-white-and-blue sign in front of the Little A-Le-Inn said EARTHLINGS WELCOME. I pulled into the parking lot and went inside the building, which was actually a double-wide house trailer. The only people in the room were a stout, pretty, dark-haired barmaid and a guy in a baseball hat who was playing the slot machine. The jukebox had a few recent pop tunes augmenting its staple diet of Hank Williams, Dolly Parton, Merle Haggard, and Randy Travis. The walls were decorated with pictures of fighter planes from nearby Nellis Air Force Range, little gray aliens with big dark eyes, and local terrestrial luminaries: the science buff Bob Lazar, the pilot John Lear, the TV reporter George Knapp, the radio host Anthony Hilder, the funeral director Norio Hayakawa, and the self-proclaimed "world's foremost UFO researcher" Sean David Morton, who was shown meditating beneath a pyramid. T-shirts, bumper stickers, and U.S. Geological Survey maps of the area were for sale. On one wall was a six-foot panoramic photo of the secret base at Area 51, located twenty-five miles to the south. There was also an extensive library containing books and magazines and a stack of binders: UFO Papers and Reports, the International UFO Reporter, Skeptics UFO Newsletter, MUFON Local Chapters, Bob Lazar Paranet Printouts, Black Mailbox Magazine Articles, Newsletters and Press Releases, Roswell and General Reference, Crop Circles, Black Budget Aircraft, UFO Intelligence and International UFO Library. Most of this was the property of one Glenn Campbell (*not* the noted pop-country troubadour, who spells his name with only one N).

I asked the guy in the baseball cap if he'd ever been near the secret base. He said that one night when he was drunk, he'd crossed the boundary and been caught by the guards, but they decided to let him go. He showed me a copy of a form he'd signed admitting that what he'd done was illegal and subject to a five-hundred-dollar fine.

I went back outside and drove half a mile down the road to another trailer whose sign said AREA 51 RESEARCH CENTER. The yard was filled with cacti, cattle skulls, a miniature windmill, a pair of plastic "Smokey Sam" rockets, and a piece of airplane fuselage bearing the letters AF 51. A camper was parked in the driveway, and a bald, mustachioed man in his thirties was out in front. This was Glenn Campbell, whose voice betrayed northeastern roots when he said, "Welcome to Rachel."

I had phoned Campbell ahead of time to tell him I was coming. I had never met him, but knew him as the author of the *Area 51 Viewer's Guide*—a collection of information about the base and region, beginning with "Commonly Asked Questions" ("What is the best time to look for flying saucers?"—"What will happen if I intrude into the restricted zone?") and continuing with advice to visitors, a mile-by-mile guide to points along Highway 375, and meditations on everything from local government to extraterrestrial intelligence.

I had learned about Area 51 at a cocktail party a few months earlier. At the time, I was working on a book about the Mojave Desert; one of its chapters concerned a structure in California called the Integratron, which had served as a focal point for the UFO craze of the 1950s. When I mentioned this at the party, a woman asked if I knew about Rachel and the Little A-Le-Inn. I soon learned that the town, the bar, and the base had been featured on *A Current Affair*, in the *Los Angeles Times*, even in *Business Week* ("Little Gray Men Made My Eyes Turn Red"). Within the next few months, the subject would also find its way into the *New York Times Magazine* and onto the cover of *Popular Science*, and within a couple of years would be investigated on *Sixty Minutes*, portrayed in the movie *Independence Day*, and chosen as the location for a three-hour UFO special on *Larry King Live*. There wasn't much consistency to these dispatches, some of which focused on flying saucers while some didn't mention UFOs at all, choosing instead to dwell on issues involving government secrecy. But there seemed to be something here for everybody, all piqued by the allure (in the words of the *New York Times*) of a "base so secret that it doesn't exist."

As I pieced it together over time, the outline of the overall story went like this: Area 51 was located next door to the Nevada Test Site, where the government had experimented with nuclear bombs since 1951. Although it has never appeared on aviation charts or U.S. Geological Survey maps, a base was built in the mid-fifties alongside Groom Lake, a remote playa ringed by parched mountains, for the U-2 spyplane. After Francis Gary Powers was shot down over the Soviet Union in 1960, the place continued to serve as the test site for Black Budget (secretly funded) intelligence and defense projects, including the A-12 and SR-71 Blackbirds, the F-117 Stealth fighter, and a rumored hypersonic spyplane called the Aurora. For decades it was known to insiders as Watertown Strip or the Ranch, to aircraft buffs and military pilots as Dreamland or the Box—the latter names referring respectively to the call sign of its control tower and its off-limits status on aeronautical maps. Even Nellis fighter pilots taking part in "Red Flag" war games were grounded and interrogated if they overflew the restricted airspace. The base had also reportedly been used for Strategic Defense Initiative (SDI) research and NASA and commando training, which, combined with the Nellis aeronautical activity, sometimes rendered the local night skies a virtual fireworks display of flashing and streaming lights. Unmarked 737 flights from Las Vegas (one hundred miles to the south) and Palmdale, California (location of the "Skunk Works," headquarters for Lockheed Advanced Development Projects), dispensed a daily workforce of between one and two thousand employees, who were required to sign security oaths prohibiting them from even mentioning the place, violation subject to ten years in jail and a fine of ten thousand dollars.

In 1984, without the required approval of Congress, the Air Force seized control of 89,000 acres of public land around the base to prevent people from coming near it. This inspired a series of hearings in Washington, D.C., during which the Air Force representative, John Rittenhouse, told the chairman of the House Subcommittee on Lands and National Parks, Representative John Seiberling of Ohio, that he could explain the reasons for the withdrawal only in a closed briefing. When Rittenhouse said that the decision to take the land had been made at a higher level than his, Seiberling responded that "there is no higher level than the laws of the United States"—signifying, in the minds of some, that Area 51 was outside the control of the U.S. government and, by extension, the American people. The controversy was exacerbated by the Air Force's ongoing refusal to acknowledge the existence of any military facility in the area.

The intrigue escalated to a new and different level in 1989, when an obscure Las Vegas technician named Bob Lazar appeared on a local television news show and claimed that, on the recommendation of Edward Teller, the so-called father of the hydrogen bomb and chief proponent of SDI ("Star Wars") defense technology, he had been hired to work at Area 51. Lazar said that when he reported to the base, he was taken in a bus with blacked-out windows to another, smaller playa called Papoose Lake ("S-4" in alleged classified parlance), where he learned that his task was to research the propulsion systems of recovered alien spacecraft. With disarming lucidity, Lazar delivered a detailed recital of a fantastic story, touching off a frenzy in the UFO subculture. Seekers from around the world soon began making pilgrimages to Rachel, where they gathered at a black mailbox in the desert south of town, near the spot on Highway 375 where Lazar said he'd taken his friends to watch flight tests of the spacecraft on Wednesday nights—a misstep that supposedly led to his severance from the program. Quick on the uptake, the Rachel Bar and Grill expeditiously renamed itself the Little A-Le-Inn, declaring its candidacy as Mecca to UFO believers.

Meanwhile, back in Washington, D.C., a class-action suit was filed alleging that Area 51 employees had sustained long-term health damage from toxic materials illegally burned in open pits at the base. Claiming that any disclosures about classified activities would jeopardize national security, the government declined to address the charges, adding yet more acetylene to the inferno.

Unfortunately for the Air Force, its 1984 land withdrawal had neglected a promontory called White Sides Mountain, an unobstructed viewpoint just outside the border of Area 51. Photos of hangars, runways, and towers at the "nonexistent" base soon began appearing in magazines as curious hikers and correspondents converged on the peak. A private enterprise called Secret Saucer Base Expeditions even offered guided tours, promising disclosure of previously withheld government information on extraterrestrials. Whenever people were at large in the area, operations at the base had to be delayed or canceled, playing havoc with operations. Hence, in 1993, the Air Force filed a new application for four thousand more restricted acres, citing the need "to ensure the public safety and the safe and secure operation of activities in the Nellis Air Force Range Complex."

This time, watchdogs were waiting. Citizen Alert, an antinuclear organization in Reno and Las Vegas that had protested the earlier closure, and an ad-hoc group called the Rural Alliance for Military Accountability lobbied actively against the new withdrawal. Proponents of the neo-Sagebrush Rebellion, which holds that the federal government has no legal claim to Western lands, declared the proposal unconstitutional. Lincoln County—99 percent of which is public property and whose commissioners hadn't initially been notified of the plan—registered a formal protest. And citizen Glenn Campbell, lured by the legends, moved from his home in Boston to Rachel, where, operating from a corner table in the Little A-Le-Inn, he set up the Secrecy Oversight Council and White Sides Defense Committee, both of which consisted entirely of he, himself, and him.

In the forays along the border that culminated in his *Viewer's Guide*, Campbell succeeded in becoming a good-sized thorn in the side of the government. He furnished visitors with directions to the border and counseled them about their rights if they were challenged. He tied ribbons around Joshua trees to mark the route up White Sides Mountain; when those were removed, he spray-painted arrows on the rocks, and when those were eradicated, he replaced them with larger, more numerous ones. He dismantled motion sensors on public land along the Groom Lake access road ("a buffer zone for the buffer zone," he charged) and published the arrival and departure times for the flights that shuttled workers to the base, as well as the radio frequencies used by the Groom Lake air control tower, the security guards, and the Lincoln County sheriff. In short, he pushed the jurisdiction of the government as far as he could within the limits of the law and framework of the Constitution.

Most irksome of all to authorities, Campbell discovered an even better vantage point than White Sides Mountain: a ridgeline only a dozen miles from Groom Lake, with a bleacher-seat view of the base. In October 1993, he announced that he would lead a campout on this legal overlook, which he had christened Freedom Ridge. I had driven to Rachel in order to take part.

Inside the Area 51 Research Center, shelves and cartons overflowed with files: "Freedom of Information Act," "UFO Catalogs," "Las Vegas News-paper Articles," "Nevada Test Site & Nellis AFB." In one corner was a copy machine, in another a computer. A poster display of "Modern War-planes" adorned one wall, while a model army helicopter rested on a table. (At least once, Campbell had been sought out and sandblasted by an un-marked Blackhawk on White Sides Mountain.) Affixed to the refrigerator was the "Rachel phone book": a single sheet of paper containing thirty or forty names and numbers. The place had the atmosphere of a bunker or bivouac. In a back room, Campbell cleared a space for himself to sleep. Perusing the accommodations, I asked what had motivated him to move from Boston to a trailer in Rachel.

"I regard myself as an irritant," he explained. "I'm a lobbyist for open-ness. The military's job is to protect national security, which to them means not to let the enemy in on what you're doing. I agree that you can't let a Saddam Hussein know what you have, but wherever there are secrets, there are going to be abuses. The military is always pushing for more secrecy and more land; they could probably make a case that they need all of Nevada and the rest of the western states if we let them get away with it. But somebody has to push from the other direction. Fate has given me that job."

As we departed the trailer to have dinner, I noticed that Campbell left his door unlocked. We went back up the road to the A-Le-Inn, which in observance of Nevada custom serves a low-priced buffet on weekends. Accordingly, the place was now packed with Rachel residents, many of whom were reputedly employed at the "Test Site," a catch-all term for the conglomerate comprised of Nellis, Area 51, and the A-bomb center itself—a total region as large as Switzerland.

As Campbell and I sat down, an elderly man paused alongside us on his way to the bar. Shielding the contents from the view of others in the room, he opened his wallet to show Glenn an ID card from Wackenhut. This was the high-level CIA-affiliated security firm rumored to supply the guards who patrol the base's border.°

"Where did you get that?" Campbell asked.

The man grinned. "If I told you, I'd have to kill you," he answered.

Campbell merely laughed and nodded. "That's the traditional response to questions about the base," he told me after the man had departed. "People who work there unilaterally won't talk about it. You might catch them in an offhand remark, but if you press them, they clam up and get real nervous."

Campbell himself had a somewhat peculiar way of speaking. In the midst of explaining something, he would occasionally close his eyes, apparently concentrating while continuing to talk. His voice, however, was fluid and articulate, his eyes dark and bright in a full, square face. By contrast, his clothing—jeans, old jogging shoes, and hooded sweatshirt—was no more formal or composed than the inside of his trailer. He didn't seem much concerned with matters that weren't mental.

Campbell told me that he'd grown up near Boston, but had never left New England until he was twenty years old, at which point he "traveled everywhere," transferring from one college to another (Brown University, the University of Alaska, the University of Southern California) as a way of getting funded to explore contrasting environments. In the summers he'd worked for the National Park Service, though his tenure there had been controversial. For one thing, he'd tried to organize an employees' union in Glacier National Park.

"When I was twenty-two, I worked on the north rim of the Grand Canyon. I was hired to be a stock clerk, but they also gave me the job of putting out the employee newsletter, which was called *As the Rim Turns*. I changed it to the *North Rim Guardian* and began agitating in favor of things the employees needed, like toilet paper. The Park Service came down on me for publishing an unauthorized newsletter, and finally fired me for insubordination. Another time, when I was working in an office-supply store, I wrote the manager a note suggesting ways to improve the business and retard shoplifting. He went ballistic, but since I was

---

° Just prior to this, the security contract was reportedly transferred to EG&G—Edgerton, Germeshausen and Grier, a worldwide company that provides technical services to the Nevada Test Site and Nellis Air Force Range.

just a young kid, he let me keep my job. So I started acting according to my knowledge and squirreled away enough office supplies to last several years."

As a boy, Glenn had been interested in computers before he ever touched one. "I was very fond of Hal in *2001*," he said. Later he got a job programming the Apple II, and after that the IBM PC. Eventually he joined a start-up software company, designing a program that enabled bank treasuries to track their commerce efficiently. "At one point we were down to only two people—the boss and me," Campbell said. "I lived at the office and got paid in stock instead of money. Later the company became successful and expanded to about twenty employees. But I'm not a long-term company man, so when it became an organization I phased myself out, collected back salary, and sold all my stock."

Faced with the resulting "excess of funds," Campbell needed a new project. "I'd been interested in UFOs when I was a kid," he said. "I was introverted and unhappy as a teenager, but I was into science fiction and really liked Kurt Vonnegut. I drank up all the popular UFO books, but it was really just escapism—I was hoping the saucers would relieve me of this mortal coil. Eventually I realized that they were irrelevant: even if UFOs *were* orbiting the planet, I still had to live my life here on Earth. But in '91 or '92, I realized that the subject represented an intellectual challenge, a way to explore the nature of truth. The field is full of nuts and ridiculous folklore, but that doesn't mean there isn't some truth hiding behind it. The situation is intriguing precisely because there's no physical evidence. It's so vague and ambiguous, Sherlock Holmes would love it. UFOs are like a Rorschach test: When people look at a light in the sky, what they see indicates something about what's inside them. And Rachel is the place to look at people looking at UFOs."

Campbell said he first visited Rachel because of Richard Boylan, a psychologist who said he'd witnessed unexplainable phenomena there. Glenn had also heard Sean Morton proclaim on a videotape that in Rachel you could see saucers flying on a timetable basis. "I went out to the Black Mailbox and saw some hanging golden orbs," Campbell remembered. "After a couple of nights, though, I realized they were just military flares. The Nellis Range is the nation's premier testing and training area for aviation warfare, so there are all kinds of things in the sky around here. By the time I went home, I could explain every sighting of Boylan's except one: dots that jumped through space a quarter of a mile at a time. I decided I had to come back, and when I did, I met the aviation writer Jim Goodall and John Andrews, the model designer for the Testor Corporation who had come out with the first replica of the Stealth—reputable people who, I was surprised to learn, considered Bob Lazar to be credible."

Though he had no interest in aircraft technology, nor any evidence of extraterrestrial craft, Campbell began to see potential in Area 51. "I don't have any means to investigate what the aliens might be up to," he said. "But what the *government* is up to—the land grab, the cover-up—that's something I can relate to. From the beginning with the Groom Lake base, I said: This is something I can have fun with, something that can drive a creative structure. I'd begun noting mileage markers and collecting data as soon as I got here; after all, if you're looking for UFOs at night, what do you do during the day? So I started compiling the *Viewer's Guide* and cataloguing the culture of the area. The base was the core, the kernel that it was all built around. But even that's really just a sidelight—an excuse to explore these subjects and see how society works."

Between sentences, Campbell cleaned his plate of the A-Le-Inn's steam-table fare: stir-fried vegetables, Salisbury steak, chicken à la king. "If it turned out that UFOs were real," he said, "it would certainly be a turning point for humanity. But my real interest would be in helping people adjust to it. It would be like discovering another culture in Africa—the aliens might know things we don't know, but once we learned them, we'd just say, 'Oh, we should have seen that before.' I'm not into UFOs; I'm into humanity and philosophy. I'm a philosophical warrior. I have the existential view that as soon as you're born you're faced with problems and the purpose of life is simply to solve them as efficiently as possible. In the process, I try to go about shooting down icons as best I can."

Outside, the last light threw the Sand Springs Valley into otherworldly relief, a rosy sunburst shooting up behind the range that concealed the base. As Campbell and I went back toward the Research Center, I asked him how he liked the West.

"This is where I belong," he said. "There's a great deal of optimism here. The cities and towns are all brand-new, so they're very efficient. It clears the mind of extraneous stuff." As he pushed open the door to his trailer, he said, "There's no clutter."

I leafed through the *Viewer's Guide* while Campbell set about binding copies, each one numbered and editioned (the latest computer version being 2.0). It was an entertaining, intelligent work—a bemused but stubborn inquiry into the local mysteries, infused with and informed by common sense. Campbell's attitude toward both the base and the UFO business was skeptical and irreverent, but evenhanded and admirably humanistic. With regard to sheriff's department employees, he wrote: "Standing up for your rights does not mean that you have to be rude or argumentative toward the officer. . . . just because your professional goals conflict with his is no reason you can't find common ground as human beings." He cautioned readers that the "most dangerous hazard on Route 375 is not alien spacecraft or U.S. security forces but terminal encounters of the bovine kind. Since most of the highway is open range, stock wander freely across the road. . . . As one Rachel resident explained to me, 'They got black ones for the night and tan ones for the day.'" In a supplemental visitor's guide to Las Vegas, Campbell revealed: "To me, UFOs and Las Vegas go together naturally, and I now find it hard to do one without the other. Apart from being the logical staging area for expeditions to the Black Mailbox, Las Vegas also offers many sobering lessons concerning the fallibility of human perception." In a list of movies pertinent to Area 51, Campbell included *Monty Python's Life of Brian*, in which "An obscure and unwilling messiah is pursued by fanatical followers who worship him relentlessly and interpret even his shoe as a sacred object. Accurately predicts the role now played by Bob Lazar." With regard to UFOs, he warned visitors not to decide what they will find before they arrive, since "Like Christopher Columbus, who went to his death believing he had sailed to Asia, they often miss a more interesting truth because they have already made up their minds about how the universe ought to be. . . . If you understand how the Groom Lake base can continue to 'not exist' in spite of all the obvious evidence to the contrary and how thousands of workers can be kept from talking about it, then you will see that almost anything could be kept secret here, even craft from other worlds."

The telephone rang. After Campbell answered it, saying, "Hi, this is Glenn," he announced upon hanging up that a ufologist named Erik Beckjord was coming over. "He's been feuding with Gary Schultz," Campbell said. "But they're both paranoid."

Schultz and Beckjord had both been speakers at "The Ultimate UFO Seminar" held in Rachel a few months earlier. Among other things, Schultz was a conspiracy theorist who believed that a network of underground bases was concealing alien secrets from the public. He had also advanced the popular idea that the early-morning 737 employee flights to Area 51 were UFOs.

When Beckjord arrived a few minutes later, he described himself to me as a kind of curator. "I'm collecting stuff for a cryptophenomena museum," he explained. "I take pictures of Bigfoot and the Loch Ness monster and things like that." A big guy with a red face and shaggy blond hair, Beckjord was wearing jeans and a short-sleeved cowboy shirt over a beef-and-whiskey belly. He'd brought along a bottle of Black Velvet, whose contents Campbell declined to share, cleaving instead to a can of Mountain Dew. Beckjord also had a bunch of signs for people to tape to their cars the next day: U.S. TAXPAYER, they said. "Connie at the Little Alien Inn [sic] thinks the cops are uptight," he told Campbell. "They might give us a hard time tomorrow."

"Oh, I don't know," said Glenn without looking up. "I think it's going to be pretty low-key. The cops probably won't even be there."

Beckjord seemed unwilling to accept this. "You should have guides," he insisted. "Keep everyone together in a group. Leave contacts with the media. You really need to get this organized."

Campbell continued binding copies of the Viewer's Guide. "This is pre-organizational," he said, looking up and closing his eyes.

After spending the night under the camper shell of my pickup truck, I learned more about Beckjord's opinions when I gave him a ride to the hike in the morning. As we drove south on 375 across Coyote Summit, gaining a view of the Tikaboo Valley where so many strange things had occurred, Beckjord told me that, one time while visiting the area, he'd seen an orange ball shoot five thousand feet straight up in the air and explode, sending smaller lights in all directions, each one followed by a chase plane.

"I've seen the morning UFO a few times, too," he said. "To the eye it's a shower of sparks, but on film it looks blobby." He also divulged that his girlfriend had been abducted by aliens from the Little A-Le-Inn: "White creatures with four fingers said, 'Come with us.' They took her in a room that went sideways, probably to Groom Lake. She had had a hysterectomy, which disqualified her, but they might have taken some eggs. Afterward she had a red two-by-six inch welt across her buttocks. Later they came to her in L.A. and put something up her nose."

At the risk of seeming insensitive and/or overly intellectual, I mentioned two schools of thought I'd heard about aliens: the so-called "West Coast" view, which made them out to be peaceful and friendly, and the "East Coast" attitude that they were rapacious Reptilians after our DNA.

"There are all different types of aliens from different parallel worlds coming through at different times," Beckjord explained. "There may be fifty different kinds, and they may all be messing with us. My other theory is that human beings create these things out of their own minds, but it does in fact exist—it has hair and blood, but disappears when you wake up." Later I was told that Beckjord also subscribed to the belief that there were faces on Mars—enormous likenesses of Elvis, JFK, and Tammy Faye Bakker, a regular Rushmore for readers of the *Weekly World News*.

Nineteen miles south of Rachel, we passed the famous Black Mailbox. It stood mysteriously in the middle of nowhere, Joshua trees dotting the desert beyond it all the way to the Groom Range, topped by nine-thousand-foot-high Bald Mountain. The box actually belonged to Steve Medlin, a rancher who needed a security clearance just to graze his cattle. Medlin's life had been made even more difficult by Bob Lazar's revelations, what with tour buses disgorging sightseers who went through Medlin's mail. Not far beyond the mailbox on the highway was the turnoff for the Groom Lake road, a dirt strip running a dozen miles straight west to the horizon. At the intersection, Campbell had parked his car: a white Toyota covered with travel stickers from around the world (Ireland, Antarctica, Tijuana, Honolulu), its dashboard decorated with all manner of crucifixes and other religious artifacts. He'd taped a sign to the inside of the window:

SECRET BASE   →

Then, alongside it:

TIP TOP SECRET CAMP-OUT
SATURDAY NOON

And finally:

DON'T MESS WITH THIS CAR!
USE OF DEADLY FORCE AUTHORIZED

"It looks like the cops are stopping people up ahead," Beckjord observed, gazing into the distance up the road, where dust clouds rose from moving vehicles. Nevertheless, we turned off and drove west in the Tikaboo Valley, heading for the forbidden zone.

As it turned out, the cops weren't even around. But after we'd gone about ten miles on the high-speed, well-graded thoroughfare, I did notice a white Jeep Cherokee in my rearview mirror. I suddenly realized with a thrill that I was losing my Area 51 virginity: I was being shadowed by the Cammo Dudes—the anonymous security guards with whom Campbell played cat-and-mouse along the border of the base.

There existed a considerable body of folklore about these well-armed gentlemen, who traveled about in pairs, wearing desert camouflage with no insignia or nametags. It was hinted that they were Navy Seals or Delta Force veterans, and that they sometimes threatened visitors with guns, shot out the tires of passing vehicles, and even gassed unsuspecting campers to render them unconscious while secret tests were performed. Normally they kept a discreet distance, merely alerting the local sheriff if visitors set out on foot along the border, though one night while camping on Freedom Ridge, Campbell was awakened by one who asked permission to go through his pack. (Glenn refused.) Another time, returning from an excursion with a pair of journalists, Campbell had come upon a lone cammo-clad man—"a good-looking guy in his twenties or early thirties," carrying a pair of binoculars but no weapon—sitting on some rocks; when Glenn asked him what he was doing, the man said that he was counting antelope. When Campbell suggested the alternative answer that he might be bird-watching, the man said yeah, that was it, he was bird-watching. Later, Glenn requested identification from another anonymous guard on Freedom Ridge, and the man produced a card that said he worked for the Lincoln County sheriff.

"Like everything else in the Black world, the truth may be convoluted and murky, and even people who think they know where the money and authority [for the guards] comes from may not really know," Campbell had written in the *Viewer's Guide*. "In any case, the sentries themselves admit only that they work for a 'civilian entity,' and it is a safe bet that they are paid by a private company. . . . If there is an unpleasant job that needs to be done, but for some legal or political reason the government itself can't do it, it can simply turn the problem over to the private security firm and ask no further questions."

Eleven miles from the highway, we entered a range of low hills. As the road began to twist and turn, we came to a sign that said:

WARNING

THERE IS A RESTRICTED MILITARY INSTALLATION TO THE WEST

—IT IS UNLAWFUL TO MAKE ANY PHOTOGRAPH, FILM, MAP, SKETCH, PICTURE, DRAWING, GRAPHIC REPRESENTATION OF THIS AREA, OR EQUIPMENT AT OR FLYING OVER THIS INSTALLATION.

—IT IS UNLAWFUL TO REPRODUCE, PUBLISH, SELL, OR GIVE AWAY ANY PHOTOGRAPH, FILM, MAP, SKETCH, PICTURE, DRAWING, GRAPHIC REPRESENTATION OF THIS AREA, OR EQUIPMENT AT OR FLYING OVER THIS INSTALLATION.

—VIOLATION OF EITHER OFFENSE IS PUNISHABLE WITH UP TO A $1000 FINE AND/OR IMPRISONMENT FOR UP TO ONE YEAR. 18 U.S. CODE SEC. 795/797 AND EXECUTIVE ORDER 10104.

FOR INFORMATION CONTACT:

USAF/DOE LIASON (*SIC*) OFFICE

PO BOX 98518

LAS VEGAS, NEVADA 89193–8518

Since one picture of the secret base was already on display in Rachel and others would soon be gracing the pages of national magazines, it was hard to grasp the efficacy of this announcement, though the sign certainly served the purpose of putting one on alert.

A moment later we saw the group that was gathering for the hike. Campbell had parked his camper in a dirt spur off the main road; it was accompanied by an assortment of other vehicles ranging from high-clearance four-wheel-drives to little low-slung sedans. In the background was White Sides Mountain, its identity evident from the pale streaks that ran down its flanks. The surrounding hills were etched by dry water-courses, studded with Joshua trees, composed of khaki-colored gravel and copper-toned rocks decorated with dark desert varnish.

About twenty people had assembled. Some were sitting in lawn chairs; others stood around in down jackets eating Dinty Moore beef stew. Perhaps inspired by their example, Beckjord produced a can of tuna, consuming the contents using his fingers. Though the group contained a couple of women, it consisted mainly of men. Some had come looking for flying saucers; some for feature stories; some for secret airplanes, though this group knew enough not to expect very much. Still, the specter of the alleged Aurora continued to cast a shadow. When I mentioned to one of the hikers that I'd visited the Integratron in Landers, California—epicenter, as it happened, of the 7.6-magnitude southern California earthquake of June 1992—he informed me that the temblor had been touched off by "the Aurora going too fast."

In fact, the U.S. Geological Survey had blamed an unidentified high-altitude plane for a series of "airquakes" that had been shaking southern California since 1991. Rumors of a hypersonic spyplane had been stimulated in 1989 when a British oil engineer (and ex–member of the Royal Observer Corps, a group of expert aircraft spotters), saw a black, wedge-shaped plane refueling over the North Sea. A year later, the U.S. Air Force retired its SR-71 spyplane, saying that it would be replaced by satellites. Two years after that, a photographer took a picture of a strange jet contrail in the sky over Amarillo, Texas; resembling "doughnuts on a rope," it augmented reports of a pulsating roar (comparable to "the sky ripping open") heard in the vicinity of Groom Lake.

In 1985, in an apparent oversight by some censor at the Pentagon, the name "Aurora" had appeared on a budget request along with the SR-71 and (still in use) U-2. The following year, its financial appropriation was eight million dollars; the year after that, it jumped to more than two *billion* before disappearing from sight. While the term was later said to refer to the B-2 bomber, the Federation of American Scientists—a private anti-secrecy organization in Washington, D.C.—concluded that, during the 1980s, the government had spent between ten and fifteen billion dollars on this program (plus two other line-item projects referred to as "special updates"). For that amount, FAS military analyst John Pike believed, only one or two prototypes had been built, though Bill Sweetman, author of a book on the Aurora, guessed at a maximum of ten or twenty. Reportedly powered by liquid methane, the plane was said to weigh 170,000 pounds, two-thirds of which was attributable to fuel.

Aside from flying saucers, at least eight secret projects were thought to be under way at Area 51. In addition to the Aurora, they included a flying wing referred to as the TR-3A or "Black Manta" (a tactical high-altitude reconnaissance platform operating in tandem with the F-117) allegedly manufactured by Northrop-Grumman; the diamond-shaped "Pumpkin Seed" (a quiet, low-observable attack plane able to fly at both high and low, ground-hugging speeds while carrying a scad of miniature warheads); an air-launched, hypersonic, highly maneuverable glide weapon; a double-delta-shaped, vertical-takeoff-and-landing craft for special operations forces; a number of unmanned air vehicles (UAVs), variously outfitted with microwave, electromagnetic pulse, radiation-confusion, and anti–nuclear-proliferation equipment and guided weapons; and a long-rumored stealth technology demonstrator and precursor to the B-2 bomber (reportedly capable of flying along the forward edge of battle without being detected on radar while relaying reconnaissance back to a command center and scrambling incoming electronic signals to confuse the enemy), nicknamed "Shamu" because of its resemblance to a killer whale at Sea World.* The National Security Agency and National Reconnaissance Organization, which (respectively) intercept electronic communications and oversee spy satellites—and whose combined annual budget amounted to $15 billion—were also assumed to have business at the base.

Most if not all of this alleged activity was funded via the notorious Black Budget, the government's (at last count) $30 billion secret fund for military and intelligence spending. This fiscal subterfuge is achieved through thousands of deletions and false line items in the budgets for such activities, identified through acronyms or code names or as "special access programs." The only informed authorities are individual members of House and Senate committees who have a "need to know"; the programs are thus immune from congressional debate or oversight, with not only the projects themselves but even their funding figures kept hidden from tax-payers. The secret sums can be estimated, though, by subtracting the amount of *un*classified funds from the total budget.

This policy, which was born with the CIA Act of 1949, exists in obvious

---

* The Air Force declassified this aircraft in 1996, revealing its former code name to be "Tacit Blue."

violation of the U.S. Constitution (Article I, Section 9, Clause 7), which says that "No money shall be drawn from the Treasury but in consequence of appropriations made by law; and a regular statement and account of the receipts and expenditures of all public money shall be published from time to time." As a result, at intervals over the last twenty years, various over-sight and investigatory commissions have tried to at least bring the finan-cial sleight-of-hand to an end. But the mantra of "national security" has always held sway, and with the inauguration of Ronald Reagan, the urge for reform effectively vanished. In *Blank Check*, his book about the Black Budget, Pulitzer Prize–winning reporter Tim Weiner revealed that, during the 1980s, the Pentagon's classified spending for research and develop-ment increased sixteenfold (from $626 million to $10.27 billion),* with the total clandestine government outlay increasing 800 percent, to $36 bil-lion—"bigger than the federal budget for transportation or agriculture, twice the cost of the Education Department, eight times more expensive than the Environmental Protection Agency. It was bigger than the military budget of any nation in the world, except the Soviet Union." To a large degree, the unaccounted-for money was spent on computerized satellites and other equipment and installations intended to win a nuclear war. But the situation was not much ameliorated by the demise of the Soviet Union nor by the advent of a Democratic presidential administration: The Black Budget for the first year of Bill Clinton's second term was estimated at upwards of $30 billion for both intelligence and defense spending—a barely perceptible decrease in the wake of the Cold War.

We stood around for some time, getting acquainted and awaiting strag-glers. Glenn Campbell was nowhere to be seen—initially because he was inside his camper, but then, upon emerging, because he was dressed in desert camouflage: jacket, cap, and cargo fatigues evoking not only the Cammo Dudes but memories of Operation Desert Storm. After a while, he led us up the road to the border of the base. On a ridgeline to the south, we could see the silhouettes of two sentries observing us through binocu-lars. There were also closed-circuit surveillance cameras mounted on tripods in the scrub.

The road curved downhill to the right. At the bottom of the ravine we came to yet another sign: NO TRESPASSING BEYOND THIS POINT, with—

---

* The Black Budget includes 30 percent of the Navy's $6.1 million and 40 percent of the Army's $3.1 million budget for tactical warfare, and 95 percent of the Air Force's budget for intelligence and communications research.

yes—DEADLY FORCE AUTHORIZED to ensure compliance (not to mention a fine of five thousand dollars, though Glenn said it usually amounted to six hundred). There were no fences or gates in sight—only a succession of orange posts marching away up the hill. These marked the border beyond which, Campbell had written, "there are no rights."

Tales of dire consequences to violators were predictably colorful. One story told of a federal marshal who pursued a fugitive across the line; when intercepted by the guards, the lawman was allowed to remain, but only with an escort and a bag to put over his head if a siren sounded. Should he dare to look up, he was warned, he would be shot. A longtime observer of the base later told me that "ten or fifteen guys on motorcycles" could probably overwhelm the security forces, though he added that "it wouldn't take very long before the cavalry arrived, and then you'd be in deep shit." As for the airspace overhead, it was defended by a fleet of fighters backed up by surface-to-air missiles. Surprisingly, there were no stories of fatal altercations, though there had been some close calls. One civilian Cessna pilot, approaching the restricted zone without responding to radio warnings, was simultaneously over- and underflown by a pair of F-111s, which had permission to shoot the plane down but succeeded in turning it around and escorting it to McCarran Airport in Las Vegas. Another time, a hot-air balloon on a round-the-world trip was being blown toward Area 51, but the wind changed at the last minute, preserving the passengers' lives.

In time, Campbell would fashion a rough road to the top of Freedom Ridge. At this stage in its development, however, the route led straight uphill on foot. Undeterred, we set out.

It was a cool, overcast day. Estimated time to the viewpoint was only three-quarters of an hour, but as I watched the hikers ahead of me, I wondered how many would make it that far. The group seemed unlikely to be featured soon on the cover of *Outside* magazine; it was a decidedly ragtag lot, hauling its lawn chairs, oversized bedrolls, and gallon water jugs by hand. Even Glenn, who gave the impression in the *Viewer's Guide* of having covered every inch of the region, somehow inspired little confidence when it came to the question of desert survival. While he professed to be at home in the West, his interest in Area 51 did not appear to have arisen from a love of the outdoors.

The sun came out and the watchmen went away as we climbed the ridge. The going got easier near the top, from which we could see the guard shack where clueless motorists were commonly arrested on Groom

Lake Road. Campbell had tied ribbons to Joshua trees in order to mark the north-south route; they prescribed a gentler path than the straight line followed by the border, which rose and fell at right angles to east-west gullies and canyons. Here and there, dessicated trunks lay rotting where trees had been uprooted. As we continued to climb, the wind that had blown them down began buffeting us—we'd crossed to the west side of the ridge and were thus exposed to the prevailing gale from the direction of the Test Site. I wondered how much plutonium was present in the suspended dust.

Chrome-colored globes now began to appear, suspended atop twelve-foot-tall posts. Though they bore the ominous aluminoid aspect of fifties science-fiction films, they looked too tall to be the fabled "ammonia detectors"—most fanciful of the rumored array of bugs and sensors hereabouts, alleged to be able to discern the difference between human and nonhuman perspiration. One aspiring infiltrator had reportedly planned to beat this system by crossing the border in a rubber wetsuit; if apprehended, his plan was to say that he'd heard there was "a lake out there" and wanted to go scuba diving. Other rumored devices included concealed microphones, vibration sensors, and the big white radar dome on top of Bald Mountain, which may have been reading my mind at that very moment.

As the group strung out across the plateau, I noted that Glenn, our guide and leader, hiked by himself. The others struggled gamely on, despite their accoutrements. After crossing a rocky divide, we made the final open ascent to the top of Freedom Ridge, comprised of stony outcroppings above the sandy slopes. East of the crest was an expansive view of Tikaboo Valley, culminating in the Timpahute Mountains. To the west was Area 51.

Despite having gone behind a cloud, the sun was sending a beam of rays directly onto Groom Lake, causing its surface to gleam like a plate beneath a spotlight. The distinctness of the base itself was obscured by the lowering angle of the sun, which backlit the entire scene. We would have to wait until the next morning for this arrangement to be reversed, floodlighting the place from the foreground to illuminate every nook and cranny. For the moment, though, one fact was obvious: For a nonexistent base, this was a very extensive installation, with scores of structures littering an area of more than fifty square miles.

The rest of the afternoon was occupied with setting up camp: sleeping sites, telescopes, a fire pit, a latrine. Campbell designated one rock as the official register, where attendees were invited to sign their names (in code or otherwise) with black Magic Marker. The desirability of lawn chairs soon became evident, as did the utility of a good sleeping pad in the rough and steep conditions. I found a reasonably level spot on the east side of the ridge, where I couldn't see the base but neither would I be blasted by the wind. As I lay there on my back, looking up at the sky, I noticed numerous UFOs. Similar in appearance to bacteria or bicycle chains, they were described in the *Viewer's Guide* as "floaters": white-blood and dead receptor cells in the vitreous humor of my own eyes. I amused myself with them for some time, manipulating their progress across my field of vision by moving my eyeballs—looking up, down, left, or right to keep them from drifting out of sight.

Many other such phenomena had confused people in these parts. Some, like the floaters, originated in the eye itself—for example, the so-called bumblebee and strobe effects, which made lighted objects jump about in the dark. The desert night sky, free as it is of clouds and street-lamps, can seem a cornucopia of flashing and/or shining lights, with planets, galaxies, meteors, and satellites all on constant display. Moreover, as previously noted, there was the plethora of airborne flotsam associated with the Nellis Range—golden orbs (magnesium flares), blue streaks (engine exhaust), red dots (aircraft lights), and twitching specks (lightweight exo-atmospheric particles), to name only a few.

At sunset I noticed some others, including a hot-pink cloud above the Timpahutes that appeared altogether inflamed if not necessarily radioactive. As night descended, the glow of Las Vegas appeared on the southern horizon. I was startled to see bright lights bobbing in the sky above Papoose Mountain until I realized that they were flashlights held by my fellow campers, making their way along a near ridgeline. Some were just settling down to dinner, which for Campbell meant hot dogs and an MRE (a "meal-ready-to-eat") obtained from a surplus store in Las Vegas—a staple of the reconnaissance regimen. "Like candlelight and a fine French wine, they lend the appropriate romance to any camping experience," Glenn had written in the *Viewer's Guide*. In addition to the entrée, this precooked repast in a plastic pouch came with a tiny bottle of Tabasco. "That looks like a Barbie bottle," one female camper observed.

She was one of several, I learned as the evening unfolded, who were here because they'd seen UFOs elsewhere. One—a fellow missing several teeth, who had wrapped himself in his sleeping bag and gone to bed before dark while playing an audiotape of Bob Lazar—claimed that he (not his girlfriend) had been abducted by aliens. Others, such as Matt Coolidge, a young guy wearing a cowboy hat and leather jacket, had been drawn by the magnet of a no-man's-land where "people can project their imaginations and fantasies." In this regard, one astute commentator labeled Area 51 a "big laundry hamper" for every imagined modern conspiracy from the invention of AIDS to the destination of kidnapped children, who were supposedly subjects of medical experiments in an underground lab. According to some sources, the base had twenty-two subterranean levels and was connected by underground tunnels to other facilities through-out the Southwest. Mind-control beam weapons were being developed within our line of sight (though not right now; it was Saturday). The base was overseen not by such earthbound lackeys as Congress or the Presi-dent or even the Air Force, but by the Bilderbergs/Council on For-eign Relations/Trilateral Commission/One World Government/New World Order—different names for the clandestine cabal operating within/outside the military-industrial complex. These renegade powermongers would stop at nothing to achieve their aim, which was no less sinister or ambitious a goal than worldwide domination. All excellent and appropriate ideas to take to bed beside the base.

It sprinkled a bit during the night; perhaps this was the threatened gas. In any case, when we arose in the morning, Area 51 looked like a telephoto picture on fine-grain, large-format film. In other words, details were clearly on display: clusters of hangars, radar facilities, satellite dishes, a control tower, four water tanks on an east-facing hillside, a fuel-tank farm at the southern end. There were lots of other, less imposing buildings, but towering over everything was an enormous yellow hangar. Likened to "an auto assembly plant or a really huge Kmart" by one observer, it was rumored to house a "transatmospheric" aero-spacecraft with an orbital speed and global range. The lakebed supported two major runways, each one long enough to accommodate the space shuttle.

The documented background to this scene was less exciting than the previous night's scenario, but fairly provocative in itself. Since the late 1970s, throughout the Reagan-Bush years but continuing into the post–Cold War era, the size of the base had doubled. To enliven the exis-tence of isolated workers, there was a commissary, a theater, a swimming pool, a baseball diamond, a gymnasium, and some tennis and racquetball courts, the latter located alongside a saloon. The buildings at the north end of the base were foreign-technology hangars, housing MiGs and other air-craft used to teach pilots about enemy capabilities. The quartet of water tanks was relatively recent, as were the tank farm and the big yellow hangar, which was as long as a football field and five stories tall. The second runway had been built while the main one was being extended from fifteen thousand to twenty-seven thousand feet, making it one of the longest airstrips in the world.

Much of this was open to inspection on a Russian satellite picture taken in 1988, available from select domestic photo agencies and included with the Testor model kit of the Aurora. Moreover, within a few months, twenty-three other countries—Belarus, Belgium, Bulgaria, Canada, the Czech Republic, Denmark, France, Georgia, Germany, Greece, Hungary, Iceland, Italy, Kyrgyzstan, Luxembourg, the Netherlands, Norway, Poland, Portugal, Romania, Russia, the Slovak Republic, Spain, Turkey, the United Kingdom, and Ukraine—would gain the privilege of overflying and photographing the base, courtesy of the Open Skies Treaty, negotiated in 1992 between members of NATO and the former Warsaw Pact. Since the flights would be rigorously scheduled and controlled, they'd present little problem to classified operations, as secret stuff could still be concealed in the customary "scoot'n'hide" sheds designed to frustrate passing satellites. What it meant in light of the land withdrawal, however, was that, in the words of one camper, "everybody except American taxpayers can look at the base."

"And that I can't dump motor oil on my own property, but the Air Force can burn toxic waste on government land," someone else observed.

This was a reference to a lawsuit recently filed against the Lockheed corporation by one Helen Frost, the widow of a former Area 51 employee. Mrs. Frost claimed that her husband had been exposed to poisonous chemicals in smoke emitted from toxic waste burned in open pits at Groom Lake; she had a list of fifty-five witnesses who claimed to have either seen the pits or suffered such problems as peeling skin or cirrhosis of the liver, both of which had plagued her late spouse. Though Mr. Frost's tissue was found to contain unusually high levels of dioxins and dibenzofurans, a federal judge dismissed the suit, ruling that Mrs. Frost failed to prove that the fumes were responsible for her husband's death. The case had since been taken up by Jonathan Turley, head of the Environmental Crimes Project at George Washington University, who was preparing a citizen-action lawsuit against the Air Force.

Any environmental reports of tests performed at Area 51 were, of course, classified—as was the name of every person, item, or substance that had ever been employed there. When no longer needed, anything used at the base (except for the people, presumably) was either burned or buried on the premises. According to one ex-worker, during development of the Stealth fighter, Kenworthy trucks arrived from California every Monday and Wednesday, unloading fifty-five-gallon drums into pits fifteen feet deep and three hundred feet long, drenching them with solvents or jet fuel, and setting them on fire. The burning allegedly continued for hours, filling the base with acrid smoke. Workers were required to stand close to the burning waste, sometimes even to enter the trenches and sift through the smoldering remains to make sure that all classified material had been destroyed. Requests for protective clothing were reportedly met with derision by guards; the workers were allowed to wear masks or gloves that they bought themselves, but more elaborate equipment was prohibited by security regulations. The people were later tormented by headaches, blackouts, skin rashes, eye irritations, breathing problems, and chest pains. Purportedly, three thousand such barrels had been incinerated during the 1980s.

When these stories were made public, Lockheed issued a statement from its headquarters in Palmdale, California, explaining that the company "on occasions in the past has had requirements for removal of materials from our factory that our customer, the U.S. Air Force, deemed to be classified materials. In those instances, Lockheed followed instructions from its customer as to how the materials were to be transported away from the factory location. When the materials were trucked away, the destination of the trucks and the eventual disposition of the classified materials were determined by the Air Force."

The same ex-worker who described the burning told the *Las Vegas Review-Journal* that he'd seen charts in the base comptroller's office that showed the Area 51 budget to fall between $93 million and $115 million per month. On top of the secret experimental technology and employee shuttle flights, he said that the money went toward such supplies as prime rib, king crab, frog legs, and filet mignon. Flights would occasionally land on the runway to deliver shrimp from Florida, while one especially discriminating colonel requested twenty-five-dollar grapefruits from Israel and twenty-six-dollar cans of tuna from South America. The base's bottled-water bill was fifty thousand dollars per month (after all, this was the desert). The saloon, supposedly called Sam's Place after the last CIA commander of the base, was a carpeted nightclub with a bar as big as those in the Las Vegas casinos.

"The stories I hear from inside the test site aren't about the Aurora or Stealth," said Campbell. "They're about waste and mismanagement, people spending years on programs that never work or get used. Most companies don't enjoy the privilege of keeping their operations secret, but it turns out that the military does—so there's no way to find out if our tax dollars are being spent wisely." This problem has of course been illustrated again and again, from toilet seats in the Pentagon to the two-billion-dollar B-2 stealth bomber (which skyrocketed from $400 million as its cost was concealed from Congress) to the National Reconnaissance Organization, which in 1996 was revealed to have amassed some four billion unsupervised dollars through "excessive secrecy, financial incompetence, and a lack of accountability," according to senior intelligence officials. By most estimates, secrecy adds between 15 and 25 percent to the price of a classified program; as *New York Times* reporter Weiner pointed out, the cost of classifying government information ($2.2 billion) was higher than the budget for the entire State Department, while the expense of reimbursing contractors for complying with secrecy regulations came to a cool $13.8 billion a year. At the same time, the contractors themselves— seduced by the temptation to do business any way they liked—had been fined millions of dollars for bribing clients and lying to the government.

As all of this was going on, poor Lincoln County received hardly any revenue from the billion-dollar base within its borders. The federal government can't be taxed, but if a company uses a government building for profit, the building can be assessed as if it were private property—and "Groom Lake is an entire city full of facilities like that," said Campbell. "A single hangar or assembly building used by Lockheed or Northrop might be worth millions, but the local tax assessor isn't allowed to enter the base, so the Air Force has the luxury of deciding what its own facilities are worth." In the coming year, Campbell would find that the Air Force paid the county $65,000 in taxes, based on a total property assessment of $2.5 million.

As the sun got higher, the light grew flatter. Singly and in groups, the campers began to wander away, packing up their paraphernalia and trickling back downhill. No security guards were encountered on the return; no deputies awaited us by the cars. A few months later, however, camera film would be confiscated from a *New York Times Magazine* photographer and reporter who cornered a Cammo Dude on Groom Lake Road, and in April 1994, an ABC-TV news crew would have $65,000 *(coincidence?)* worth of video and sound equipment seized on a search warrant.

The following summer, Glenn Campbell himself would be arrested for locking the doors of a TV news vehicle to prevent a sheriff's deputy from entering it. At that point, his humanistic relationship with local law enforcement would appear to have worn thin, as would his welcome at the Little A-Le-Inn. That was still far in the future, however. By then, many other odd things would have occurred along the border of the base that didn't exist, the place whose name was never spoken, the "remote operating location in the Nevada desert" where the world's most advanced aircraft were developed and a secret satellite government was said to be tinkering with technology that was, in the words of one observer, "literally out of this world."

TWO

Paradise Ranch

Nineteen fifty-three was a hot year in the Cold War. Joseph Stalin died of a bleeding brain brought on by hypertension and was replaced by Nikita Khrushchev as first secretary of the Soviet Communist Party. General Dwight D. Eisenhower succeeded Harry S. Truman as President of the United States; the Korean War came to a close, but the Russians detonated their first hydrogen bomb, dwarfing the atomic version they'd exploded four years earlier. Ethel and Julius Rosenberg were executed for passing atomic secrets to the Soviets, and Senator Joseph McCarthy prepared to convene a series of hearings accusing the U.S. military of susceptibility to Communist subversion. Defense spending reached a record peacetime level of $52.8 billion, up from $13.7 billion in 1950. Since Russia had obtained the Bomb, the official policy of the United States government—articulated in a classified 25,000-word document called

"NSC-68"—was that massive rearmament was the only way to withstand a voracious Soviet threat.

A chief beneficiary of this bloat was the Strategic Air Command (SAC), which amassed a thousand atomic bombers where three years earlier there had been only thirty. Nevertheless, Washington was petrified that America might be falling behind the Russians in nuclear air power. Implementing a curious strategy, it directed bombers over the USSR to photograph secret military installations, trying to assess the strength of the Soviet force. In a secret war that escaped notice by the press of either country, a hundred American servicemen disappeared as these menacing planes were shot down, threatening to start a war on appearances alone.

At Wright-Patterson Air Force Base in Ohio (the place where alien bodies and hardware were allegedly transferred from the UFO crash at Roswell, New Mexico), a development officer and aerospace engineer named Major John Seaberg envisioned a way to spy on the Soviets without endangering Americans. He recommended the pairing of a new generation of high-speed jet engine (specifically the Pratt and Whitney J57) with a wing design capable of taking an aircraft to higher altitudes than ever before. If a plane could soar to seventy thousand feet, it could exceed the range of existing air defenses and overfly Russia with impunity. To encourage efficiency, Seaberg bypassed big contractors when he issued a call for designs; ignoring the likes of Lockheed and Boeing, he offered the job to three smaller companies: Bell, Fairchild, and Martin. He hadn't counted, however, on the stubbornness of Lockheed's chief designer, the legendary Clarence L. "Kelly" Johnson, who had recently overseen the development of the world's fastest airplane—the so-called "missile with a man in it," the Mach Two XF-104 Starfighter. When Johnson heard about Seaberg's request, he submitted his own uninvited design: an F-104 body, essentially, with a seventy-foot wingspan and unpressurized cockpit but no weapons, landing gear, or ejector seat. Seaberg promptly dismissed it, pointing out that the fuselage was too small for the Pratt and Whitney engine—and again failing to reckon with the irascible determination of Johnson, who had also taken the liberty of presenting his plan to the people directly responsible for the spying.

The Central Intelligence Agency was then six years old. It had been created in 1947 (the same year as the Roswell crash) by the National Security Act, which also gave birth to the Department of Defense and the president's National Security Council. In replacing the disbanded Office of

Strategic Services, which had directed Allied espionage during World War II, the CIA combined spying operations and intelligence analysis under one roof. The character of its conduct in the postwar climate was defined two years later, when the CIA Act of 1949 stipulated that not only the agency's work but its budget would be classified. The precedent for such secrecy was the Manhattan Project—during World War II, it had carried out research on the atomic bomb with a clandestine budget cloaked in code names and nonspecific appropriations. At the time, of course, the rationale was that security was a matter of survival, and now that the war was over, the reasoning was no different. The Cold War was considered every bit as real and infinitely more perilous. Accordingly, the CIA Act declared that any department of the government—not just defense but housing, commerce, transportation, et al.—could transfer funds to the intelligence agency "without regard to any provisions of law." Moreover, as ordered by the president, CIA operations would be "so planned . . . that if uncovered the U.S. Government can plausibly disclaim any responsibility for them."

With this in mind, Eisenhower decided that overflights of Russia should be handled by the CIA as an unarmed "civilian" operation that could be disowned by Washington if necessary. Partly on the advice of Dr. Edwin H. Land—the Polaroid Land Camera scientist, who saw that new film bases and camera lenses could produce extraordinarily detailed pictures even from thirteen miles up—the contract was awarded to Johnson of Lockheed, who promised not only to accommodate the J57 engine but to have the plane ready in eight months. The initial cost of aircraft, training, and operations was $22 million, to be provided from the secret budget of the CIA, which assigned the code word "Aquatone" to the project. This was later changed to "Idealist," but within Lockheed, both names were subordinate to a moniker inspired by the celestial nature of the airplane's mission: "Angel."

Kelly Johnson had a collection of words to live by. His professional motto was "Be quick, be quiet, and be on time," and his favorite acronym was KISS, for "Keep it simple, stupid." At the so-called Skunk Works—the experimental arm of Lockheed, so named when one of its employees (a *Li'l Abner* aficionado) answered the phone with those words—he had achieved his dream of a small, streamlined department where designers, engineers, and production people worked cheek by jowl. To meet the eight-month deadline for the new plane, Johnson drove his staff twelve hours a day and six days a week, not one minute of which could be acknowledged or discussed off the premises. As the design of the aircraft evolved, the fuselage was lengthened and widened to fit the J57 engine; to save weight, the aluminum skin was only two one-hundredths of an inch thick (tantamount to "Reynolds Wrap" in the opinion of the crew). The plane was powered by the only fuel that wouldn't freeze at seventy thousand feet: a type of kerosene that was suspiciously similar to Ronson cigarette lighter fluid.

When it came time to test the design, Edwards Air Force Base—formerly Muroc Army Air Field, the customary test site for high-speed aircraft—was considered insufficiently secure for such a top-secret project. To find a more secluded site, Johnson called on Lockheed's chief test pilot, Tony LeVier, an ace who had flown the F-104 and P-38 and had once bailed out of a P-80 as it split in half when its engine exploded.

Today LeVier lives in La Cañada Flintridge, a tony Los Angeles suburb not far from Pasadena. Some time after my trip to Freedom Ridge, I visited him at the house that he and his wife have owned for four decades at the foot of the San Gabriel Mountains. Now eighty-four years old, LeVier was a big and balding man with a shrill, gravelly voice; wearing aviator-style eyeglasses—naturally—he sat me down in a darkening living room. The sun had just set when I arrived, but LeVier didn't bother to turn on any lights; apparently comfortable with cryptic conditions, he plunged into his story.

"Kelly Johnson called me into his office in January 1955," LeVier said. "He said, 'Close the door.' Then he asked, 'You want to fly my new airplane?' I said, 'Well, I don't know. What's it like?' He said, 'I can't tell you. If you don't want to, get the hell out of my office.'

"I said all right, and he fished out a drawing with these big, long wings that stretched out forever. I laughed and said, 'First you got me in an F-104 with no wings. Now this?' He said, 'Don't say a word to anybody about it.'

"Kelly's favorite crew chief was Dorsey Kammerier, a terrific guy who was a mechanical genius but could also handle men. Kelly said, 'I want you and Dorsey to dress up like hunters, take our single-engine Beechcraft Bonanza, wipe the Lockheed identification off it, and find me a place to fly this airplane.' He left it completely up to me—he just wanted it to be somewhere in the Southwest.

"Well, I knew right away what I wanted: a damn good dry lake. In the early jets, we had nothing but problems with flameouts and things like that, and I was making dead-stick landings on dry lakes all the time—I'd flown at Muroc before the military was even aware of it. So I got out my maps and chose a course through Arizona and Nevada. We took off from Palmdale and headed toward Mexico, saying that Lockheed had some special deal there; then we changed direction.

"We landed on at least a dozen lakes. We took photographs and wrote a report on each one, rating them from one to ten. The last one we came on was Groom. It was round, about three and a half miles in diameter; it had been used for target practice during World War II, so it had a lot of rubbish on it—shell casings, machine-gun links, odds and ends. Walking over the lakebed, you'd come across a funny, twisty path like the trail of a sidewinder leading to these pumice stones. When it rained, the mud got slippery as hell and the rocks moved around. But it was a nice surface, and it was really out in the boondocks. Outside of Nellis, there wasn't anything—they used to go out there and drop bombs and fire weapons with impunity. The only thing of any importance nearby was the AEC Proving Ground,* but we figured the fallout would keep people away. It was ideal, far better than any of the other sites.

"We took our report back to Kelly. A week later he told me: 'You better get Dorsey and go find another place. We can't use yours.' They'd seen it was right next to the Proving Ground and said, 'We don't want to be anywhere near that place.' But a couple of days after that he told me, 'Forget it. We're gonna use yours after all.' They'd talked to the AEC, who said, 'No sweat—we'd be glad to have you as neighbors.' "

I had heard a story that, before he'd landed on Groom Lake, LeVier had dropped a sixteen-pound shotput from his plane onto the playa to test the solidity of the surface. Another version held that the site, which was part of the Las Vegas Bombing and Gunnery Range, had actually been suggested by Air Force Colonel Ozzie Ritland, who'd noticed it during his involvement with nuclear testing, and subsequently flew out to inspect it with LeVier, Johnson, and Richard Bissell, the CIA official in charge of the

---

* The name was later changed to the Nevada Test Site by the Atomic Energy Commission, which itself was superseded by the U.S. Department of Energy.

program. Johnson himself reportedly recalled flying back over an atomic bomb perched on its test tower a few hours before detonation—not a very likely story, since air traffic over the Proving Ground was rigorously restricted.

LeVier dismissed all of these tales. He did, however, remember flying Johnson and Bissell to the site. "My wife made us a hell of a picnic," he said. "I recommended setting up a camp on the southwestern corner of the lake. There was a dirt road into that area, so it was practical."

The dirt road led toward Yucca Flat, the Proving Ground's primary test site only twelve miles away. Groom Lake lay directly in the downwind fall-out path from the atomic tests, which were then proceeding at their peak of aboveground activity. In 1953 alone, 252 kilotons—the equivalent of twenty Hiroshimas—had been detonated there, spreading radiation over western Nevada and Utah. In its rationale for spewing fallout into the region, the AEC had referred to the area as "virtually uninhabited." There was no Rachel then, no Highway 375; the nearest settlement was the town of Alamo thirty miles to the northeast. There was, however, a lead mine in the mountains alongside Groom Lake, operated by the Sheahan family, who were periodically evacuated by the AEC; sometimes their work was shut down for two weeks in a row. Other times, they were unexpectedly awakened by explosions that broke their windows, threw open their doors, and shook sheet metal from their walls. Fallout swept over the mountains like a storm, raining radioactive debris. Cattle, horses, sheep, and deer died with beta burns on their backs. Dan Sheahan would eventually sue the AEC for loss of his home and livelihood; his wife would develop cancer.* But Lockheed and the CIA were welcome to move in, since the security of the Proving Ground was considered a plus for the program. The AEC air closure was expanded to include Groom Lake, which was thereafter referred to in government documents as Watertown—the name, as it happened, of CIA director Allen Dulles's hometown in New York State. Kelly Johnson, going his own way as usual, simply called it the Ranch—an abbreviation of "Paradise Ranch," his sardonic name for a site that the army had described as "a damn good place to dump used razor blades."

Amid these remote, rugged, and radioactive conditions, a functional air base had to be built within a few months. Lockheed wasn't licensed to

---

* According to historian Gary Paine, "The government denied [Sheahan's] claims, and the case was dismissed because of the statute of limitations."

build on the site, nor did the CIA desire to reveal its own participation, so a make-believe construction firm ("CLJ"—Johnson's initials) was invented as a front. One of the authorized test-site contractors it hired, in putting parts of the job out to bid, was warned to be careful about CLJ—which, it was said, lacked any rating in Dun and Bradstreet. Crews labored throughout the spring and hundred-degree desert summer to create the secret compound, about whose aim the workers were kept completely in the dark.

At a summit conference in Geneva that July, President Eisenhower proposed to the Soviets that each superpower allow the other to openly overfly and photograph its military installations. When Russia refused, Eisenhower gave the final go-ahead for a clandestine operation.

"In July," LeVier told me, "Kelly said, 'Pack up, we're going out there.' Well, my God—now they had big hangars, a mile-long runway, a concrete ramp, a control tower, a mess hall, motor homes, a sewer system, and a source of water. It was a red-hot program—I mean, they went in there with *zest*. I cleared off the entire lake myself, going back and forth with a pickup truck every morning for an hour or more. I took tons of shit off that lake, including the front end of an old streamroller. I drug it with a line to the edge of the lakebed, then cracked the whip, and it went ass over teakettle out into the desert. It's probably still out there somewhere.

"They selected Bob Matye to be my backup pilot. They wanted us to socialize together and not fraternize with anybody else and spill the beans. We all went by aliases, so I chose my mother's maiden name—Anthony Evans. We had to go back east to be fitted with partial pressure suits; this was the beginning of the age of high-altitude flying, and breathing oxygen was a problem in itself in those days—we'd get the bends. I had to go into the decompression chamber at Wright Field, where they'd blast you up to seventy thousand feet in a second. It wasn't something you were used to at all. We were on the edge of disaster all the time; looking back on it today, I don't know how we survived.

"We had a C-47 for transporting people and stuff to Groom Lake," LeVier remembered. "We'd stay there for a week or more, then get a break and go home for a weekend. At one point I decided to scoot around to the other dry lakes nearby to get a look at 'em and learn more about the area. Lakebeds can be deceptive if you don't know how to deal with them;

if there's nothing for your eyes to focus on, you can't tell if you're five or fifty feet above the surface. I wanted to mark the runways so you could tell where the lakebed was. I asked a guy at the AEC who seemed to be able to get things done, and he said he could do it for four hundred and fifty dollars. But Kelly said, 'Nope, we haven't got the budget.'

"Anyway, we piled a bunch of guys into a C-47 and flew around to eyeball the other lakes for use as emergency landing sites. For security, we named all the lakes after fish and all the mountains after birds. When we were coming back, I asked this Air Force colonel who was the base commander if he wanted to handle the landing. He said he'd never landed on a dry lake before, so I told him to come in gradually and make sure he knew where the ground was. Well, he dumped the nose and cut the power when we were still pretty far up off the surface—he had no idea how high he was. I jammed the throttle forward and yanked back on the steering control and just barely pulled out of it. Even then, it made a hell of a bounce."

The first prototype of the secret plane was called Article 341. Disassembled and wrapped in cloth, it was flown on a transport from Burbank to Groom Lake on July 24, 1955. As it approached the Ranch, however, the local commander refused permission to land. Afraid that the surface was too thin for such a heavy load, he suggested landing at another base, from which the material could be trucked in by dirt road—a plan that would set the schedule back by a full week. Adhering to his motto, Johnson offered to reduce the air pressure in the airborne transport's tires so as to soften its impact upon landing. When the reply remained negative, he went over the commander's head, calling Washington from the air and getting permission to bring the plane in—quickly, quietly, and on time. Once again, the aircraft designer had refused to be restricted by the reasoning of the Air Force.

The first taxi test occurred a week later. "Kelly told me to take it up to fifty knots," LeVier recalled. "When I did, I found out that the brakes were no good. I coasted to a stop and told him I could hardly feel the damn things. He said, 'You have to burn 'em in. Go east and take it up to sixty.' So I did, and when they caught up with me about two miles later, Kelly said, 'Go back to the barn and take it up to seventy.' Same routine, but this time when I looked out at the wings, they were lifting. So I rolled it a little from side to side, and I realized the damn thing was in the air! None of our other planes could get airborne before you hit a hundred knots, or even two hundred.

"I had no idea how high I was. I was in idle, so I jammed the power in, but a jet engine takes a while to spool up, and the plane went into a stall buffet. I managed to keep it under control, but when it came down it hit really hard—blew out both tires and set fire to the brake lines. The crew came roaring up and had to put it out with fire extinguishers. Apparently, as I'd been taxiing across the lake, I'd disappeared in a cloud of dust; when they saw the plane rise up above it, Kelly almost fainted.

"The next day he asked me, 'How much was it for those runway lines?' I said four hundred and fifty dollars, and he said, 'Okay, we'll do it. And we'll put double brakes on each wheel.' "

The first real flight test of Aquatone took place on August 4. The plane was scheduled to attain an altitude of eight thousand feet. At first the engine wouldn't start; then the chase plane was delayed in refueling; then the wind direction changed, forcing LeVier to reposition the aircraft. The afternoon weather was ominous, with thunderstorms brewing over the Great Basin. Finally, at almost four o'clock, Article 341 took off.

"It went up like a homesick angel," LeVier recalled (though at the time, he'd radioed Johnson that it "flew like a baby buggy"). LeVier circled the lakebed, testing the landing gear and flaps and stalling out a few times on purpose. After just fifteen minutes, rain began to streak the windshield.

"We had to cut the flight short," LeVier said. "The plane was very fragile, and there was a limit to the number of G's you could pull—if you hit turbulence, the wings might break off. So this was a real no-monkey-business type of situation."

Similar to a glider or bicycle, the plane had only two landing wheels: fore and aft. On takeoff, the wings were supported by props, but these fell away as the craft became airborne. "I had talked to B-47 pilots that had a similar two-point configuration," LeVier said. "They told me never to land on the nose wheel—it could bounce you right into a wreck. But that was how Kelly wanted to do it; he was fearful that the engine would stall because of the high-aspect ratio of the wing. We argued about it, but I agreed to give the nose landing a try.

"I didn't have the guts to really spike it. That's not the right way to land an airplane, though it was common with ones that were cranky. I brought it in as gently as I could, and as soon as the nose wheel touched down, sure enough, it started to porpoise. I pulled up again, and Kelly told me on the radio to come in lower and slower.

"The second time, it porpoised again. Now it was really starting to rain, and I had to land the damn thing. Kelly wasn't thinking too clearly along about that time, and he told me to bring it in on the belly. I said: 'I'll land it my way before I do that.' So I came in nose high and set it down in a perfect two-pointer. Right after that, the rain just started pouring—the lake got flooded with two inches of water."

In his book, *Dark Eagles: A History of Top-Secret U.S. Aircraft Programs,* Curtis Peebles writes that, when LeVier climbed out of the cockpit and saw Johnson, he " 'saluted' him with an obscene gesture and accused Johnson of trying to kill him. Johnson responded with the same gesture and a loud, 'You too' "—bestowing upon Article 341 the name it would carry into history. I liked this story so much that I didn't ask LeVier to confirm or deny it. He did indicate, however, that their test of wills continued after touchdown.

"That night we had our usual first-flight celebration," LeVier said. "We all got pretty well schnockered, and like a fool, I took Kelly on in arm wrestling. He played with me for a while, and then he slammed my arm down so hard that he damn near broke it. The next day it was all bandaged up, and when Kelly saw it he said, 'What happened to you?' He'd been so smashed that he couldn't even remember."

LeVier went on to make twenty flights in the U-2, including the first-ever ascension to sixty thousand feet. "My contract was over in October 1955," he said. "They didn't want me to continue because of my age; I was forty-two. I became director of flight operations for Lockheed, but I was out of the U-2 program—and I've never been back to Groom Lake since the day I left. They say they can't take me there any more because I don't have a security clearance, but I think that's chickenshit. They should grandfather me in and show me a good time."

Recruitment of CIA U-2 pilots—all of whom were first-rate F-84 officers with top-secret clearances from SAC bases—began about the time that LeVier left the program. At first the men were told only that an interesting job was available; later, in interviews held at motels, that they would be paid handsomely but would be overseas for eighteen months without their families. Those who remained interested were then given the galvanizing details, in addition to medical and lie-detector tests. The twenty-nine pilots ultimately chosen resigned from the Air Force and signed on with the CIA—a practice known as "sheep dipping." Like LeVier, they assumed aliases upon reporting to the Ranch. (Francis Gary Powers, who would become the most famous U-2 pilot, was known as Francis G. Palmer.)

In *Dark Eagles*, Peebles describes the routine that ensued:

Training operations followed a pattern. The pilots arrived at Groom Lake on the Monday morning flight. They turned in their IDs, which gave their true names and described them as pilots with Lockheed, then assumed the cover names. Each pilot would make two or three U-2 flights per week. Then, on Friday afternoon, the pilots left the site to spend the weekend in Los Angeles.

While at the Ranch, the pilots lived in trailers, four in each. Powers called "Watertown Strip," which was the pilots' name for the site, "one of those 'you can't get there from here' places." The population had grown from about 20, at the time of the first flight, to around 150 air force personnel, Lockheed maintenance crews, and CIA guards. A third hangar had been added, as had more trailers. The Ranch was still a remote desert airstrip. The growing number of U-2s were parked on the hard-packed dirt on the edge of the lake bed; there was no concrete apron. U-2 takeoffs and landings were made from the lake bed. The whole facility was temporary; it was never built to last.

Amusements were limited. There was no PX or Officers' Club. The mess hall, however, was likened to a first-class cafeteria. The food was excellent and second helpings were available. The mess hall also had several pool tables. A sixteen-millimeter projector provided nightly movies. Given the isolation of the site, the pilots were forced to create their own entertainment. Alcohol was freely available and consumed in abundance. Marathon poker games were also organized by the pilots. The first group of pilots scrounged up gunpowder, woodshavings, and cigar tubes to build small rockets. They made a satisfying "whoosh" when launched, but the fun ended when one nearly hit a C-131 transport in the landing pattern.

From time to time, official visitors would come to Groom Lake. In December 1955, Defense Secretary Charles Wilson was shown around the Skunk Works and the Ranch. Allen Dulles also visited the Ranch and met with the first group of pilots.

The only "outsiders" allowed into Groom Lake were the C-124 transport crews, and they did not know where they were. The production U-2s were not built at Burbank, but in the small town of Oildale, California, near Bakersfield. The factory was a tin-roofed warehouse called "Unit 80." During 1956 and 1957, the aircraft were completed, then disassembled, covered, and taken to a local airport, where they were loaded on the C-124s.

It was important that no one know the Ranch's location, so the flights were made at night. The crew was instructed to fly to a point on the California-Nevada border, then contact "Sage Control." The radio voice would tell them not to acknowledge further transmissions. The C-124 would then be given new headings and altitudes. Soon the crew would be contacted by "Delta," who would tell them to start descending into the black desert night. The voice would then tell the transport's crew to lower their flaps and landing gear. Yet their maps showed no civilian or military airports in the area, only empty desert. Then the runway lights would come on, and Delta would clear them to land. Following the landing, the runway lights would be turned off and a "follow me" truck would direct them to a parking spot. The buildings were visible only as lights in the distance. A group of tight-lipped men with names like "Smith" would unload the U-2.

After several months of training, the pilots began making flights as far as the Allegheny Mountains and back. Such missions, which covered four thousand miles and lasted eight hours, were as demanding as if made in a Volkswagen at night during a hurricane. The U-2 was so fragile and finicky that, at high altitude, the difference between its top and stall speeds was only ten knots; if the maximum were exceeded, the plane would disintegrate. The solo pilot thus had to maintain an unwavering grip while simultaneously navigating a course and operating the camera. During the training period, several U-2 pilots crashed and died; one parachuted to safety in Arizona after his oxygen supply expired. Others had close calls when their engines flamed out. One such plane landed at Palm Springs Airport; another came down at Kirtland Air Force Base in Albuquerque when its engine failed over the Mississippi River. Upon landing, the "articles" were quickly covered with tarps. The unpainted aircraft bore only the markings of the National Advisory Committee on Aeronautics, for which they were said to be performing a tried and untrue mission: weather observation. The pilots' uniforms had no nametags or insignia.

At Groom, however, they did wear dosimeters to measure their radiation exposure. During 1955 alone, fourteen nuclear detonations occurred at the Test Site; whenever a blast was scheduled (and even if it was ultimately postponed), Watertown had to be evacuated and U-2 testing and training suspended, sometimes for as long as a month. Between April and October 1957, Operation Plumbob blew up twenty-four bombs, the first of which was a "safety experiment" designed to find out if an accident might produce a nuclear yield. This test—"Project 57"—distributed plutonium over nine hundred acres in Area 13 five miles northwest of Groom Lake. After the test, the area was fenced off, but no effort was made to clean it up for another twenty-four years.

An informal agreement between the government and the Pentagon forbade the use of fusion weapons on American soil. But in July 1957, just such a thermonuclear device—a seventy-four-kiloton hydrogen bomb called "Hood," the sixth shot in the Plumbob series—was detonated from a balloon fifteen hundred feet above Yucca Lake. The most potent airburst ever exploded in the continental United States, its shockwave splintered windows and deformed doors at Watertown before dispensing its burden of fallout. Ten days later, the Ranch was used as a laboratory to measure radiation from seventeen-kiloton Shot Diablo. Normal background levels of radiation are between .02 and .04 milliRoentgens per hour; when the cloud from Diablo passed over Groom Lake, numbers as high as 80 and 90 were recorded inside the buildings. One truck parked in the nearby desert received 1,420. Within a few weeks, U-2 training, conceived in order to assess a peril that existed not twelve but twelve thousand miles away, resumed.

The first U-2 overflight of the Soviet Union took place on July 4, 1956. Two more followed within a week, immediately extinguishing with their pictures the Pentagon's fear of a bomber gap, which had been based on nothing more than paranoid speculation. The overflights—carried out "alone, unarmed, and unafraid"—were immediately detected and attacked with futility (but with increasing accuracy, owing to newly developed surface-to-air missiles) by the Russians; they continued sporadically until 1960, when U.S. intelligence suggested that a missile site capable of nuking New York was being built near the Ural Mountains. President Eisenhower, scheduled to visit Moscow after a Paris summit in late May, authorized two more U-2 missions, with the mandate that they occur no later than than April 25.

Poor weather forced an extension of the deadline until May 1. On that day, Francis Gary Powers took off from Peshawar, Pakistan, intending to cross the entire continent and land in Norway. At seventy-two thousand feet, however, the shock wave from a Soviet missile flipped his airplane upside down, tearing off its wings. Parachuting to earth from fifteen thousand feet, Powers was captured immediately. The U-2 program had begun and ended on holidays celebrating American democracy and the spread of communism.

Facing the irrefutable evidence, Eisenhower admitted authorizing the overflights but declined Khrushchev's demand to apologize for them. The Paris summit conference collapsed, and a month later the Soviets walked out of disarmament talks in Geneva. Powers ultimately confessed to spying and was condemned to ten years in a Russian prison; on the day he was sentenced, film from the first successful American spy satellite revealed more information about Soviet military installations than all twenty-four U-2 flights combined. (It showed, for example, that a supposed missile gap was just as imaginary as the bomber chasm.) After seventeen months in jail, Powers was swapped for a Russian spy; he returned home to work for Lockheed as a U-2 test pilot (the plane would later be used to discover Soviet Missiles in Cuba and was still flying at the time of the Persian Gulf War), but even before his capture by the Russians, Project Aquatone had been moved away from Watertown. The Ranch was needed for the next generation of secret spyplane.

Even before Powers was shot down, work had begun on a supersonic reconnaissance aircraft that could fly higher and faster than the U-2. Since it supplanted the fondly named "Angel," Lockheed naturally called this one "Archangel" and numbered it A-1. (The CIA, perhaps reacting against the grandiosity, called it Project Oxcart.) By the time the design was finalized, ten more versions had evolved into the A-11 "Blackbird": a long, sleek jet with a sharp nose, black paint job, titanium body, one seat, and two engines that used eight thousand gallons of fuel per hour, enabling the aircraft to attain an altitude of ninety thousand feet and speed three times that of sound. The plane's propulsion engineer, Ben Rich, who would later succeed Kelly Johnson as director of the Skunk Works, declared that "the U-2 was to the Blackbird as a covered wagon was to an Indy 500 race car." He called it "the wild horse of the stratosphere." To Norman Nelson, the CIA's watchdog within the Skunk Works, it was "a twenty-first century performer delivered in the early 1960s."

For all of that, Eisenhower also wanted it to be undetectable on radar, a task that was tackled at Watertown, where a full-scale model A-11 was perched on a pylon. Despite its ongoing utility and rustic charm, however, Paradise Ranch was dismissed as a feasible flight-test site for the project. For one thing, the new plane required a runway of nearly nine thousand feet where Groom Lake's was merely a mile. Moreover, the Ranch had rude accommodations for only a hundred and fifty workers while Oxcart needed *fifteen* hundred. Ten other bases targeted for shutdown were evaluated as potential test sites before it was again concluded that only one place on the continent could conceal such a secret project. Four months after Powers's capture, construction crews began working double shifts to convert the Ranch into a small town.

To explain all the activity this time, Watertown was officially described as a radar test range. Workers were transformed into government "consultants" so that their identities wouldn't have to be divulged, as was required by Nevada state law. The manufacture of airplane parts was funded by front companies, as were the rented warehouses where the components were stored. Phony businesses and third parties were even able to procure titanium from the Soviet Union. Ironically, amid all the subterfuge, many Oxcart blueprints were unclassified, based on the belief that such status would attract undue attention.

Nevertheless, when the first Archangel prototype (numbered A-12, owing to final adjustments in its radar cross section) was ready in February 1962, it was concealed inside a wide-load trailer and trucked out of the San Fernando Valley at three o'clock in the morning. Before the trip, the route had been driven in a pickup truck with two protruding bamboo poles as high and wide as the trailer; whenever the poles hit a road marker, the driver got out, sawed off the sign, and then braced and bolted it back together. When the actual convoy came through, the lead car dismantled the doctored sign and the tail car reassembled it. Most awkwardly, after the caravan reached the desert, a passing Greyhound got scraped by the A-12's trailer. Then and there, the bus driver received $3,500 to ensure that no insurance report was filed.

As the Archangel approached the Ranch, its ingress was eased by eighteen miles of newly resurfaced roads. When it arrived, its stay was sustained by three surplus navy hangars and a hundred dismantled dormitories that had been shipped to the site and rebuilt. When it came time to take off, it was empowered by a new fuel-tank farm containing more than a million gallons, not to mention an 8,500-foot runway consisting of 25,000 cubic yards of concrete. The base would soon boast a new movie theater, a new baseball field, and a new saloon; it was only fitting that it should also have a new name. Since the adjoining Test Site was carved up into nondescriptly numbered zones—Area 11, Area 12, Area 13, etc.—Groom Lake subtly followed suit. Beginning in 1960, it was referred to in government documents as Area 51.

While it wasn't possible to maintain utter secrecy on Project Oxcart indefinitely, the CIA tried. At first, when the A-12 was on the runway, everyone unconnected to the program was ordered to go inside (and presumably cover their eyes). Its flight path was fashioned to direct the sound away from the town of Alamo, but even in the remote desert mountains, a pack train of mules startled by the sonic boom reportedly tried to leap from a cliff. The early test flights lasted only an hour—but in those sixty minutes, the plane could cross most of the continent. It was, after all, capable of traveling three thousand feet per second; it used up eighty-six miles merely in making a turn. On one late-stage test flight, an A-12 that took off from Groom Lake flew north to Wyoming, east to Minnesota, south to Florida, west to Oregon, east again to Tennessee, and finally home to Nevada. The ten-thousand-mile trip lasted six hours. If a pilot didn't like the first sunrise he saw on such a day, he could watch a couple more before landing, with at least one of them taking place in the West. A Blackbird pilot named Jim Wadkins testified that this sort of thing constituted "almost a religious experience."

In 1962, the sonic boom from an A-12 thirty thousand feet up collapsed a chimney on the ground in West Virginia, killing two people. Under such circumstances, detection of the odd, unpainted aircraft was far from unheard of. Nor were official explanations terribly sophisticated.

When an Edwards Air Force captain, patrolling a runway at dawn, saw an A-12 overhead and asked the control tower, "What was that airplane?" the reply was simply: "What airplane?" When an A-12 stalled and crashed in Utah, the Air Force was instructed to report the loss of an F-105. Nellis spokesmen, following orders, tried their best to mouth these words without scratching their heads. As much in the dark as anybody else, even they were mystified by activities at Area 51.

In 1962, the restricted airspace above the Ranch was expanded to six hundred square miles with Groom Lake occupying the bull's-eye of the no-fly zone. Nellis mapmakers marked it down on their aviation charts with the call sign of its control tower, which seemed to sum up the expanding image of this enigmatic neighbor: "Dreamland."

That same year, at the request of the Air Force, Lockheed began working on a version of the A-12 that had room for two crew members. Initially designed as an interceptor, it ultimately became a reconnaissance plane that could peer into the Soviet Union from high altitude without transgressing the border. Thus, it was code-numbered RS-71, for "reconnaissance strike." In early 1964, three months after the assassination of John Kennedy, President Lyndon Johnson—who had been briefed about Oxcart soon after taking office, and expected to face a rabid anticommunist as his Republican opponent in November—wanted badly to show a talon (i.e., a hawklike hand). Since supersonic technology was, moreover, considered commercially valuable, Johnson, after conferring with the National Security Council, elected to announce that the world's most advanced jet aircraft had been developed by Democrats. To obfuscate its antiradar design as well as its secret location, he told the media on February 29 that "several A-11 aircraft are now being flight tested at Edwards Air Force Base in California."

Unfortunately, none had ever been there. To head off the storming press, a pair of planes were promptly powered up at Groom and launched through the air toward Edwards. Upon landing, they taxied into their new hangar, where their exhaust activated the building's overhead sprinklers, which were authorized to be shut off by only one person on the base. Security prevented him from entering the hangar for half an hour, during which time the place was flooded—along with Republican hopes for the White House. The secret of Area 51, however, remained secure.

Four months after the A-11 announcement, Peebles writes, ". . . there was another. According to legend, Johnson asked an aide what the RS-71 was for. The aide responded, 'strategic reconnaissance.' Thus, when he announced the existence of a new reconnaissance aircraft on July 24, 1964, President Johnson called it the 'SR-71.' As a result of switching the letters, twenty-five thousand drawings had to be changed." From that moment until 1990, when it was retired by the Air Force, the existence of the SR-71 was openly acknowledged, while its progenitor, the A-12, remained a covert CIA spyplane overflying North Korea and (most notably and frequently) North Vietnam. Skunk Works's price for delivering the first five A-12s, originally estimated at $100 million, had eventually risen to $161 million (a pittance compared to the $600 million cost of developing the plane's *engine*, which had been funded from the secret budget of the CIA). On this investment, which did not include improvements and operations at Area 51, the final fleet of ten A-12s helped the U.S. fight the war in Vietnam for a little over a year. Future missions over Southeast Asia, Cuba, Korea, Libya, the Eastern bloc border, and the Persian Gulf would be handled by the SR-71 at an annual cost of about $260 million.

By the time Project Oxcart was terminated in 1968, the main Groom Lake runway had again been extended, this time by ten thousand feet. The northern part of the base had a radar complex, a reservoir, sewage ponds, and an RCS test range; the southern section ("Baja Groom Lake") had a commissary, dormitories, a water tower, a fire station, the fuel tank farm, recreation facilities, and Lockheed's company hangars. Daily flights had been established between the base, Burbank, and Las Vegas; the population of Area 51 was 1,835. The Ranch was no longer a ramshackle outpost in the middle of nowhere: The Blackbird had transformed it into the nation's premier test site for top-secret aircraft.

When the A-12 was retired, a ceremony was performed at Area 51, at which time the pilots' wives (presumably flown in while blindfolded) were finally apprised of what their husbands had been doing away from home. The airplane was subsequently replaced on Groom Lake runways by the ill-fated D-21 Tagboard—a relatively low-priced, "low observable reconnaissance drone," or unmanned spyplane, which made four abortive overflights of Communist China before being axed—and an assortment of Soviet MiGs, acquired through various means of skullduggery and used (under the code names Have Doughnut and Have Drill) in mock dogfights on the Nellis range. The first MiG 21 was obtained in a trade with Israel, which had gotten it from an apparent oxymoron: a Roman Catholic Iraqi pilot, who had decided to defect. Imaginatively numbered 007 and repainted with a Star of David, it provided enough expertise for Israel to shoot down thirty-seven MiGs in the Six Day War of 1967. In search of commensurate wisdom, by the mid-1980s the United States had amassed a mock-Soviet force that included two dozen such airplanes. But by then, the crowning achievement of Black R&D had taken over the Ranch.

Ever since the U-2, the Pentagon had been striving to develop an invisible aircraft—a dream that consisted of reducing the plane's radar cross section, or the amount of surface area that reflected radio signals. No plane had yet been able to escape detection altogether; despite a coat of radar-absorbing ferrites and plastics, the Blackbird and D-21 still relied on speed and altitude to avoid harm's way. In the Yom Kippur War of 1973, however, Israel experienced a reversal of its earlier success with MiGs: Sending a fleet of F-4 Phantoms (state-of-the-art American fighter-bombers) against the Arabs' Soviet missiles, the Israelis lost more than seventy airplanes in two days. A few months later, the Pentagon assigned the concept of "stealth" its top aviation priority, embarking upon Project Harvey (named for the invisible rabbit of the same name).

As it had been for the U-2, Lockheed was initially overlooked when the call went out for designs. Now in his mid-sixties, Kelly Johnson was semi-retired; the company hadn't produced a fighter—the intended platform for this project—since the Korean War. Moreover, much of its antiradar work had been so successfully cloaked that it was (surprise!) little-known. But the new Skunk Works chief, Ben Rich, Johnson's former right-hand man, had apparently learned his lessons well. Just as Johnson had done twenty years earlier, Rich went to the CIA for permission to be included in the competition. To refresh the short memory of Lockheed's longtime partner, the emissary sent by Rich was Johnson himself. Duly admitted to the race, the Skunk Works team trampled all contenders with a breakthrough in aeronautical design.

The keys to stealth were stashed in research dating back to the nineteenth century, when Scottish and German physicists had predicted the ways in which radar signals would be reflected by simple surfaces such as plates and spheres. In the 1960s, this work had been distilled—again ironically—by a Soviet scientist named Pyotr Ufimtsev, who applied it to more complicated shapes such as discs. The leap that Lockheed made was in breaking down the shape of an airplane into a collection of flat surfaces, each of which would deflect waves away from a source rather than back toward it. Since the resulting object looked like a diamond, the concept was called "faceting" and the name for the project within Lockheed became "Hopeless Diamond"—reflecting not merely radar signals but those emitted by Kelly Johnson, who believed that the future of airborne "defense" lay entirely in missiles, not airplanes. According to Rich, Johnson literally kicked his ass when he first saw the stealth design; senior Skunk Works scientists preferred the idea of a flying saucer to an arrowhead-shaped diamond, but Rich complained that "the Martians wouldn't tell" him how to fly one. Johnson predicted that Hopeless Diamond would be no more stealthy than the D-21, but he was forced to eat his words when a full-scale model was tested at White Sands, New Mexico. The radar operator detected it only when a crow landed on top, and even then, all he could see was the animal. As had happened with the first test of the "You too," Johnson was embarrassed (if not humbled) by the bird.

Like aeronautical designs, code names were now being created by computers. The prefix assigned to aircraft projects was the word "Have," so Hopeless Diamond, which no longer seemed so hopeless, turned into "Have Blue." Initially unclassified, it soon became the most top-secret program since the development of the atomic bomb. Johnson had warned Rich that such security would make his life miserable, and Rich quickly concluded that he was right. Nobody was allowed to be alone in a room with a Have Blue drawing; if two engineers were discussing a diagram and one had to take a leak, the Have Blueprint was locked up until he returned from the john. Even Skunk Works coffee cups, which bore a cartoon of the airplane's nose sticking out from behind a cloud with a skunk's tail at the other end, were classified top-secret. Safe-lock combinations had to be memorized (not written down), and every worker with access to the project was subjected to a background check that went on for months, during which he had to be paid for irrelevant busy work. Such requirements added at least 15 percent to the cost of a secret project. What was more, Rich would write, "It was like working at KGB headquarters in Moscow."

The first Have Blue prototype arrived at Area 51 in November 1977. When it was beheld by its pilot, Bill Park, he thought it "looked like something that flew in from outer space." The dark, inscrutable, angular craft did bear a decided resemblance to Darth Vader, who was introduced the same year. Park himself had a history worthy of *The Right Stuff*: He'd once bailed out of an SR-71 that flipped upside down while taking off, and during Project Tagboard had ejected from an M-21 a hundred and fifty miles off the Pacific coast. He was rescued, but his launch systems officer drowned at sea. Park was being paid a bonus of $25,000 for the Have Blue test series.

In May, on the plane's thirty-sixth flight, Park hit the Groom Lake runway rather hard while landing. Instead of veering off the tarmac, he pulled up and began another pass, at which point he discovered that his landing gear had jammed. Trying to bang it loose, Park intentionally brought the plane down hard once again, but without success in freeing the gear. Then, as he climbed back skyward, one of his engines flamed out. He was running out of fuel.

With typical test-pilot aplomb, Park radioed the tower that he was "gonna bail out of here unless anyone has any better ideas." He got the okay, but as he punched out, his helmet hit the plane's headrest, knocking him cold. Peebles writes that Park's "parachute opened automatically, but he was still unconscious when his limp body hit the desert floor. Park's leg was broken, he suffered a concussion, and his mouth was filled with dirt as the parachute was dragged across the desert by a strong wind. By the time paramedics reached him, Park's heart had stopped. The paramedics were able to save him, but Park never flew again." Instead he was named Lockheed's director of flight operations, the same position that been awarded to the aging Tony LeVier.

The aftermath of the crash of Have Blue 1001 signaled the Area 51 public-relations policy of the future. The wreckage was buried at Groom Lake, but the crash had attracted outside attention; when officials were queried for an explanation, however, they simply declined to provide one, deferring to "national security" strictures. A year later, when a second prototype crashed and burned north of Groom on its fifty-second flight, the tack was similar. A rescue truck from the Tonopah Test Range, racing toward the crash site, was intercepted and run off the road by an F-15 fighter roaring in from the Ranch; the Have Blue pilot, who had parachuted to safety, was picked up by a helicopter. Again the wreckage was buried within the boundaries of Dreamland, where nobody from the corporeal world could dig it up and figure it out.

Nonetheless, vague information about stealth leaked out in newspapers and on television. In the election year of 1980, President Jimmy Carter decided to try and repair damage to his image in the Defense Department. Already wounded by his cancellation of the B-1 bomber (which he killed after his national security chief, Zbigniew Brezinski, was treated to a look at Have Blue inside a guarded hangar at Groom Lake) and the botched Iranian hostage rescue (also said to have been rehearsed at the Ranch), Carter's secretary of defense, Harold Brown, admitted in an August press conference that the United States had indeed been successful in developing stealth technology. He and his undersecretary for research and engineering, William Perry, went on to define the informational lines that would and wouldn't be breached, with Brown offering the rationale that, "In the face of . . . leaks, I believe that it is not appropriate or credible for us to deny the existence of this program."

Such candor would evaporate as soon as it took form. Republicans accused Carter of election-year expediency; Congressmen complained that the press conference revealed more to the public than they'd known themselves (!); Admiral Elmo Zumwalt, former chief of operations for the navy, suggested that the administration itself had initiated the leaks that led to the ultimate disclosure. Soon thereafter, Ronald Reagan was elected president, and the rest is stealthy history.

The culmination of the Have Blue program—the celebrated F-117 stealth fighter, code-named "Senior Trend"—made its first flight from Groom Lake on June 18, 1981: Ben Rich's birthday. The inherent instability of its madhouse avionics was rendered serene by a bevy of onboard computers that corrected the craft's control surfaces thousands of times per second. In the next few months, four more F-117s would join this first full-scale development model on the flight line. Unfortunately, the following year, a technician mistakenly reversed the wires controlling pitch and yaw on the first production plane, and upon taking off from Groom Lake, the $43 million debutante fighter turned upside down and disintegrated. (The pilot, Bob Riedenauer, survived.) Lockheed quickly established new safeguards and inspection procedures and wrinkles were ironed out of the other planes while, just to the north, the Tonopah Test Range—previously dedicated to nuclear drop tests—was equipped with double fencing, motion detectors, and winterized trailers picked up for a song (a mere million dollars) from Chevron. This would become home base for the Nightstalkers, Goatsuckers, and Grim Reapers—tactical squadrons of stealth fighters, which, after a shaky first mission chasing General Manuel Noriega in Panama, went on to glory in the Persian Gulf. After their famous first night of bombing Baghdad, every single F-117 returned to its point of origin untouched.

In the decade that passed between the first flight of the Stealth and the first night of Desert Storm, the U.S. defense budget had more than doubled from $142 billion to $300 billion. (As Ben Rich would write, "The open secret in our business was that the government practiced a very obvious form of paternalistic socialism to make certain that its principal weapons suppliers stayed solvent.") Under the Reagan administration, the Air Force upped its original order for eighteen F-117 fighters to fifty-nine. The B-1 bomber was revived, and Congress also gave a green light to a B-2 *stealth* bomber—which, built not by Lockheed but Northrop (though both companies were riddled with indictments for fraud and conspiracy), had, at last count and without entering service, risen in cost from four hundred million to *two billion* dollars per plane, a situation permitted by the fact that, for a full decade, the project's budget had been concealed from Congress. As this debacle was developing, the Soviet Union disappeared, while the base at Groom Lake continued to grow. Housing from the 1960s had been torn down and replaced with modern dormitory units; a second three-mile runway was built; there were new water tanks, a new fuel tank farm, and the enormous new yellow hangar, now said to house the stealth cruise missile. USSR or no USSR, Area 51 was going strong.

In 1983, in order to protest Reagan's nuclear buildup, members of the environmental group Greenpeace infiltrated the Nevada Test Site to disrupt a routine blast. While making their way through the mountains, they reportedly got a glimpse of an F-117, whose spectral countenance made the group's "hair stand on end." The following year, armed guards began barring hikers and hunters from the Groom Range for unspecified reasons pertaining, as usual, to national security. Despite the fact that this was illegal, the closure was (eventually) approved by Congress until June 15, 1988. When that day arrived, however, a debate was still under way in both Nevada and Washington, D.C., as to whether the land withdrawal should be extended. Hence, on June 16, local activists staked a gold-mining claim on Bald Mountain, overlooking Area 51.

Congress reauthorized the land closure the next day. The following month, the "miners" returned to "work" their "claim," at which time they were arrested and later convicted of trespassing by the Lincoln County justice of the peace. A higher court would reverse the decision four years later, but by that time the group had allowed its claim to expire. In any case, the events showed that the Cold War ethos that had served to shield Groom Lake from view, begun under Allied commander Eisenhower and culminating with CIA boss Bush, was no longer fully operational. The Gulf War notwithstanding, Vietnam and Watergate had indelibly altered the attitude of the public—as had the sheer weight of the national population, which had (among other things) transformed Nevada into the fastest-growing state in the union. The Ranch no longer qualified, as it had under Ike, as the most isolated spot in the continental United States. But as the government chose to deal with this problem by denying the very existence of the base, the place became even more evocative in its role as Dream-land, gaining a worldwide reputation as the site of every sordid scheme since World War II.

In 1953, when both Eisenhower and the U-2 program were inaugu-rated, the former five-star general himself pointed out that the cost of one bomber (forty years before the two-billion dollar B-2) was equivalent to that of two hospitals, a pair of power plants, or a couple of dozen schools. He warned against "a burden of arms draining the life of all peoples," cau-tioning that what the Cold War offered was "not a way of life at all," but rather "humanity hanging from a cross of iron." Now that the long standoff was ending and the Evil Empire evaporating, however, Americans still found themselves oddly uneasy. Just as Ike had feared, the country's social and economic framework (simultaneously enlivened and endangered by a growing electronic onslaught that he could not have foreseen), had indeed been eroded by "deficit socialism," applied not to societal needs but toward the kinds of extravagant gadgets hidden inside Area 51. To justify the secrecy as well as the debt, the national mind continued to require an outside threat.

Despite his qualifications for the position, Saddam Hussein was only one man. With the approach of the year 2000, the stage was set for some-thing more sweeping—some kind of staggering revelation about what had gone on behind closed doors for half a century. The prophet, when he appeared, wouldn't be some boring pacifist; in the age of Powell and Schwartzkopf, that image was passé. Instead, the whistle-blower would come from within the modern program: He would be a personable young techie from Los Alamos and Las Vegas who liked to build jet engines, drive fast cars, consort with prostitutes, and blow things up.

To kick-start the millennium, along came Bob Lazar.

THREE

Lazar

I have never met Bob Lazar. At this point, within the world of ufology, meeting Bob Lazar is tantamount to meeting Bob Dylan. Lazar is similarly a reclusive superstar and a legend in his own time; if not exactly the voice of a generation, he has nonetheless had a defining impact on popular consciousness, and finding himself (also like the fabled singer-songwriter) overexposed to onrushing masses with whom he had no desire to associate, he subsequently retreated from public view, assuming a notorious role as an enigma.

This is not to imply that it is impossible to encounter Bob Lazar. He continues to reside in Las Vegas, where he reportedly has a lively social circle and a handful of small businesses (though one of these—repairing alpha probes for radiation laboratories—is reportedly "going down the tubes" with the cessation of nuclear weapons testing). For a brief period in 1995, Lazar even had his own radio show, during which he and his friend/partner/flack Gene Huff took telephone calls from listeners. No hermit by nature, Lazar convenes an annual party on a dry lake in Nevada, where he kicks back with his fellow fireworks and weapons enthusiasts and displays his homemade jet car against a backdrop of beer, guns, and loud rock music. Invitations to the shindig (called "Desert Blast") are not easy to come by, however. A video trailer describing it—scripted and circulated, like most of Lazar's public communiqués, by Huff—warns: "If you don't know where it is, you're not invited."

For years it has been rumored that New Line Cinema was about to begin production on a movie telling Bob Lazar's tale about his experiences near Area 51. At one time, the attached director was reportedly Chuck Russell, who had had commercial success with *Nightmare on Elm Street*. Under these circumstances, it's easy to understand why Lazar would want to shield his story from indiscriminate circulation. If the price or situation seems right, he will still grant an occasional interview to a carefully selected journalist, but in order for this to become possible, the applicant first has to get past Huff, a combative and corpulent real-estate appraiser with a manner so insultingly off-putting as to repel nine out of every ten applicants for the honor.

I myself stand as a member of this undistinguished 90 percent. Midway through my research, I contacted Huff by telephone and electronic mail (the latter a venue where he has carved out a considerable reputation for himself) to say that I was writing a book about Area 51 and was therefore interested in interviewing Lazar. In one of these solicitations, I left a message from Glenn Campbell's telephone—a fatally naive misstep, as it turned out.

"No, Bob Lazar and I won't be available for any interviews," Huff (eventually) e-mailed me in response. "We get solicited by mainstream journalists all the time and none of them stay at Glenn Campbell's and that is the main reason you were turned down." (Later I learned that Huff refers to Campbell by the mysterious nickname of "Goober.") I had provided him with a list of people I'd already interviewed, suggesting that he contact them if he wanted to check my credibility. Declaring in his e-mail that only two of the people on my list were worth talking to, Huff further divulged: "I actually spoke to a couple of your references and neither of them gave you a thumbs up." Curious as to why not, I called one of the two that he had mentioned—only to learn that the man had not been contacted by Huff about me. I asked this person to call Lazar himself on my behalf, but instead he called Huff, who relented to the extent of asking for written questions before he would reconsider my application.

I have not complied with this request. The fact of the matter is that, aside from procedural convention, I've never considered it especially important to meet Bob Lazar. In addition to producing his own sensational videotape, he has already told and retold his story to a number of interviewers, notably George Knapp of KLAS-TV in Las Vegas, Timothy Good for the book *Alien Contact*, Michael Lindemann and Ralph Steiner for the book *UFOs and the Alien Presence*, Michael Hessemann for the "documentary" video *Secrets of the Black World*, and in an onstage appearance at the "Ultimate UFO Seminar" in Rachel in 1993, transcribed by Glenn Campbell. Working from these transcripts (as well as Huff's own synopsis of his friend's experiences), one can assemble a highly detailed chronicle—one that I wouldn't expect to change if I met Lazar face-to-face. And anyway, it would be a shame if it did. As Glenn Campbell observed in an essay entitled "Lazar as a Fictional Character":

> Maybe Lazar is a fraud, and maybe his tale is no more real than Alice in Wonderland, but that doesn't mean we can't learn something from him. . . . If Lazar's story is fiction, it's great fiction, filled with a richness of plausible details and complex philosophical dilemmas that you can't find in most popular novels. . . . a lot more tangible fiction about our origins than most religions seem to offer [and] far superior to most science fiction in creating a world that could be true.

At this writing and in photographs and videotapes, Robert Scott Lazar is a thin, thirty-eight-year-old man with high cheekbones, wide lips, aviator-style eyeglasses, and a wry, intelligent, ironic air. He was born (it is believed; the circumstances of his birth are one of many mysterious elements in his history) on January 26, 1959, in Coral Gables, Florida, but says he grew up with adoptive parents and graduated from high school on Long Island, New York, in 1976. Two years later his parents moved to southern California, where Bob took an electronics course at Pierce Junior College. He also claims to have attended California State University at

Northridge and to have obtained master's degrees in electronic technology from the California Institute of Technology (CalTech) and physics from the Massachusetts Institute of Technology (MIT), though no record exists of his having attended any of these institutions.

In 1980, Lazar married a woman named Carol Strong, who was seventeen years his senior. After Bob spent some time working for Fairchild Industries, the couple found its way to Los Alamos, New Mexico, where Lazar says° he worked as a research physicist at the Meson Physics Facility of Los Alamos National Laboratories (LANL). Here he was awarded a top-secret security clearance for classified defense work, reportedly involving particle-beam accelerators as part of the Strategic Defense Initiative (a.k.a. "Star Wars") program.

On June 27, 1982, a front-page feature story in the local newspaper, the *Los Alamos Monitor*, confirmed that Lazar had by then begun his hobby of powering automobiles with jet engines. L.A. MAN JOINS THE JET SET—AT 200 MPH, the headline proclaimed, followed by an article whose photographs show a converted Honda with air scoops and a license plate that read JETUBET. The story explained that the car's engine, made of stainless steel and titanium, ran on liquid propane with a kerosene afterburner capable of generating eight hundred pounds of thrust. Lazar reported that he had driven the vehicle over two hundred miles per hour on a dry lake near Los Angeles.

As it happened, the day after this article appeared, Dr. Edward Teller—chief proponent of SDI, so-called father of the hydrogen bomb, and, according to some, the model for Dr. Strangelove in the Stanley Kubrick film—was speaking against the nuclear-freeze movement in Los Alamos. Arriving early for the talk, Lazar saw Teller sitting outside the lecture hall, perusing the jet-car story in the paper. "That's me you're reading about," Lazar announced by way of an introduction. The famous physicist politely told the young technician that he found the article "very interesting." In the time remaining before Teller's speech, the two repaired to a nearby coffee shop for a science chat.

Three years later, while vacationing in Nevada, Bob and Carol purportedly purchased a partial interest in a brothel called the Honeysuckle Ranch. Not long afterward they bought a house in Las Vegas, though Bob

---

° Since many of Lazar's claims remain unverified (for reasons that he says are attributable to official expungement of his records), I will simply repeat much of his story as he and Huff tell it, leaving most of the questions for later.

continued to spend time in Los Alamos, where for unknown reasons he had left his job at LANL. He and Carol subsequently started a film-processing business out of their house, catering largely to the Las Vegas real-estate industry, which was enjoying an economic boom; in the 1980s, Sin City was the fastest-growing metropolis in the country. Lazar became known as "Bob the photo guy" among the community of local appraisers, which included Gene Huff.

Carol died in 1986, and Lazar married another woman named Tracy Murk, whom he had met in Los Alamos. Like Bob, Tracy (whose looks have been described by Huff as "model quality") lived there because of the national laboratory, where her father, Don, worked on detonation charges for A-bombs. In any case, two months after Carol died, Lazar declared bankruptcy, listing among his reasons for financial hardship "loss of spouse" and "loss of business." Nevertheless, he continued making photo deliveries in his jet-powered Honda, piquing the curiosity of a good many observers, including Gene Huff. The down-to-earth appraiser considered his eccentric film processor "somewhat of an egghead," but as he got to know Bob better, he grew impressed with Lazar's knack for things scientific—not just jet propulsion but computers, electronics, explosives, et al.

One day, Lazar made up a batch of nitroglycerine while Huff sat talking to him at the kitchen table. Then they took it out in the desert and blew it up. Eventually the fascinated Huff asked Lazar, "What's the difference between you and a scientist?" When Bob divulged that he had degrees in physics and electronic technology, Gene asked why he hadn't mentioned this before. "What did you want me to do?" Lazar responded. "Say, 'Hey, man—I'm a scientist'?" He shook his head and stalked away.

As it happened, Huff was also friends with the son of William P. Lear, the man who designed the Learjet and eight-track stereo. John Lear, for whom Gene had appraised some property in Las Vegas, was an accomplished pilot in his own right: He held every airline certificate ever issued by the Federal Aviation Administration, had flown 160 different types of aircraft in fifty countries, owned seventeen Learjet speed records, and had carried out secret missions around the world for the CIA. He had also run for the Nevada state senate and—apparently beginning in 1986, when he met some Air Force "personnel" who'd witnessed a UFO landing in England—become convinced that the U.S. government was in cahoots with a race of extraterrestrial biological entities, or "EBEs." Between 1969 and 1971, Lear believed, a deal had been made between alien visitors from outer space and the Majestic-12 committee that had been ordained by President Truman: In exchange for advanced technology, the government agreed to overlook an ongoing wave of human abductions. Unfortunately, unbeknownst to the earthly authorities, who considered the kidnappings relatively benign, the abductions were being conducted to create human/alien hybrids, control the victims through artificial implants, and maintain a supply of organs that the abductors needed to replenish their own dysfunctional digestive systems. The desired effect was reportedly obtained by extracting an enzyme or hormone from the abductee, mixing it with hydrogen peroxide, and applying the resultant solution to an EBE's body. In a pinch, beef could be substituted in the recipe for human body parts, which also explained the mysterious plague of cattle mutilations infesting the western range: Ranchers had been finding livestock corpses with no eyes, tongues, throats, or genitals, their rectums cored out up to the colon with "surgical precision" and no spillage of blood. According to Lear, the body of one Sergeant Jonathan P. Louette had been discovered in this same condition on the White Sands Missile Test Range in 1956, three days after he'd been abducted by a disc-shaped object at three in the morning. The operations, performed while the victims were still alive (if not kicking), were said to supply several underground laboratories, one of which was located at Groom Lake.

"Between 1979 and 1983," Lear revealed on the ParaNet computer network in December 1987, "it became increasingly obvious to MJ-12 that things were not going as planned." While the organization had "subtly promoted *Close Encounters of the Third Kind* and *E.T.* to get the public used to 'odd-looking' aliens that were compassionate, benevolent, and very much our 'space brothers'. . . . quite the opposite was true."

In 1979, a group of people investigating the situation were supposedly trapped inside a joint CIA-alien underground complex at Dulce, New Mexico. A special armed-forces unit was dispatched in a rescue attempt, resulting in the deaths of sixty-six soldiers. In the wake of these catastrophes, the modern-day members of MJ-12 (including the insidious likes of former Secretary of State Henry Kissinger, former CIA director Richard Helms, and former head of Naval Intelligence and the National Security Agency Bobby Ray Inman), meeting at "the 'Country Club,' a remote lodge with private golf course, comfortable sleeping and working quarters, and its own private airstrip," began arguing about how to salvage the situation. One faction thought that the government should simply come clean with the public about its misjudgment of the predatory (and heretofore unannounced) aliens, but the majority wisely believed that such a revelation would create mass panic. Instead, they undertook to develop a weapon to fight the EBEs—a program that was proceeding under the smokescreen of the Strategic Defense Initiative, which had nothing whatsoever to do with its advertised aim of intercepting Russian missiles. As a matter of fact, Lear divulged, in a desperate push to save humanity from the aliens, at that very moment "Dr. Edward Teller [was] in the test tunnels of the Nevada Test site, driving his workers and associates, in the words of one, 'like a man possessed.'

"And well he should," Lear revealed, "for Dr. Teller is a member of MJ-12."

By the time Gene Huff introduced Bob Lazar to John Lear in 1988, Lazar had already dismissed Lear as a complete crackpot. A year earlier, Jim Tagliani, a friend of Bob's from his days at Fairchild, had invited Lazar along to hear "a guy named John Lear speaking about aliens and the government" at the Spring Valley Library in Las Vegas. Lazar had called Tagliani "a blithering idiot" for wasting his time on such garbage, though Tagliani later returned to report that the place had been packed.

By the time he met Lear, Lazar was growing bored with his film-processing business. Thinking that he might try to resume his scientific career, he sent résumés to government labs. Just for the hell of it, he sent an extra one to Edward Teller with a note reminding him of their meeting six years earlier.

One day soon thereafter, Lazar's telephone rang. When he picked it up, there on the other end was Dr. Strangelove himself. Teller told Lazar that he now functioned primarily as a consultant, but gave him a number to contact in Las Vegas. When Bob followed up,* he was invited for an interview at the EG&G administrative building at McCarran Airport.

Edgerton, Germeshausen and Grier employs more than thirty thousand people around the world, providing management and research support for the likes of NASA and the U.S. Departments of Energy and

---

* In another version of the story, Lazar has said that about ten minutes after his talk with Teller, the third party contacted *him*.

Defense. Much of its technical work is carried out at the Test Site and Nellis Air Force Range, where its Special Projects Division deals with "programs of a sensitive nature." The people who interviewed Lazar did not work for EG&G, however.

The first question Bob was asked was: "What is your relationship with John Lear?" Deducing that this was a sensitive matter, Lazar answered that Lear was merely an acquaintance, and, moreover, a guy who "sticks his nose into places where it doesn't belong." Apparently satisified, the interviewers dropped the subject, confining the rest of their questions to the types of technical topics with which Lazar was comfortable. Curiously, even though they knew he'd been involved in top-secret weapons research at Los Alamos, the questioners seemed most impressed when Bob told them that he had a particle accelerator in his bedroom.

Lazar thought he'd done well enough in the interview to get whatever job they had to offer. As it turned out, they considered him overqualified but later called him back about an opening for a "senior staff physicist" in a classified research program. From their remarks, Lazar guessed that the work involved some kind of field-propulsion system. When he demonstrated familiarity with concepts in gravitation, they told him that he'd find the work "very interesting." Thus, while his personal background was being checked, his "Q" clearance from Los Alamos was reactivated and he was told to report to the EG&G terminal at the airport, where a man named Dennis Mariani would accompany him to the job site.

Mariani was a medium-built guy in his late thirties, militaristic in attitude and appearance, with blond hair and a close-cropped mustache. As Mariani ushered him aboard one of the Boeing 737 "Janet" flights that ferry workers to Groom Lake, Lazar—who knew about Area 51 from his Las Vegas residency and classified defense work—was excited to infer that he was going to work there. When the plane landed, Mariani took him to an office where he was asked to sign a security oath, a waiver of his right to a trial if he violated his pledge, and consent to have his telephone tapped and home and car searched without warning. This was considerably more than had been required of him at Los Alamos, but Bob was sufficiently intrigued with the situation to agree to the unusual demands. Only when he and Mariani went back outside, boarded a bus with blacked-out windows, and began driving away from the base on a dirt road, did it dawn on him that maybe he wasn't going to work at Area 51 after all.

They rode south through the desert for about half an hour, passing through a range of mountains and eventually coming to a stop on another dry lakebed. When they got off the bus, Lazar saw a series of hangars built into the slope at the edge of the playa, angled at about thirty degrees and camouflaged to resemble the mountainside. He and Mariani were met by a security guard and escorted through a hangar, where Bob noticed a lustrous disc about thirty-five feet in diameter.* Taken aback by the sight, his mind reeled through a rapid-fire series of suppositions. This explains all the UFO stuff, he thought; we built them and have been testing them here; it's some sort of super-secret weapon. As he passed by the object, he ran his hand along its edge and felt that it was made of metal. Glancing inside, he noticed that the seats were very small. The guard told him to keep moving with his eyes forward.

Inside the subterranean building, Bob was administered a kind of medical exam: A grid was placed on his arm and his skin was pricked with chemicals to determine any allergies. Several blood samples were taken, and he was told to drink a cup of liquid that smelled like pine—which, under the circumstances, he assumed was an anti-allergenic. He was also issued a security badge bearing his photograph, the words "U.S. Department of Naval Intelligence," a Department of Energy contract number (E-6722MAJ), a magnetic strip, and a number of project area codes including "D5," "ETL," and "WX," with a star punched through the one that said "S4." The magnetic strip was needed to open doors throughout the facility. Bob noticed that security personnel in the place seemed to outnumber civilians by about three to one; some of the guards were dressed in desert camouflage, but most wore dark blue uniforms.

After the preliminaries, Mariani took Lazar into a closed briefing room and gave him a file containing more than a hundred blue-covered folders. Explaining that the purpose of the documents was to "bring him up to speed," Dennis left Bob alone to study the material. When Mariani shut the door behind him, however, Lazar noticed that it bore a peculiar poster. Pictured in the air above a dry lake was a disc like the one he'd seen in the hangar. Below it were the words: *They're here.*

In the first folder Bob found, to his unfolding astonishment, eight-by-ten glossy photographs of nine flying saucers. One looked like the object in the hangar and poster; the others differed in shape from one to the next.

---

* Contradictions also exist here with some of Lazar's other recollections. He now says that the diameter of the disc was not thirty-five but fifty-two feet, and in some interviews he has said that he didn't see the craft until a later visit.

There were also photos from an alleged autopsy that had been performed on one of the crafts' original operators, sarcastically called "the Kids." Lazar would later describe the figure as a "typical" gray alien: short and hairless with a large head, small nose and mouth, and big, dark, almond-shaped eyes. A single organ, apparently capable of performing several bodily functions, was exposed within the carcass.

The reports revealed that both the Kids and the discs had come from the Zeta Reticuli star system, which can be seen from Earth's southern hemisphere. Zeta Reticuli is binary, meaning that it contains two suns; the visitors reportedly hailed from the fourth planet out from the second sun—i.e., "Zeta Two Reticulum Four," where a day is ninety hours long. Since this system is located more than thirty-seven light-years from Earth, the question had naturally arisen as to how the craft could cover such distances, a topic that was being researched at S-4 under the heading of Project Galileo. Two other secret programs were also being carried out on the premises: Project Sidekick, involving a beam weapon with a neutron source focused by a gravity lens, and Project Looking Glass, concerned with the physics of seeing backward in time.

Reportedly, the Kids had cooperated with this research until 1979, at which point there was a fatal altercation. A military guard ignored an EBE order not to bring live ammunition into an area where a field was being generated, and as a consequence, a number of humans died with head wounds. (None of the aliens was killed.) More recently, in 1987, another accident had apparently resulted in Lazar's hiring. Trying to determine how a disc's propulsion system operated, some Galileo scientists cut into a reactor at the Test Site and the device exploded, killing the researchers and creating the vacancy that Lazar was selected to fill. Lazar's task at S-4 was to be part of a "back-engineering" team—taking apart the propulsion system to figure out how it worked.

Among the briefing documents that Lazar looked at was a curious volume that on one side appeared to tell the history of Earth (referred to therein as "Sol Three") and on the other dispensed information about Reticulum Four. It reminded Bob of anatomy books that contain a series of transparent pages, each exhibiting a different life system—bones, blood vessels, organs, etc. According to this chronicle, some sixty-five genetic alterations had been performed on *Homo sapiens* in the course of human evolution, with some supposedly taking place more than ten thousand years in the past. In the course of modern human history, three spiritual leaders, including Jesus Christ, had been artificially created by alien engineers. Oddly, any reference to people in the pages was replaced by the term "containers," though the book never explained exactly what human beings contained.

Lazar hardly knew how to react to the material in the folders. Previous to this exposure, he had considered the whole idea of flying saucers to be bunk; he placed instinctive trust only in "hardware"—things that he could see and touch. When he went home that night, however, he could hardly sleep.

While his clearance was being updated, Lazar kept going back to S-4 (which turned out to be situated at Papoose Lake, fifteen miles south of Groom) on an intermittent basis. During the day, he continued operating his photo business; if summoned for duty at night, he'd go to the airport at 5:00 P.M. and take a Janet flight to Area 51, returning to Vegas around midnight. Operating in this fashion over a period of five months, Lazar saw and touched enough hardware to change his mind about flying saucers— and ultimately (despite the secrecy he'd sworn himself to) make him a folk hero among the UFO cultists he despised. This latter trick was achieved through a series of appearances on television and radio, and the 1991 release of *The Lazar Tape and Excerpts from the Government Bible*, a commercial video whose contents rival *Star Trek* for attention to fantastic scientific detail, to say nothing of its implications for traditional religious thought.

As he explains on the tape, Lazar eventually learned that the discs at S-4 propelled themselves via energy generated by a mineral that doesn't occur naturally on Earth. He labels this element "115," referring to the atomic number (of protons) that it would occupy on our periodic chart, which currently extends only as far as 112. Describing the substance as soft and heavy and burnt-orange in color, Lazar says that its power resides in the fact that it generates gravity waves beyond the perimeter of its atom, where the energy can be accessed and amplified to distort space and time. We on Earth have already witnessed space/time distortion in sending atomic clocks to high altitudes, or in looking at stars that should be blocked from our view by the Sun—phenomena that occur because of changes in gravitational fields acting upon the observed objects.

Declaring the theory of gravitons (subatomic particles exerting the force that we call gravity) "total nonsense," Lazar says that gravity actually breaks down into two types of (electromagnetic) waves, unsurprisingly labeled *A* and *B*. The latter constitutes "big gravity"—the kind that holds the Earth to the Sun, and the moon and satellites and ourselves to the Earth. By contrast, Gravity *A*, although much stronger than *B*, operates on a much smaller scale. Referred to in mainstream physics as the "strong nuclear force," it holds protons and neutrons together.

Lazar argues that the character of matter found in any solar system reflects the conditions that applied during the creation of that system. Since most solar systems in the Milky Way have more and/or larger suns than ours, it stands to reason that their elements have more mass and energy. Hence, the binary Zeta Reticuli system contains heavier elements—for example, 115—than those found on Earth. As elements become heavier, he says, they exert gravity *A* waves so intense that the atoms possess their own force fields. The harnessing of this power is the key to interstellar travel.

The saucer that Lazar worked on at S-4 boasted three gravity amplifiers and a reactor. The latter, which was about the size of a basketball, contained a small particle accelerator, in which a chunk of 115 was bombarded with protons. When a new proton plugs into the nucleus, it becomes an atom of Element *116*, which decays instantly; in doing so, it radiates antimatter, which in colliding with gaseous matter in the reactor detonates an annihilation reaction 100 percent effective in converting mass to energy (and thus far more powerful than either fission or fusion, the nuclear reactions that take place in atomic and hydrogen bombs). Amplified by this awesome force, which is converted into electric current by a (similarly 100 percent efficient) thermoelectric generator, the Gravity *A* wave is channeled through a guide and focused on some distant point where the operator wants to go. The resulting gravitational field is strong enough to warp space and time between the two points, effectively pulling the destination to the craft without any passage of time. Analogously, if we view space as a rubber sheet, we can bring points closer together simply by stretching and/or pinching the surface.

For such travel, the craft turns on its side with all three gravity amplifiers employed in the so-called "Delta" configuration. When the disc enters the external gravitational field of some planet or other large body, only one amplifier is activated and the Gravity *A* wave is phase-shifted into the *B* type exerted by the Earth. This is called "Omicron" mode, in which the craft floats on a gravitational field like a cork and can thus be affected by local weather. In this configuration, the idle amplifiers could conceivably be used to pick up people or cattle or anything else that UFO stories describe being picked up (though Lazar says that, in the model he worked on, there was no bay door on the bottom to receive any such cargo). Because of its sleek appearance, he nicknamed this craft the "Sport Model"; other shapes in the fleet included the "Top Hat" and the "Jell-O Mold." Of the nine discs at S-4, Lazar says, about half were functional. One had a hole in the fuselage that looked like it might have been made by a bullet.

At least once, Lazar was able to watch the Sport Model hovering in Omicron mode above Papoose Lake. As he later described it to TV reporter George Knapp:

> It was just about dusk. I came out of the door that was outside the hangar, which led to a hallway . . . and the disc was already outside. Whether they carted it out or flew it out, I don't know. It was sitting on the ground. Right off to the side there was a guy with a scanner. The first thing I was told was to stand by him and not go anywhere else. . . . The disc sat out there for a period of time, then the bottom of it glowed blue and it began to hiss, like high voltage does on a round sphere. It's my impression that the reason they're round and have no sharp edges is to contain the voltage. . . . It lifted off the ground, quietly, except for that little hiss in the background, and that stopped as soon as it reached about twenty or thirty feet. It shifted over to the left, shifted over to the right, and set back down. I mean, it doesn't sound like much, but it was incredibly impressive, just—mind-boggling. It's just magic!

The reference to "no sharp edges" is consistent with Lazar's claim that the entire craft seemed to be cast out of one piece of material, as if it were injection-molded or made of wax and melted down. Even the junctions of the walls, floors, and ceilings were rounded, as were the edges of every object or device in the vehicle. There were no nuts, no bolts, no wires, no lights, and no physical connections between different parts of the propulsion system, which worked like a Tesla coil, with a transmitter and receiver.

The amplifiers were located on the lowest of the craft's three levels, which Lazar was allowed to inspect only once. As he told Michael Lindemann and Ralph Steiner:

> The panel was taken off, and I kind of squeezed down there. It's such a small hole, obviously it wasn't made for a human to go poking around down there. But once you wedge in there, you're isolated and sealed off. It's kind of claustrophobic in there. That in itself was an ominous experience, because you can see . . . I can't even describe it . . . the amplifiers hanging down, and it just looks powerful and awesome.

Lazar never got to see the saucer's uppermost chamber, but surmised that it was a navigation cockpit. He did get a quick look at the main (middle) level, whose pewter-colored interior had sloped archways "similar to Spanish-style architecture" and a column that rose straight up from the reactor through the middle of the craft. This was a wave guide, surrounded by three "consoles" or amplifier heads, each of which was accompanied by a Kid-sized chair. Lazar says that when the disc was energized, one of the archways became transparent except for a mysterious "form of writing unlike any alphabetic, scientific, or mathematical symbols" he had ever seen. Moreover, when the amplifiers were running at full power, the saucer itself was invisible from underneath. Such distortion apparently explained why UFOs are often said to disappear, or to make ninety-degree turns while traveling at speeds of several thousand miles per hour.

Lazar says that, at the point when he went to work at Papoose Lake, little progress had been made in back-engineering the propulsion system. He believes this was partly due to the caliber of the program's scientists, whose lackluster credentials he attributed to the prohibitive security demands. Of twenty-two researchers at S-4, none (including him) could be called top-notch; since Bob himself was not an expert in any of the fields they were researching, he was frankly mystified as to why he'd been hired, unless it was due to the Teller connection or to the fact that the program needed fresh ideas. Historically, Lazar says, he has distinguished himself in scientific jobs by coming at problems from "out of left field," or radically new directions. In fact, he says, he was the person who identified Element 115 as the power source for the propulsion system. Before he arrived, not much attention had been paid to this question; the focus was on duplicating the hardware and, he suspects, employing the technology in some kind of superbomb. Though his badge and paycheck made reference to the Department of Naval Intelligence, Lazar heard that S-4 funding came from the Strategic Defense Initiative. He doubted that even NASA knew what was going on there.

The apparent fact that the research was military-controlled and weapons-related was the major reason, Lazar believes, for the oppressive level of secrecy and security. Bob was allowed to speak to no one at work except for his supervisor Dennis and a work partner named Barry; he was required to have a guard escort him wherever he went, even to the bathroom. Sometimes, immediately after he talked on the telephone to his friend Jim Tagliani—who during this period went to work in the stealth fighter program on the Tonopah Test Range—security agents would appear at Lazar's house with a transcript of the conversation, demanding a detailed explanation of its contents. As time went on, this sort of thing, along with the fact that so little progress was being made on a matter of such historic and scientific magnitude, cramped Bob's style.

"It's just unfair not to put it in the hands of the overall scientific community," Lazar later said. "There are people that are much more capable of dealing with this information, and by this time would have gotten a lot further along than this select small group of people working out in the middle of the desert. They don't even have the facilities, really, to completely analyze what they're dealing with. . . .

"I did not believe that this should be a security matter," Lazar said. "Just the concept that there's definite proof and we even have articles from another world, another system . . . you can't just *not tell everyone*."

Around this time, KLAS-TV in Las Vegas was airing a documentary series about UFOs hosted by George Knapp. Huff and Tagliani were constantly talking about it while Bob kept dutifully mum. One day, as Huff and Lazar were going down Alta Drive in Gene's car, with Huff rambling on about the likelihood of flying saucers, Lazar decided that he was tired of holding everything back. Point-blank, he told his (suddenly speechless) appraiser that he'd been back-engineering alien discs near Area 51.

With this disclosure, Bob and Gene became permanent confidants. Since they couldn't discuss anything on the telephone, the two exchanged information only in person, even going so far as to make up code names for themselves. Since the Central and Mutual UFO Network organizations were abbreviated "CUFON" and "MUFON," Lazar and Huff began calling each other "Gufon" and "Bufon." Huff, for his part, started reading everything he could find about flying saucers.

One evening in March 1989, after he'd had time to do some homework, Gene dropped by Bob's house after work. The problem with all the most important UFO sightings, Gene lamented, was that they'd taken place in the past. If these things were real, why shouldn't we still be seeing them? Bob, who until that moment had seemed preoccupied, looking up at the sky, suddenly leveled his gaze at Gene and asked him what he was doing next Wednesday night. That, he said, was when the discs at S-4 were flight-tested. If the two of them drove up 375 toward Rachel that evening, they might be able to see one from outside the base.

Sure enough, just after dusk on March 22, from a vantage point along Groom Lake Road, Huff and Lazar watched a bright light rise from behind the mountains, maneuver up, down, back, and forth, stop, hover, and disappear. The following week, they came back with Tracy and Tagliani; this time, after the light came up and moved around for a few minutes, it sped down Tikaboo Valley toward them in a rapid-fire series of jumps. Huff (who's afraid of flying in airplanes) found this quite alarming, especially since the object was glowing more brightly than anything he'd ever seen. At one point he feared that the object was going to explode, though Lazar explained that it all had to do with the way the disc was energized and distorted space and time. In the end, the sighting constituted the thrill of Gene's lifetime.

The following week, they returned for what was now becoming a Wednesday-night ritual. This time they brought along Tracy's sister Kristen, in addition to none other than John Lear, who'd gotten wind of what they were doing and owned an arsenal of optics to boot. While the group was waiting for dusk to descend at the turnoff for Groom Lake Road, they noticed more security vehicles than usual patrolling the distant desert. When it got dark, the interlopers drove in with their headlights off, but as soon as the driver (presumably Lear) touched the brakes, the car was spotted. As one of the security vehicles started coming in their direction, the group turned around and, according to Lazar, "really hauled ass" back toward the highway. Then they saw another set of headlights blocking the road ahead.

Figuring they were trapped, Lazar got out and ran into the sagebrush to hide. Lear began feverishly setting up his telescope; when the guards got out of their vehicle and approached, John told them that he and his friends were out "looking at Jupiter." Saying that they'd prefer it if the group went back to the highway, the guards wrote them out a warning, got back in their vehicle and departed—though unbeknownst to Lazar's crew, they stopped a few hundred yards up the road, where they continued to monitor the group's movements through nightscopes.

Lazar emerged from the desert and the band drove back to the highway, where they spent some time cursorily watching the western horizon. (As it turned out, their incursion aborted the scheduled test.) Almost as soon as they decided to call it a night and return to Vegas, however, a Lincoln County sheriff's squad car pulled up alongside. Apparently alerted to their presence by the guards, the deputy asked to see everyone's ID.

Lear's wallet was in the trunk. When he obligingly popped open the compartment, the cop saw his video camera, telescope, and Geiger counter. Moreover, where the guards had initially reported that the group contained four people, the deputy now counted five. He therefore detained them for some time, radioing data from their IDs to the security guard post. After almost an hour had passed (the maximum time that was allowed in lieu of an arrest) he let them go.

As it happened, Bob was scheduled to work at S-4 the next day. When he arrived at the airport, however, Dennis Mariani told him that they wouldn't be flying to Groom Lake after all. Instead, they drove up Highway 95 to Indian Springs Auxiliary Air Force Base south of the Nevada Test Site. When they arrived, a man with an FBI badge was waiting, along with the security guards from the previous night. Point by point, a guy in an apparent position of authority went over the security agreement that Lazar had signed. He concluded that, based on Bob's membership in the previous night's reconnaissance, he could now be jailed for espionage. Figuring there was no use in denying that he'd been there, Lazar answered that he and his friends had merely been stargazing on public land—to which the man responded that a judge would sooner believe government employees than Bob and his sleazeball friends from Vegas. He asked sarcastically if Bob thought that "top secret" meant to bring his pals out to see what was going on.

Unappreciative of the line of questioning, Lazar—who has never

exhibited an overdeveloped respect for authority—casually asked the man
if he was referring to "the flying saucers." At that, the eyes of the security
guards widened, indicating to Bob that they weren't aware of what they'd
been guarding. The FBI agent ushered the guards out of the room, where-
upon the pressure guy went at Lazar with even more gusto, positioning his
face a few inches from Bob's and even holding a gun to his head, shouting
that he had the power to kill him right then and there for disclosing classified information. Under his defenseless circumstances, Bob broke into one
of his ironic grins; this seemed to exasperate the strong-arm man, who,
casting about for another threat, suggested that they could also do a number on Bob's wife. In closing, he told Bob that if he didn't mind his p's and
q's, he'd end up in a loony bin or six feet under the desert topsoil.

Lazar says that even after this turn of events, he wasn't fired from his
job at S-4. Instead, his supervisors denied his final security clearance,
telling him that he could reapply in six to nine months.° He says he was
actually called back to work at Papoose Lake one more time, but fearing
for his safety, he declined to go. He was asked if he was officially refusing,
to which he responded, "Yes."

One day shortly thereafter, Bob was at John Lear's house when George
Knapp called. Apparently tipped off about Lazar by Lear, Knapp asked if
Bob would appear on camera for his TV series *UFOs: The Best Evidence*.
At first Bob demurred, but Knapp—excited, to say the least, by the idea of
getting someone with direct experience to confirm longstanding UFO
rumors about Area 51—kept calling back until Bob agreed to appear
unidentified in silhouette. A few days before the show aired, Bob was
house-sitting for a friend in Vegas when his friend Jim Tagliani was pulled
out of work at Tonopah; among other questions about Lazar, Tagliani was
asked if he knew how to get in touch with Bob so that he might be given
some "help."

Knapp's interview with "Dennis" (Bob's inside joke on his S-4 supervisor) was broadcast in May 1989. Shortly thereafter, it would also be televised in Europe and Japan. As soon as the Las Vegas broadcast ended,
Lazar's telephone rang. On the other end was Mariani, asking Bob if he

---

° In some interviews, Lazar has said that his security clearance was *not* withdrawn.

had any idea what they were going to do to him now. Shortly afterward, Lazar found out: As he was turning onto Interstate 15 from Charleston Boulevard in Las Vegas, a white car pulled up alongside him. Its window came down, a pistol poked out, and a bullet went through Lazar's rear-wheel, severing the brake line and blowing out the tire. Bob aborted his turn onto the freeway, careening onto a gravel shoulder in a cloud of dust. The other car sped up the onramp and disappeared.

After this incident, Lazar decided to go on the air with Knapp again, this time as himself so that if anything happened to him, everyone watching would know why. Assuming that his overseers were listening in, he and Huff began telephoning friends and circulating Bob's story, intimating that they'd notified others through the mail. In December Lazar also appeared on a Las Vegas radio show, during which he informed the southwestern United States and southern California that Wednesday nights were the best time to view flying saucers from Nevada Highway 375. With these appearances, Bob immediately became a cynosure in the UFO cosmos, and Area 51 catapulted to notoriety among legions of people who had never before heard of the place.

Lazar and Huff later surmised that Mariani may have paid for such a spillage of beans. After the excrement interfaced with the wind machine, Dennis called to tell Bob that he'd like to meet with him "on a personal level." Lazar took Huff and Joe Vaninetti, a friend who was visiting from Los Alamos, with him to the Union Plaza casino in downtown Las Vegas at eight o'clock on a Saturday night, ensuring a crowd of onlookers for the engagement. Lazar went into the building first; Huff and Vaninetti entered a few minutes later, then sat down to play slot machines while keeping an eye on Lazar.

At first Mariani was nowhere to be found. Eventually Bob saw him coming through the crowd, but as he approached, Dennis walked right past him without even acknowledging his presence. Just then, against a far wall, Lazar caught sight of another security agent he recognized from S-4. Bob strolled back past his two friends and, without looking directly at either one, whispered what was going on.

Separately, Lazar and Huff went into a different part of the casino, where they now saw Mariani sitting at a blackjack table. According to Huff, Dennis was smoking "a slender cigar" and oddly declining to glance up from his cards at either of "two very attractive, very buxom women" flanking him at the table, though he did sneak a look at Lazar as Bob walked along the bar nearby. Finally, from behind a bank of slot machines, Huff watched Lazar march up and confront Mariani at the table.

"Well, Dennis," Bob said. "You said you wanted to meet me. Here I am."

Mariani didn't look up.

"What the hell is going on, Dennis?" Lazar demanded, but Mariani just kept staring down at his cards.

Lazar went back to Huff and suggested that, when Mariani got up to leave, Gene or Joe should follow him and get his license plate number. They conferred for only a few seconds, but when Lazar returned to the blackjack table, Mariani was gone. Bob, Gene, and Joe proceeded to comb the casino for him, including the rest rooms, but Mariani had disappeared—apparently for good.

As Huff would later put it, "We could only surmise that maybe Mariani was there to speak on a personal level [that was what he'd said] and that the other security guy that Bob had spotted was a surprise to everyone, including Dennis. No one has seen or heard anything from Dennis Mariani since that night."

The body of Bob Lazar's story fit with various arms of flying-saucer folklore. Lazar himself observed that the so-called Sport Model resembled an airborne disc photographed by Swiss UFO witness Billy Meier. Zeta Reticuli had been identified as the origin of alien visitors by abductees Betty and Barney Hill and ufologist Bill Moore, who in 1983 had received a set of "secret" documents explaining, among other things, that the U.S. government had recovered several extraterrestrial aircraft, that at least one EBE had been kept in custody at a base in New Mexico, and that an effort to study and test-fly alien discs was proceeding in Nevada. In 1988, Moore and his fellow ufologist Jaime Shandera had interviewed a pair of undercover "informants" (code-named Falcon and Condor) who had gone into considerable detail about the covert research program (which they said was so compartmentalized that other government agencies were unaware of it) and the alien visitors (who reportedly had few internal organs, each performing multiple body functions). Falcon maintained that a history of the whole episode was locked up at CIA headquarters in Langley, Virginia, and referred to by insiders as "the Bible." An ex-counterintelligence officer from the Air Force Office of Special Investigations named Richard C. Doty (suspected of being Falcon) had shown a purported presidential briefing paper to filmmaker Linda Howe, reiterating many of the above allegations and adding that several "DNA manipulations" had been performed on *Homo sapiens*, including the creation of a nonviolent spiritual leader two thousand years ago. Then, of course, there was John Lear with his rousing tales of underground bases, Edward Teller, and the SDI smokescreen. The question, for anyone who cared or wondered if Lazar's story might be true, was whether the congruency between it and other accounts was attributable to their collective authenticity, or merely to a careful scenarist's incorporation of existing material into a fresher and more audacious framework.

Of course, the first issue to be raised about any such incredible claims is the credibility of the claimant himself. When George Knapp checked out Bob's background for the TV special, he came up rather short. Though Lazar said he had degrees from MIT and CalTech, both universities denied any record of his attendance. The same thing was initially true of Los Alamos National Laboratory, where Bob claimed he'd worked in 1982.

"They're trying to make me a nonperson," Lazar immediately countered, divulging that even he was now unable to obtain his own birth certificate from the hospital where he'd been born. He did produce a 1982 telephone book listing him among LANL employees, and he provided Knapp with the names of some LANL coworkers who confirmed that Lazar had been there. The laboratory administration continued to deny it, however, until Knapp learned that Bob had actually been paid by a subcontractor called Kirk-Mayer—which, in accepting the baton for the runaround, said that Lazar's alleged period of employment preceded the year to which the company kept back records. Knapp ultimately enlisted the help of Nevada Congressman Jim Bilbray, whose office (according to Knapp) "stated that this was one of the strangest cases their office had ever dealt with, and that all of the agencies it had contacted for Lazar's records had stalled every step of the way."

Lazar did have a nice piece of "evidence" in the form of a W-2 from the Department of Naval Intelligence. Blank W-2 forms, however, are easy to obtain—and what's more, no such department officially exists within the U.S. Navy. Inquiries about Robert S. Lazar directed to the *Office* of Naval Intelligence (ONI) and *Department* of the Navy extracted the usual absence of information, though a ufologist named Bob Oechsler, a former

NASA mission analyst, learned that the zip code on Lazar's W-2 did correspond to one used by an ONI station in Maryland. Oechsler also found that the first two digits in the form's employer ID number (46) were affiliated with a South Dakota division of the Internal Revenue Service, though information about the rest of the number (1007639) was confidential. Meanwhile, the Office of Management and Budget (OMB) number on the form (E-6722) was confirmed by a Department of Energy official as consistent with the 6700 series of contract numbers managed out of Albuquerque, New Mexico. (Not surprisingly, the affiliation of the "point of contact" designation—MAJ—was unidentified.) The Social Security Administration Office in Baltimore showed no entries in Lazar's account since 1983, when he says he left his job at Los Alamos; an attempt to track the name of his last employer there (presumably Kirk-Mayer) met with the prohibitive message "SECURITY VIOLATION"—apparently corroborating Lazar's claim that he'd been involved in classified work.

When Knapp proposed that he submit to a series of lie-detector tests, Bob readily agreed, but the results were inconclusive. Two examiners found he was telling the truth; another thought he was lying; a fourth suspected that he was parroting information passed along by someone else. Lazar says he thinks that part of his memory was erased by drugs and hypnosis at S-4—and in an effort to re-create it, he consulted a licensed hypno-therapist, who determined that his subconscious mind believed everything he was saying. Knapp also arranged a meeting between Lazar and an electrical engineer who had worked at Area 51 during the 1970s; the man quizzed Bob on questions like, "What does the cafeteria look like?" and "How do employees pay for their meals?" Lazar reportedly passed the exam with flying colors.

Bob also remembered a security agent named Mike Thigpen who came to the house to investigate Bob's background for his clearance. Sure enough, Knapp said he found an operative under that name at Las Vegas's (unlisted) Office of Federal Investigations, which conducts background checks on people who work at the Test Site and Nellis Range. Thigpen told Knapp that he didn't remember anybody named Bob Lazar, though he surmised that he might have consulted Bob about his friend Jim Tagliani, who was employed in the stealth fighter program at the Tonopah Test Range.

When Lazar appeared on the radio, a phone-in caller who said he worked for the Reynolds Electrical and Engineering Company (of EG&G)

claimed he had helped build the hangars at Papoose Lake. He told Lazar that his coworkers were "meeting in small groups and . . . trying to organize support for you to back you up." He said that two people were planning to come forward but others were "scared to death." No such workers ever materialized, though as time went on, others appeared to elaborate on Lazar's S-4 scenario. Retired Air Force Colonel (and ufologist) Wendelle Stevens—the person who'd collected the story that one visitor to Area 51 was required to put a bag over his head and threatened with death if he dared to look up—videotaped a gaunt and nervous young man supposedly named Derek Hennesy, who claimed to have worked as a security guard at S-4. Hennesy said the facility was divided into four levels, one of which housed alien corpses in large, liquid-filled cylinders. "Their eyes are shrivelled like prunes," Hennesy recalled. "Otherwise, they look like typical Grays."

Over time, George Knapp compiled a long list of reputedly more reliable witnesses, none of whom would agree to appear on camera, since many said they'd been threatened for talking to him in the first place. They allegedly included

- a security guard who said he'd seen Lazar at Area 51;
- an engineer who inadvertently walked into a hangar at Area 51 and saw a disc concealed under a tarp;
- a golf pro taken into confidence by an Air Force colonel who told him that hardware from the Roswell crash was stored at Area 51;
- a tax preparer who handled returns for some Area 51 employees, who told him "in no uncertain terms" that recovered alien discs were housed there;
- a flight engineer who told an elected official of Knapp's acquaintance that he had seen not only alien craft but alien bodies at Area 51;
- a former worker for defense contractor Holmes and Narver, who sat in on "meetings between high-level executives and military personnel" while they discussed recovered alien discs (which the witness said were controlled not by the military but by a private company);
- a former Test Site photographer who had seen metallic discs in the air above Area 51, and was told by a German physicist named Otto Krause that researchers there were trying to duplicate the

propulsion system of an alien craft recovered from a crash in New Mexico;

- an EG&G electrical engineer named Doug Schroeder, who before dying "mysteriously" of a heart attack told Las Vegas TV producer Bob Patrick that he'd photographed tests of alien discs, which he said had come to Area 51 from "a base in Ohio";

- a "prominent biologist" named Dan Crain, reportedly well-known in southern Nevada, who told Knapp that he had documents proving he'd worked with alien tissue samples, but subsequently dropped out of sight and was later said to be working as a security guard for a Las Vegas hotel;

- a man named John Harbour, who told an acquaintance of Knapp's that he had worked as an Air Force security officer at Area 51 in the late 1980s, and that the alien presence was being concealed because it would throw our institutions into upheaval and people might quit paying their taxes;

- an investigative reporter and lawyer named Andrew Basiago, who wrote a story for *MUFON Journal* about a former CIA operative named Marion Leo Williams, who before dying of cancer told his family that he had helped Lockheed provide parts and supplies "to a supersecret laboratory in Nevada dedicated to exploiting the technologies of crashed UFOs and studying the biologies of their occupants," that "American government researchers are busy conducting genetic studies of intact alien corpses recovered from crashed alien spacecraft," and that "design principles deduced from the saucers have been utilized in the stealth bomber";

- Knapp's apparent favorite, a "member of a prominent Nevada family [with] a proven, documentable work record including high-level contacts with top-secret military research dating back to the early fifties." This man, who wasn't prepared to go public but promised to provide Knapp with a videotape to be released after his death, said that "he was directly involved with the alien technology program even before Area 51 was built"; that "the U.S. has stored alien technology in Nevada since the early fifties"; that "private contractors, paid in cash, handle the program for the military"; that "they didn't know what the alien discs were made of and had little success in trying to fly the craft well into the

1960s"; and intimated that "a live alien had been in the custody of the government for a number of years, confined near Area 51."

Lazar himself had a story along those lines. He said that one night, while being escorted down a hallway at S-4, he'd glanced through a window into a hangar and seen a pair of men talking to a small figure. At first Bob thought it was a child, but then he noticed that it had rather long arms. Predictably, he was immediately told by a guard to keep moving, but came away with the impression that he'd glimpsed an EBE.

Lazar later downplayed the incident, theorizing that he might have seen a mannequin fashioned to fit into the spacecraft, or maybe even a doll designed to test the reactions of passersby. Huff, however, says that at the time, Lazar was so sure of what he'd seen that he telephoned Gene as soon as he got home. As it happened, Huff had the flu and didn't answer the phone, but when his answering machine came on, Bob said, "Gufon, this is Bufon. Pick up the phone."

When Huff complied, Lazar told him he wanted to meet him about "those baby pictures." Since the two had no such business between them, Gene recognized this as some kind of code, and told Bob he'd call him right back. When he did—repeatedly—Lazar failed to answer until about the sixth call, at which point he told Huff that he was talking to "some people from work." As Bob would later divulge, a pair of security agents had appeared at his door immediately after the first call, demanding to know the meaning and identity of Gufon.

The final chapter of the Bob Lazar story is perhaps best told by Gene Huff himself.

In his on-line synopsis, Huff says that, "After losing his wife* and the most important job a scientist could ever have, Bob was pretty much a broken man." However, "when he had recovered enough to go out in public" (that is, after going on TV in eight countries on three continents) . . .

. . . he sought comfort with a hooker. Now I don't know how this looks and sounds elsewhere in the world, but in Nevada this is no big deal. Prostitution is legal in the state of Nevada, but illegal in the counties that house Las Vegas, Reno, and Lake Tahoe. However, this is just for show and it's common knowledge that brothels

* Bob and Tracy Lazar were divorced in 1990.

and hookers in the form of escort services exist in these cities also. The police pretend to passively pursue this, but along with gambling, drinking, and entertainment, prostitution is part of the package.

Bob called a number out of the newspaper and happened upon a 40 to 45 year old madam/hooker who ran 2 to 4 girls out of a condominium project in the southeast part of town. This was an upper line condo project so don't envision some dark sleezy [sic] place engulfed in red lights. Bob went there and did his business, but before he left, the hookers were having some problems with a stereo or something like that and, naturally, Bob came to the rescue. He fixed it for them and they invited him back for a freebie.

Well, Bob went back more than once and, in time, all of the girls loved him. Bob has this unique manor [sic] about him in which he treats everyone equally. When you interact with Bob, he never gives you the feeling that he's a scientist and you're not so you're not worthy. He treated the hookers with respect, like friends and equals, and this was a breath of fresh air to them considering the attitudes they get from some people. The madam° explained to Bob that she had an ongoing affair with a member of Las Vegas Metro Vice and that as long as she didn't do outcalls to the hotels, vice would turn their heads and allow her to operate. It is unknown whose interest these cops were protecting in the hotels. The madam also told Bob that she was an FBI, DEA, and Las Vegas Metro informant. Bob felt a sense of security because of all of this and proceeded to tell the madam how he could streamline her operation by installing computers, security cameras, and other electronic equipment. This appealed to her and she financed her brothel's entrance into the computer age. During all of this, something bad happened. The madam fell in love with Bob. She offered him fifty percent of the business to stay around, but once the electronics were installed, he was no longer interested. Since he wasn't really interested in her, it was a drag for him to be around and he detached himself from her and the brothel. To say that she didn't take this very well is an understatement.

So now television sweeps rolled around and George Knapp

°Toni Bulloch by name.

thought it would be a great idea to give his audience an update on what the now famous Bob Lazar had been up to since his exit from the program at S4. KLAS had set ratings records with George's previous UFO special about Bob Lazar and they were interested in doing that again.

When George did the interview Bob said, amongst other things, that he had installed a computer system for a local brothel. That was a bad idea. The fact that Bob had broadcast this on television reflected his naivety [sic] about the ramifications of his actions. The Las Vegas cops now had a problem. Here was a guy stating that he knew where a local brothel was and all they had to do was ask him it's [sic] whereabouts and then bust it. The problem was compounded by the fact that the brothel was run by one of their informants and they were aware of her operation.

The madam's vice buddies explained to her that they had to bust her operation because of Bob's televised admission. After all, the entire vice department didn't know about this, just a couple of vice cops she knew and did business with. They busted the place and she blamed the entire operation on Bob, probably under their advice. She had a client list of some very high level Las Vegans, including cops, and they weren't about to force her to make that public. They let her off with a misdemeanor called, "Keeping a Disorderly House," which is a Nevada statute from the early 1900s. I don't think anybody even knows what that's supposed to mean. They then charge Bob with six felonies.

These cops thought they could just hang this whole thing on Bob and be done with it. They soon found out that Bob Lazar had a large following and hundreds of thousands of people were scrutinizing this story. Naturally, most following Bob's story thought this was a setup by the federal government to discredit him, and they may have been involved, but that is unknown to this day.

Anyway, under some of the most incompetent and questionable legal advice in history, Bob plead [sic] guilty to pandering and they dropped the rest of the charges. We all urged Bob to fight it but he didn't want to spend the money. This is part of his "I can do everything myself" attitude because his dad is a wealthy L.A. businessman and money would have been no problem. Bob simply won't depend on anyone, even those that love him and want to help him.

Prior to sentencing Judge John Lehman questioned how it was possible that a guy with no previous criminal record, like Bob, would have plead [sic] guilty under these circumstances. He also couldn't understand how the madam of the brothel wasn't in front of him as a codefendant. After all, in the madam's original statement to the police she admitted having become a prostitute in 1971 when Bob Lazar was 12 years old. The judge wasn't buying that Bob coerced HER into anything. All of the judges [sic] questions and apprehensions were stated on the record, ON CAMERA, and George Knapp still has a copy of the raw footage.

Bob was sentenced to 3 years probation and community service.* Ironically, he completed his community service by installing yet another computer system, this time for Clark County, Nevada. The guys down at probation would jockey for position to see who got to go visit Bob so they could talk to him and ask him UFO questions. He's now off probation and we're currently investigating the possibilities for a pardon.

The whole thing was one bad dream and somewhat of a joke because there have only been a handful of pandering convictions in the history of Las Vegas and the others weren't scientists with no criminal record.

According to the *Las Vegas Review-Journal*, Lazar "admitted that he had recruited a local known prostitute and encouraged her to solicit customers." Police records maintained that Bob took a 50 percent share of the madam's fees, expressed interest in recruiting other women into the operation, videotaped customers in the waiting room, and maintained records of their license-plate numbers. For reasons that were not disclosed, two apartments used in the brothel were connected by a hole through the wall. Perhaps most pertinently in light of Lazar's "unusual" treatment for a first-time offender, Bob had also tapped into state motor-vehicle records in order to identify undercover cops.

In the eyes of many observers, this fiasco was the end of the line as far as Lazar's credibility was concerned. Sympathetic umpires who'd turned a blind eye to Bob's bankruptcy, jet cars, unconfirmed jobs, and disappearing

---

* The judge also recommended, in light of Lazar's "negligent circumstances," that he consult a psychiatric counselor.

degrees finally felt compelled to cry foul when he admitted to being a pimp. It made some of them look more squarely at the fact that, for all its vaunted consistency, Lazar's story still begged considerable explanation, even when taken on its own terms. For a few examples:

If the S-4 operation was "the most top-secret program in history," why was Lazar allowed into it before his security clearance was finalized?

If secrecy was so important, why would a reference as well-known as "MAJ" appear on the security badges?

Why was Lazar, with only a standard "Q" clearance, allowed to see what he describes as "an *extremely* classified document dealing with religion"?

When Lazar violated his security oath, why wasn't he fired? If he'd signed away his right to trial, why wasn't he jailed?

If Bob was hiding in the desert when security guards questioned his friends on the night that they got caught, what good did it do for Area 51 authorities to summon those guards to Indian Springs to identify him the next day? If the guards had seen Bob through their nightscopes, why did they radio the sheriff's deputy that the party contained only four people?

If Bob decided to go public because of the freeway shooting incident, why didn't he save the shot-out tire?

If he was on "the lowest rung of the ladder" at S-4 in terms of credentials, and only worked there intermittently over a period of five months, why does he refer to himself on his videotape as a "senior staff physicist"?

If, in fact, he worked there so briefly, how did he manage to figure out that Element 115 was the reactor fuel? If his coworkers hadn't grasped that fact before he arrived, how had they gained any knowledge of the workings of the propulsion system?

If the saucer tests were so tentative, with so little known about the craft, how did it perform such sophisticated maneuvers on Wednesday nights?

If alien visitors had at one time been cooperating with the program, why hadn't they shed some light on the technology for us?

If extraterrestrials had engineered the human race with evolutionary "adjustments," why did they even need to consider cooperating with us?

Perhaps predictably, *The Lazar Tape* also leaves a good many scientific questions unanswered. While the basic concept of long-distance travel via space-time distortion is at least theoretically plausible under the principle of general relativity, curvature of space due to gravity would *increase* rather than decrease distance. Bob never explains exactly how gravity A waves are accessed and electrically amplified; why it's true that such waves extend beyond the perimeters of heavy atoms (an effect many orders of magnitude greater than anything that has been observed on Earth about the strong nuclear force); how an accelerator housed inside a basketball-sized reactor succeeds in guiding such ornery and unruly particles as protons toward the nuclei of atoms; where the accelerator obtains the considerable power that would be required to do that, or to maintain a magnetic field to keep antimatter from colliding with the matter in the walls of the "tuned vacuum tube" it's stored in. Lazar says that the annihilation reaction between matter and antimatter releases heat, which is converted into electricity by a thermoelectric generator in the reactor, but most of the energy in an annihilation reaction takes the form of gamma rays. Although such reactions are, as Lazar says, theoretically 100 percent efficient in converting mass to energy, the amount of antimatter released by a decaying atom represents only a tiny fraction of that atom's total mass, bringing about a commensurately small release of energy. Lazar maintains that, in the case of Element 115, the amplified reaction is strong enough to distort space-time over distances of many light-years; if the gravitational field generated by the reactor is that powerful—much stronger than our sun, which distorts space only by a few degrees—then why doesn't it destroy the spacecraft, or even the reactor itself, by pushing or pulling the molecules apart as soon as it's turned on? For that matter (so to speak), why doesn't it pull every object between itself and its destination into the craft? And by the way, isn't it awfully convenient that the same element serves not only as the system's source of fuel (gravity waves) but also as the source of energy (antimatter) needed to amplify the energy of that fuel? Most basically of all, if we apply the pesky formula $E=MC^2$ to the amount of Element 115 (223 grams) that Lazar says the reactor uses in *twenty to thirty years*, it would, if completely converted to energy, provide approximately enough power to run all the households in the United States for about a year and a half. That ain't bad, but it's probably still not quite enough to bend space and time over a distance of two hundred trillion miles (the gap separating Earth and Zeta Two Reticulum Four).

Of course, nearly all of these questions can be answered: *This is a form of technology several centuries beyond anything in our experience. Our knowledge of physics isn't advanced enough to understand what these things are, much less how they work.* Along with the absence of physical evidence attending UFO legends (including the one advanced by Lazar, who says he "obtained" a chunk of Element 115 for home experimentation but claims it was later stolen from his house), that's part of the tautological beauty of flying-saucer folklore. Another is the ongoing dissonance between the high and low views that extraterrestrials must hold of our humble species. Whereas, on the one hand, we appear to be mere dust beneath their technological boot heels, the fact remains that these unimaginably advanced creatures apparently find us so fascinating that they're willing to travel umpteen zillion light-years just to be around us. The discordancy in this attitude harmonizes rather nicely with humankind's love-hate relationship with itself.

As far as questions about alien motivations (or those of his S-4 supervisors) are concerned, Lazar's customary response—in keeping with his hands-on-hardware philosophy—is a candid "I don't know." This *nolo contendere* posture actually serves to enhance his credibility, considering the customary need of the common everyday charlatan to guarantee the logic of every detail in his account, no matter how far-fetched. In his videotape and TV interviews, Lazar displays the charming habit of chuckling over parts of his own story, assuming a kind of Everyman persona that's just as amused by his weird observations as anybody else. Maybe this is the egalitarian quality that Huff and the hookers so admired in him. "I don't expect anyone to believe me," Bob admits with a shrug and a grin, immediately enlisting the benefit of a skeptical listener's doubt.

Well—not every skeptical listener. After investigating Lazar's claims about his educational background, physicist/ufologist Stanton Friedman (author of *Crash at Corona* and *Top Secret Majic*) was unhesitant to label him a fraud. On the other hand, astronomer/computer scientist/ufologist Jacques Vallee, in *Revelations: Alien Contact and Human Deception*, offered the theory that Lazar may have actually worked at the place he described, but that everything he saw there was "pure theater," designed to implant and distribute disinformation.

"Criticisms of Lazar's story are many, and many are deserved," George Knapp would ultimately admit in a MUFON lecture. "There are many gaps, many things that don't make sense. But too much of what he says *does* make sense to merely dismiss it." While Knapp admits that the vanished degrees constitute "the weakest part of Lazar's story," he believes that, since Bob apparently did work at Los Alamos, "it must have meant he went to school somewhere." (As Huff puts it: "You don't know what [Bob] knows by taking one electronics course at Pierce Junior College.") Knapp points out that Lazar not only knew what the Area 51 cafeteria looked like, but also knew that EG&G was the prime contractor, that Boeing 737s shuttled workers to and from Groom Lake, and that an agent named Mike Thigpen conducted background checks for security clearances on the Nellis Range—all of which turned out to be true.

With regard to Lazar's colorful personal history, Knapp ultimately seemed to subscribe to a theory advanced by Bob himself. "Lazar may have been exactly what [the supervisors of the program] were looking for: someone who was technically qualified but who could be discredited if it became necessary," Knapp hypothesized. "Perhaps discrediting him was what they had in mind all along, as a way of discrediting the entire Area 51 story. . . . By picking someone like Bob for their program, by letting him see certain documents even before his clearance had been upgraded, by messing with his mind, they had a perfect built-in safety valve. By discrediting him, you give UFO luminaries an excuse to attack [flying-saucer allegations about Area 51] as well, you give the lunatic fringe something to embrace and embellish, and you almost guarantee that no official in his right mind would get anywhere near this mess to find out what really was going on."

You might not repel another kind of operative, however. In fact, you might very well attract someone who was neither an official nor a lunatic nor, for that matter, gainfully employed (or very grown-up), but was motivated solely by insightful curiosity. As it turned out, this profile didn't describe one personality but many, most of whom were in electronic contact with one another. As the Bob Lazar story had gained currency, so had the Internet—and through this miracle of modern communications, Dreamland aficionados everywhere became not only acquaintances but cooperatives, dedicating their collective wits to the topic of Area 51 and its geo-psycho-sociopolitical environs. Resisting the covert impulse of the Black force that had drawn them, they positioned themselves in the interstices between democracy and secrecy, disinformation and intelligence, public servant and private contractor, fact and fiction, gravity and infinity. Applying a differently directed version of the maverick creativity that characterized their sullied prophet, they loosed themselves upon Las Vegas and its no-longer-so-secret surrounding desert, earning the name that attached itself to their role and strategic mission.

FOUR

The Interceptors

hen Glenn Campbell moved to Rachel in early 1993, he found a place that was spartan even by rural Nevada standards. The mind-boggling emptiness of the Great Basin is stubbornly dotted with tiny communities that, if not exactly deserving of the term *town*, still usually contain at least one fast-food drive-in, a couple of bars, and a motel that says "Motel." By contrast, Rachel, at the bottom of sweeping Sand Springs Valley, had only two commercial establishments: the Quik Pik gas station/convenience store and the Little A-Le-Inn. The community had no post office, no police station, no bank, no brothel (illegal in Lincoln County), no direct TV reception, and no school. It did boast a set of radiation monitoring gauges alongside the Quik Pik, but the town had not existed when the Nevada Test Site was plastering the area with nuclear fallout in the 1950s. Having been unofficially established in 1978 (when it was named for a baby girl delivered by her father, and electric power arrived from Hoover

Dam), Rachel was absent from many Nevada maps. It was sometimes represented by the names of Sand Springs or Tempiute Village, the latter referring to a nearby mine whose silver, tungsten, lead, and mercury had attracted the Union Carbide company in the mid-seventies, along with enough workers to create the town. Almost all of the hundred-odd residents lived in mobile homes, making monthly daylong trips to Las Vegas for supplies. The county seat, the town of Pioche, was an hour-and-a-half drive, one way. Children had ridden the school bus fifty miles southeast to Alamo since 1982, when Rachel's (male) elementary-school teacher failed to return from Christmas vacation, having been previously discovered at home with several young local boys who were dressed in women's clothing. Other than that, local entertainment consisted of shooting, drinking, or listening to sonic booms sounded by jets from Nellis and Groom. Once or twice, planes had even plummeted to earth within the city limits. In 1984, a jet crashed and burned near the Rachel dump, a mile outside of town; when local men arrived at the site, guards disembarking from helicopters told them they had a minute to leave. The Air Force said the plane was an F-16, but a rumor persists to this day that it was a Russian MiG. Two years later, an actual F-16 augured in alongside a Rachel playground and trailer park. People raced to put out the fire while the pilot—a Norwegian officer participating in Red Flag exercises—parachuted to earth. A few minutes later, he came walking down a dirt road from across the highway; when a Rachel resident drove out to pick him up, the pilot raised his hands and cried out: "I didn't mean to!" Later he sent the town some squadron patches, a small Viking ship, and a Christmas card announcing that he was being made safety officer of his home air base. "Concerning the accident, the investigation board couldn't find anything to blame me," he wrote. "I was of course happy to hear that. I was also happy to hear that you doesn't hold a grudge to me." For its part, the U.S. Air Force offered the townspeople no official compensation for the inconvenience caused by the crashes, except for a free tour of Nellis Air Force Base the following year.

Prior to 1990, the Little A-Le-Inn had had a half-dozen different names, including the Oasis, the Watering Hole, and the Stage Stop Saloon. Most of its ten succeeding owners had gone bankrupt. Throughout the twentieth century, Highway 375 had undergone a gradual transition from raw desert to rural dirt route to paved state thoroughfare, but still saw only about fifty cars per twenty-four-hour day. When Union Carbide closed down its mine in 1988, half the population departed and the future seemed about as promising as that of the rotary dial telephone. But as it happened, Ladell and Harold Singer—the owners of what was then called the Rachel Bar and Grill—unexpectedly found a couple of buyers in Joe and Pat Travis, who had migrated to Nevada by way of California and the Midwest. As divorcées, they had been introduced by their own match-making children; Pat, who had come to Las Vegas with her stagehand (for-mer) husband, had been a cook her whole life, while Joe, who had grown up mainly in Michigan "and hated every minute of it," was a carpenter determined to avoid cold weather for the rest of his days.

When Pat noticed that the Rachel Bar and Grill was for sale, she men-tioned the fact to Joe without much hope of inspiring interest. After all, Rachel was three thousand feet higher, and considerably colder, than Las Vegas. When Joe surprised her three days later by agreeing to look into the situation, Pat began to feel that their lives were guided by some special force. Lo and behold, within a year of their purchase of the bar, Bob Lazar appeared like a messiah, summoning UFO believers to Rachel from all over the world. Soon the Travises added five mobile-home motel rooms to the double-wide that housed the bar and eighteen RV hookups in the dirt lot next door. Since the place no longer functioned only as a bar and grill, they also figured that they needed another new name. As circumstances would come to show, the "Little A-Le-Inn" was a public-relations master-stroke.

At first, aside from the name, the atmosphere was not much different from that of any other bar in the Nevada boondocks. Despite his South-ern/Midwestern roots, the tall, bearded, red-faced Joe Travis was a hard-drinking, cowboy-hat-wearing Westerner of the first magnitude. Though most of Lincoln County, located as it was on the Utah border, was Mormon in culture, law, and attitude, Rachel was situated in the far northwestern corner alongside Nye County, where prostitution was still legal and gov-ernment was considered the root of all evil, despite the fact that the county's tax base was overwhelmingly dependent on federal facilities such as the Nevada Test Site and the Tonopah Test Range. In this part of the West, power (as Mao Tse-tung had ironically observed) was still widely believed to issue from the barrel of a gun, the enforced registration of which was tantamount to enslavement. When the Waco Branch Davidian compound was destroyed by federal agents, sentiment at the A-Le-Inn came down squarely on the side of David Koresh, who had (it was believed) merely been exercising his right to bear arms against the Bureau of Alcohol, Tobacco, and Firearms. As far as federal regulation of those substances was concerned, the bar bore some telling bumper stickers:

WE DON'T HAVE A TOWN DRUNK—WE ALL TAKE TURNS.
THANK YOU FOR HOLDING YOUR BREATH WHILE I SMOKE.
YEAH, YOU CAN HAVE MY GUN—BULLETS FIRST.

This was the environment to which Glenn Campbell emigrated from Boston, Massachusetts, in February 1993. He planted his truck camper in the parking lot and ate his meals in the A-Le-Inn, setting up shop at a corner table where he compiled the *Area 51 Viewer's Guide*, in which he described Rachel as "a diverse place welcoming people of all political persuasions as long as they are not Liberal." He further observed that, "At first glance, Rachel may seem like a democratic, classless place, but . . . if you look carefully at the residences here, you can see that Rachel is divided very clearly into the 'Haves' and 'Have-Nots'—that is, people who have satellite dishes and those who have not." Though the A-Le-Inn did possess such a device, Campbell warned that "about the only entertainment station Joe can get with sound is the SciFi Channel. . . . Patrons and staff are treated to a steady diet of space battles, police androids, flesh-sucking aliens and creatures from beyond the grave. This can't be good for the mind." This, then, was "life at the Little A-Le-Inn: No newspapers, radio or TV news, only Scifi and Rush [Limbaugh] on the tube, aliens and flying saucers on the walls and a constant stream of UFO-minded visitors eager to discuss government conspiracies or their latest abduction experience. A few days here and you'll be asking yourself, *What is real?*"

During the day, Campbell continued making forays into the surrounding region, sometimes in the company of Jim Goodall, the garrulous aviation sleuth who was becoming his mentor. One time, the two drove out a back road that led from Rachel to a guard shack for the base. When they reached the gate, they parked their vehicle and walked along the border in full view of the guards. Up and down, up and down they went, over hill and dale, until they reached a gully where they stayed down and hid under a bush. When they failed to surface, a platoon of guards and vehicles fanned out over the desert, trying to figure out where they'd gone. They played the same game again a few months later when, scrambling around a mountainside on public land by the border, they succeeded in evading a Blackhawk helicopter for six hours—convincing Campbell that, among other things, the base's vaunted detection systems weren't all they were cracked up to be. He thus decided that he would walk the entire unrestricted (eastern) border; almost as soon as he did, he discovered Freedom Ridge with its unrestricted view of Groom Lake.

One day in April 1993, while installing a TV antenna on his camper, Glenn saw Goodall pull up in a Toyota Land Cruiser. He was accompanied by Stuart F. Brown, a technology reporter who had procured the vehicle for purposes of "product familiarization." Brown was employed as an editor of *Popular Science*, in whose pages he'd just published an article about the alleged Aurora, including a photograph of Area 51. A witty and voluble New Yorker, he had recently moved from Manhattan to Hollywood, the better to cover stories in what he called "the Fertile Crescent" of modern technology: the far Western United States, from Seattle to San Diego. As part of the package, he'd begun exploring the desert and practicing the arcane science of secret-airplane spotting.

After some direct exposure in the Antelope Valley north of Los Angeles, Brown quickly came to consider UFO believers "weird morons who live in trailers." The fact that Campbell's lodging alongside the "Little A-Le-Inn" answered to this description didn't predispose Stuart to lend Glenn much credence. But in Goodall's company, Brown was surprised to find Campbell "a bright, wry self-starter type, pursuing some sort of quasi-whimsical/quasi-serious line of inquiry out there on the back ass of nowhere. It wasn't entirely different from what I was doing, but he was in it full-time." Despite the fact that Campbell was essentially uninterested in technology, Stu was impressed that Glenn at least sought to understand its place in "the puzzle he was trying to piece together—this odd amalgam of politics, law, and mystery."

One afternoon, the three men drove out Groom Lake Road to camp on Freedom Ridge. Sometime after nightfall, Brown, using a Russian nightscope, was taken aback to see some guards watching them from nearby. Hours later, in the middle of the night, he was awakened by a flashlight shining in his face. It was held by one of the Cammo Dudes, who announced that he wanted to go through Brown's gear. Brown—a civilized sort, unaccustomed to paramilitary shakedowns in the wee hours—was petrified, but from their sleeping bags, Campbell and Goodall calmly informed the interloper that if he wanted to search their belongings, he would need a warrant. Moreover, they demanded to see his ID. The guard gave up, and in the considerable amount of time it took Brown to get back to sleep, he found himself impressed by and grateful for his companions' sociopolitical savvy.

Glenn Campbell's arrival in Rachel coincided with the advent of the first Democratic presidential administration in the town's history—a circumstance that contained a certain symmetry. As a smooth-talking, liberal, educated Easterner, Campbell fit into Rachel about as well as Hillary Clinton. On the other hand, Nevada, in addition to coming ever more under the cosmopolitan influence of California and Las Vegas, has always been constitutionally committed to living and letting live. In that spirit, Campbell was absorbed into the threadbare Rachel mosaic almost as well as any other eccentric refugee. In fact, as an articulate mouthpiece to the media, he began bringing the area new national attention, from which the Little A-Le-Inn only stood to benefit. In one corner of the saloon, he created a UFO library for the use of patrons; on the wall, Jim Goodall tacked up his six-foot-long photo of Area 51. When people came looking for flying saucers or secret bases, Campbell served them as a sort of unofficial ranger, dispensing directions, wisdom, and advice.

In this capacity, he inevitably crossed paths with some unusual people. One heavily made-up blonde woman in leopard-skin tights said she hailed from the planet Venus; she gave Campbell her business card ("weddings, exorcisms, and alignment healings") in case anyone else happened by from "the Galactic Council." Another of his passing contacts claimed to come from the Pleiades constellation. When Glenn told her that he was from Boston, she asked: "But where are you from Out There?"

The bull-goose local avowed extraterrestrial was a fortyish guy with an Abe Lincoln beard, the former David Solomon from "Miracle City" (né Silver City), Nevada. Now going by the name and title of Ambassador Merlyn Merlin II from the ancient north star Alpha Draconis, he showed up at Glenn's trailer one day explaining that he aimed to establish a Saucerian Embassy and gain a seat in the United Nations. He said he had already been officially recognized by the State of Nevada, proof of which he possessed in the form of a letter from Secretary of State Cheryl Lau, politely addressing him (in context of declining his invitation to a meeting) as "Mr. Ambassador." Unfortunately, Campbell soon learned that Ambassador Merlyn considered him a "chosen one" with respect to the coming Golden Age, when extraterrestrials would be integrated into earthly society and humans would assume a higher form. Merlyn camped out in his car in front of Campbell's trailer, forcing Glenn to resort to rude treatment to get rid of him. Merlyn's chosen ones also apparently included the employees of several Nevada brothels, although he declined to utilize their services, preferring simply to sit at the bar. This may have had something to do with the rumor that he had sexual healing powers, involving the conservation of seminal liquor through Kundalini yoga.

One night when Glenn was working in the Inn, he was approached by a longhaired, six-foot-two, two-hundred-pound, desert-cammo-clad figure. The fellow said his name was Mark Farmer; his card identified him as a "Blackworld Investigative Consultant and Information Warfare Specialist." In fact, he was a thirty-year-old veteran of the U.S. Coast Guard, in which he'd served as a navigator, rescue swimmer, and photojournalist. Farmer lived in Juneau, Alaska, where he had a job in a gun store and a Friday-night radio show called *Oil of Dog*. He had also served as deputy press secretary and audiovisual director for pro-development Alaska Governor Walter Hickel, and run unsuccessfully for mayor of Juneau on a Green Party antigrowth platform. An avid snowboarder, he'd broken his nose eleven times and two or three other bones every year. In short, he was a quick-witted thrillseeker, good-humored hustler, and inveterate hardware junkie with a solid DOD database. As a lifelong "airplane head," he'd known about Groom Lake since the 1970s; now making his first pilgrimage, he'd just completed an eighteen-hour drive from Seattle in a Chevy Sunbird convertible that he'd agreed to deliver to Las Vegas.

From the questions Farmer asked him about Area 51, Campbell guessed that he was going to try and penetrate the border. When Glenn advised against it, Mark assured him that he wouldn't risk his $1,200-per-month military pension, which he'd been awarded for a back injury incurred in the Coast Guard, entitling him to free passage on military flights. He said he was going to drop off the convertible in Vegas, from which he would take a bus back to the town of Alamo. When he asked if Glenn might pick him up there and drive him out to Groom Lake Road, Campbell agreed; the next time Glenn heard from him, however, was when he saw Farmer hitchhiking on the highway in Ash Springs several days later.

As it turned out, Farmer, after caching fifty gallons of water in various parts of Tikaboo Valley, had stopped in at the Shark Club in Las Vegas, where he'd met a woman who agreed to drive him back out to the border. There he'd risen before dawn and—whether by accident or design—crossed into the restricted zone under cover of darkness, then been spotted by the Cammo Dudes while coming back down the public part of White Sides Mountain after sunrise. Farmer was carrying a 1,250-millimeter Celestron telescope, a pair of night-vision goggles, a tape recorder with a parabolic mike, a .44 Magnum derringer, a canister of cayenne pepper spray, and combat knives on his belt and leg. Looking him over, the guards understandably inquired what he was up to. When he answered that he was looking for secret airplanes and asked if they might give him a hand, one of the sentries told him, "Either you and your equipment can be our guests, or you can walk out of here right now."

Hauling his 120-pound pack, Farmer started trekking down Groom Lake Road toward Highway 375, thirteen miles distant. The Dudes tailed him in their Bronco at a speed of two miles per hour. Pretty soon a dust cloud appeared in the road ahead; it was a Lincoln County sheriff's deputy, who had been alerted as per policy by the guards.

The deputy announced that he wanted Farmer to open his pack. Under the circumstances, Mark elected not to resist—and as things developed, his cooperation won him the officer's support. "You've got some nice stuff here," the deputy said, looking over Farmer's arsenal. Warming to the situation, the friendly freelance weapons specialist showed the admiring peace officer how to determine if film had been exposed inside a camera by examining the crimped end of the roll.

While this was going on, the Cammo Dudes were on the radio to their bosses. The cop went over to confer with them; when he returned, he said: "They want you and your equipment, but I'm not going to give you to them. I'm going to take you back to the highway and watch you hitchhike out of the county. I'd rather do that now than come get you later in a body bag."

After a while, Glenn Campbell chanced to came along in his camper, on the way to Las Vegas. He picked up Farmer, who recounted what had happened. The pair spent the next couple of hours getting to know each other, talking about the base and Lazar, forming a bond based on irritation of authority. Farmer returned to the border later, bringing a sound-activated tape recorder that he hid on White Sides Mountain, hoping to pick up the sound of the Aurora. (He got only wind.) Over the next several years, he would return again and again, camping out, talking to locals, writing articles for his personal bible, *Jane's Defence Weekly*, and a San

Francisco 'zine called *The Nose* ("I Am Your Black-Door Man"). He even used his government audiovisual contacts to become a guide for the likes of *Encounters*, *Sightings*, and CNN.

Fashioning a suitably swashbuckling image for public consumption, Farmer soon became known to the media as "Agent X." Not to be outdone, Campbell adopted his own *nom de plume:* Articulating the mission that he'd defined for himself in moving to Nevada, he now referred to himself in electronic dispatches as "Psychospy."

Soon after Campbell relocated to Rachel, the Penoyer Valley Electric Cooperative—the only autonomous local government body—raised the A-Le-Inn's electricity bill 80 percent. To make up the difference, the Travises had an idea: They determined to host a UFO conference. Paying customers would spend a couple of days listening to testimony from witnesses and experts on extraterrestrial affairs while Joe and Pat collected admission and provided meals. Rachel had nothing like an auditorium or meeting hall, but that problem could be overcome by holding the conference in a tent during the warm season. As moderators, the Travises signed up Gary Schultz and Norio Hayakawa, a couple of Black Mailbox habitués and Area 51 "researchers" from Southern California. For speakers they pulled off a coup, attracting the likes of John Lear, George Knapp, and the cosmic whistleblower himself, Bob Lazar. The Travises optimistically entitled the event "The Ultimate UFO Seminar." The fee for the weekend was fifty dollars; where the original aim had been to attract a paying audience of seventy-five, by the time of the meeting (May Day 1993) the number ballooned to two hundred—small by "normal" conference standards, but huge for the Little A-Le-Inn.

By Friday afternoon, April 30, a carnival atmosphere had taken hold in Rachel. Rows of vendors set up booths and tables, where they sold the usual fare available at UFO conferences: books, pictures, placards, posters, tapes, and T-shirts (hampered somewhat in the hawking by a howling wind). A gray-haired guy who'd been hired to tape the talks and provide interim music (ranging from Mozart to the DeVinyls, selected segments were entitled "Saucer Watchers Under Surveillance," "Sneaking into Papoose Lake," and "Deep Black Is Where It's At") turned out to have a sideline as an earth-energy dowser, traipsing about locating "ley lines." To shelter the conference-goers, Joe Travis and crew rigged up an enormous olive-drab army tent, decorated at one end by camouflage netting and at the other by red and blue tarps that, backlit by the desert sun, lent a stained-glass ambience to the interior. Several observers commented on the camp-meeting character of the milieu, which would intensify as the weekend wore on.

On Friday night, Schultz and Hayakawa outlined their respective theories on exactly what kind of conspiracy was being consummated beyond the Groom Mountains. Hayakawa, a funeral director and former head of the Civilian Intelligence Network, posited that a "technology transfer" was under way; Schultz—a diminutive fellow with a disabled arm who ran, among other things, an outfit called Secret Saucer Base Expeditions, taking curious customers on tours of suspect environs—surprised some people by saying that Area 51 was only a pawn in a wicked worldwide politico-economic game, about which he would soon go into much greater detail.

Schultz eventually yielded to John Lear, who, wearing a white shirt and black windbreaker, presented (i.e., read) his patented account of the government cover-up, going back to the crash at Roswell and proceeding through the Eisenhower administration (Ike alleged to have met with ETs at Edwards Air Force Base, disguising the rendezvous as a dental appointment) to the JFK assassination (carried out by the President's limousine driver as Kennedy was about to expose our deal with the aliens) by way of the proverbial abduction agreements, subterranean shootouts, and eighty extraterrestrial races visiting the planet Earth. Lear, whose talk elicited audible and repeated gasps from his listeners, was followed by a jut-jawed, sweater-and-sportcoat-clad citizen identified only as "Captain Eric"—a commercial airline pilot who showed aerial photographs of Groom Lake, the Tonopah Test Range, the Jicarilla Apache reservation near Dulce, New Mexico (purported site of an underground base that UFOs entered through a limestone ledge), and radar-cross-section facilities operated by Lockheed, Northrop, and McDonnell Douglas in the Antelope Valley desert north of Los Angeles, believed to conceal the sites of several secret saucer laboratories. Video presentations continued into the early morning, confirming that sleeplessness is a necessary condition for committed ufologists.

The next day it was announced that George Knapp and Tony Pelham— the latter a "professional investigative journalist" who, while documenting cattle mutilations in Lincoln County, had experienced some early encounters with Groom Lake security guards—had cancelled their appearances. This left a hole in the schedule, into which emcee Schultz seized the opportunity to leap. With a high-volume, rabble-rousing delivery that seemed to find its inspiration somewhere between a fundamentalist preacher and a television game-show host, he elaborated on his intimations of the night before, railing about a "shadow government" controlled by the Council on Foreign Relations and linking it to the Kennedy killings, the Federal Reserve, the IRS, the cure for cancer, the Karen Silkwood murder, and the Waco Holocaust. As he went on and on in this vein, the audience, most of which had paid fifty bucks to find out about flying saucers and/or Area 51, grew discernibly restive, drifting outside to browse the booths or escape the wind in the A-Le-Inn.

Around noon, this trickle turned into a torrent as Bob Lazar arrived on the scene. In case anyone held the mistaken idea that Lazar liked to keep a low profile, he showed up in a silver Corvette with a license plate that said "MJ-12." Beside him was a woman who, according to some, qualified as a bombshell but, in the eyes of others, resembled an extraterrestrial (large head, slanted eyes, pallid complexion). In his black jeans, white turtleneck, aviator glasses, and swept-back hairstyle, Lazar looked the part of a Hollywood celebrity, and following suit, Rachel was suddenly transformed into a radioactive Riviera, flanked by oceanic desert. As soon as Lazar alighted from his car, he was rushed by a camera-wielding crowd, flashbulbs going off in his face, people pressing to get his autograph or shake his hand. He accepted it all with a dutiful air, quietly doing his part on behalf of the Travises.

Lazar slowly made his way into the Inn, where he ordered a glass of wine and turned to face his followers. As he held court before a bevy of hand-held tape recorders, Glenn Campbell—who had been watching from the wings, having never before laid eyes on Lazar—slipped outside. When he returned, he was wearing a bug-eyed alien mask, from behind which he waved to Lazar. Nobody seemed to notice this except for Bob himself— who, tellingly, waved back.

After a while, Lazar moved into the big tent, where he took questions from the assembled throng. His extemporaneous performance there has been described as "brilliant" in its detail, directness, and characteristic air of ingenuousness, whether natural or feigned. As he stood patiently for two and a half hours, addressing every fine point of his story from antigravity technology to the appearance of S-4 security badges, the crowd's attention flagged only once: When someone outside yelled, "There's something in the sky," the enclosure emptied as abruptly as it had when Lazar arrived. The UFO in question turned out to be only a balloon, bearing the mocking visage of Mickey Mouse.

Actually, during his talk, Lazar continued this ufological deflation— declaring, for example, that he found ninety-nine percent of UFO stories "absolutely ridiculous." Regarding a notorious video shot from the space shuttle, he suggested that some mysterious dots were dust particles on the camera lens. He downplayed his own reported glimpse of an alien (saying that it might have been a model) and went so far as to characterize John Lear's line of assertions as "borderline insanity," explaining that his friend had "a tendency to add about fifteen percent color to stories, and if a story goes through him twice, it's thirty percent, and it doesn't stop."

At one point, someone in the audience observed, "It seems as if even knowing that we possess alien technology hasn't made you a believer." Lazar laughingly acknowledged that "That's probably true. . . . I believe the stuff I worked on, there's absolutely no question in my mind, but I think everyone can only go so far, and I just have to speculate because I hate to be wrong." He divulged that he had duplicated the gravity ampli- fiers of the craft he'd worked on and planned to patent the design since no one else on Earth had done so. Still, he said he regretted leaving the S-4 program so early because he would have liked to learn more about the technology. When someone in the bar asked him what kind of work could get him excited now, he replied, "Weapons"—adding with a chuckle, "I like really destructive things."

When Lazar finished, Gary Schultz called for a moment of silence. The conference then broke for dinner, after which Schultz, to widespread dis- may, resumed his diatribe. Attempting to outline (by unwitting example) the techniques and failings of mass mind control, Schultz continued to browbeat his listeners with pompous pronouncements on the nature of knowledge, existence, and truth, defining the latter prosaically as "an accu- rate representation of that under consideration and its relationship to all other things as it always has been in the past, is universally in the present, and will hold without a single exception in the entire future. Anything less than that is. . . . an *opinion*. It's *speculation*." The tent-revival atmosphere that had been looming all weekend now came crashingly to the fore as the firebrand evangelist took to underscoring his points with passages from the

Bible, "the only authorized version" of which he happened to have on sale outside.

Before Schultz could wrap things up by calling believers to baptism, an insurrection broke out beneath the big top. Heretics began demanding their money back, with one faction insisting that Glenn Campbell be allowed to address the crowd. Schultz had already stipulated, however, that he wouldn't relinquish the mike unless Campbell agreed to change the name of White Sides Mountain in the *Viewer's Guide* to "Pearl's Peak" after Schultz's wife. Since Glenn refused—the name White Sides appears, after all, on U.S. Geological Survey maps—Schultz said he would have to keep to the "scheduled syllabus," characterizing those who opposed him as "pinhead scoffers."

Campbell immediately went to his computer and printed out a bunch of flyers announcing a "Pinhead Scoffers Alternative Conference" for the next day. Only a handful of people showed up for it, but that seemed more than the number of Schultz's supporters by the close of the weekend, as even his co–host-and-conspiracy-buff Norio Hayakawa severed relations with him from that time one. In future editions of what had proved a no-frills religious revival and no-holds-barred New Age power struggle, the "Ultimate UFO Seminar" would instead be known as the "UFO Friend-ship Camp-Out."

As events of that weekend implied, Glenn Campbell was, in the minds of many, fast becoming the civilian authority on Area 51. He, not Gary Schultz, was the guy reporters called before they visited the area. He, not Joe or Pat Travis, was the person visitors sought out when passing through the town of Rachel. When Campbell wasn't in the field, he could usually be found at the Inn, not drinking beer or playing pool but working on his laptop computer or binding and shipping copies of the *Viewer's Guide*. As he became a fixture in the lives of the Travises, he took to calling them "Ma and Pa." The way he saw it, they were all participating in a symbiotic rela-tionship: Joe and Pat provided him with a roof and center for his activities, which in turn brought them business and increased attention.

The "family" was not fully functional, however. A couple of months after the UFO Seminar, Joe reportedly took some money out of the cash register and disappeared on a bender. Apparently he was disgruntled with conditions at the Inn; for one thing, he didn't like the extent to which it was becoming Glenn's office. Campbell now had a copier and fax machine in the corner of the saloon, which was beginning to resemble a storehouse for his boxes and books. He'd even printed the Inn's address and telephone number on his own business card. Joe and Pat had bought this place in the middle of nowhere and built it up into something viable, and now this newcomer from back East was acting like it belonged to him. Glenn had recently rented a room in one of the mobile homes out back to store some of his stuff, but that didn't change the fact that Joe was the provider and proprietor. He deserved some recognition and respect.

Travis came back from his "binge" after a couple of days and, duly chastened, went around apologizing to his family and employees. Glenn, not wanting to endorse what he saw as a hollow and self-perpetuating ritual, purposefully stayed out of the way. "I felt that Joe had thrown a tantrum and should suffer more," Campbell would later explain. In other words, the surrogate son did not approve of the family father figure. Viewed another way, the skulking interloper was refusing to recognize the authority of the Alpha male. For his part, Joe wondered who the hell Glenn Campbell thought he was.

One night just before Labor Day of 1993, after the Inn had closed and Glenn was sleeping in his camper, Joe again sat drinking in the saloon. His eye gradually came to rest on Jim Goodall's photomural of Groom Lake. In one of its corners was an inset advising interested parties—i.e., people who wanted to purchase a copy—to contact . . . *Glenn Campbell*. In return for giving these hustlers a gallery for their goods, the Travises were being cut out of the loop and the profits.

A few minutes later, Glenn was startled awake by a pounding at the door of his camper. "Glenn Campbell!" shouted a drunk and drawling voice. "You get the fuck out of here!"

Glenn immediately recognized the voice as Joe's. From experience, he also posited that Travis was armed. Under the circumstances, he thought it best not to argue. "I'm going, I'm going," he called out, pulling on his clothes. As he did so, however, he added in his usual rational way: "Any particular reason?"

"Because I hate you, you bald-faced fucker!" Travis gave Campbell fifteen minutes to get off the property.

Glenn disconnected his camper from its hookup and drove it less than a mile away, parking it in the desert out of sight of the Inn and the highway. He spent the next few days there, making "cautious forays" to retrieve his belongings and test the waters. Pat Travis soon informed him, however, that Joe's judgment, whether rendered drunk or sober, was final. She now agreed that Glenn had been "trying to take over" their business, a state of affairs that would not be tolerated. He could still keep his library, sell his *Viewer's Guide*, and eat his meals at the Inn, but he couldn't live and work there anymore. He was on his own.

"It was like a male-female relationship that goes bad," Campbell would later say. "The woman claims that the man forced himself on her; the man says he thought he had her consent. But whatever feelings people may have in retrospect, only one story is true—and the fact is, it was a good mutual relationship that worked for everyone. The real problem was that Joe was feeling useless. Pat had a choice—she could have said Joe was wrong, but instead she said I was. I became a convenient lightning rod for problems in their relationship.

"This is something I've run up against again and again in my life," Glenn revealed. "Reconstruction after the fact, justifications that allow people to avoid something inside that's more difficult to face. By placing blame elsewhere, you avoid blaming yourself. If you're not a success, it must be because of the Council on Foreign Relations.

"The bottom line is that I was too good for this place. Things will seek their own level, and I caused a disequilibrium at the Inn. I came into a situation where Joe was the boss, the man with the guns—but I was more competent than he was. It was territorial. The surprising thing isn't that I was kicked out; it's that I was diplomatic enough to get along there for six months."

Upon being disbarred from the Inn, Campbell took up residence at the other end of town ("Upper Rachel"), renting a trailer there for $215 per month. This soon became known as the Area 51 Research Center, where I met him in October 1993. Shortly after that, Glenn began clearing a jeep path to the top of Freedom Ridge; having noticed the trace of an old road in an adjacent and unrestricted canyon, blocked in only one spot (apparently on purpose) by a bunch of boulders, Glenn went at the rocks with a sledgehammer, then built an earthen access ramp up and over their remains. He was joined in the final phase by Agent X, who had come down from Alaska to sprinkle the ashes of a deceased friend over Dreamland.

Farmer also aspired to photograph the base. Hence, one afternoon when Glenn drove out to the border, Mark hid in the back of his Chevy Blazer. When the vehicle dropped briefly into a ravine where it couldn't be seen by the Cammo Dudes, Farmer jumped out and camouflaged himself under a bush, crouching among the rocks with branches sticking out of his gear. Campbell drove on ahead, got out and hammered at boulders for a few minutes, then turned around and left.

Pretty soon the guards showed up to investigate what he'd been up to. In doing so, they walked right past Farmer, "so close that I could smell their Aqua Velva." After a few minutes, he thought he heard one of them mention something about prime rib; with that, they got back in their Cherokee and drove away.

Agent X waited for dark, then climbed up the back side of the ridge. He stashed his gear just below the summit, stripped to his boots, did a ceremonial dance, and sprinkled his friend's ashes into forbidden airspace. At sunrise he took a picture of the base, then began packing up to rendezvous with Campbell. Just as he was doing so, however, an MH60G Pave Hawk helicopter appeared over the ridge, coming from the direction of Groom Lake.

The chopper started blasting the hillside, hosing Farmer down with rotowash. At times, the whirring propeller blades were right above his head. When the copter circled to make another pass, Mark launched himself down the ridge and hid among the rocks. This game continued for some time until he reached the ravine—where, sure enough, Campbell was waiting at 9:00 A.M. sharp, having driven in that morning with a mannequin in the seat beside him. Now they threw the dummy in back, along with Farmer's gear; Glenn gunned his way up the makeshift route while Mark ran ahead, clearing obstacles. Within a few minutes, the Blazer bounced out on top of the ridge before the spreading spectacle of Area 51.

Across the ridge, they could see a pair of Cammo Dudes watching from their Cherokee. Campbell and Farmer turned their scanner to the guards' frequency, where an exasperated voice was heard to mutter: "Now it's just like a damn drive-in movie." At those words, Psychospy and Agent X began jumping up and down on the crest of Freedom Ridge, celebrating the dawn of a new era in the history of Dreamland.

To advertise the opening of the "Freedom Ridge Expressway" for the public and the media, in January 1994 Campbell organized a gala ribbon-cutting and "aviation field trip." Extending an invitation through the mail and over the Internet, he attracted a bevy of luminaries, including a tightly jumpsuited Jim Goodall, his writing partner Bill Sweetman, Stuart Brown of *Popular Science*, Michael Dornheim of *Aviation Week*, a guy called "Warren the Rocket Scientist" who hosted a science-fiction program on Pacifica radio, an amateur aviation historian named Peter Merlin (no relation to Ambassador Merlyn Merlin II), and a bunch of California cops who happened to be airplane nuts.

Shortly after the four-wheel-drive caravan arrived on Freedom Ridge, as the group was reclining in lawn chairs looking out toward Groom Lake, they gradually made out a figure moving through the desert below. Clad in desert camouflage, a lone hiker was hauling an enormous backpack uphill from the direction of the base. Assuming it was a Cammo Dude, Brown flashed back to the rude awakening he'd received on his first trip. The guards were indeed monitoring the picnic from a couple of miles away, with video surveillance emanating from a camouflaged van with a five-foot-tall tower. The approaching figure, however, turned out to be Agent X, going solo and getting in late as usual.

Pretty soon a clean-cut couple also came along, wearing what Brown described as "high-tech hiking attire." Their savvy desert wardrobes included a foreign-legion-type hat (with visor and Arabian veil) for the husband, an Orange County engineer named Tom Mahood. He and his wife, Jeri, having recently learned about Bob Lazar and seen Glenn's posting on the Net, had come to explore the area in the company of experts.

The Mahoods agreed beforehand that, if they found a gathering of "saucer nuts," they'd beat a quick retreat. But Tom soon found that "it was even more bizarre than that—all these journalists doing deals, schmoozing each other to sell their photos and talk up story ideas." Farmer positioned a tape recorder between himself and Goodall, engaging him in a volley of secret-aircraft stories. Brown, a droll comic who was just finishing a feature on Area 51 for *Popular Science*, simultaneously dispensed and collected a whimsical load of technolore. Instead of sneaking around in the hope of glimpsing government secrets, the company seemed more concerned with keeping each other entertained, not least with rampant speculation, much of it supportive, about the claims of Bob Lazar. "Jeri and I had never met a group quite like that before," Tom remembers. "Bright, intelligent, interesting people who thought there just *could* be saucers out at Groom Lake. It kind of gets your attention."*

When they tired of Freedom Ridge, the field trippers repaired to Rachel and the A-Le-Inn, where Brown treated one and all to his "Famous Fartless Chili." From there, a smaller faction moved on to the north and the fenceline of the Tonopah Test Range. Even though they came in at night, they still managed to attract the authorities, who had been expecting them ever since Campbell's invitation had gone out. As the first guard approached in his truck, Glenn suddenly crouched down in the dark and darted toward the vehicle; he was trying to get the guy's radio frequency, but at the time, nobody—including his own companions—understood what was he was up to. Alarmed by this erratic behavior, the California cops in the group elected to abandon the scene.

"Glenn can get excitable in groups," Stuart Brown would later explain. "He's sort of antic sometimes, like a little kid when Mom and Dad invite too many friends over. He was zigzagging past this guy's truck, showing off like an eleven-year-old—but the guard was alone, and *he had a machine gun*. It was provocative, foolish behavior; sometimes, you know, you need to pause and put yourself in the other guy's shoes."

Fortunately, nothing untoward occurred. In fact, after some more guards showed up, Glenn gave them all embroidered patches that he and Goodall had designed, portraying an airplane taking off from Area 51. The next morning in Tonopah, however, the cops took the opportunity to, in Stuart Brown's words, verbally "carve Glenn a new asshole. After all, he could have gotten several people shot."

This disparity—between Campbell the incisive writer-researcher and Campbell the incomprehensible loose cannon—was gradually making itself known among Area 51 aficionados. After reading the *Viewer's Guide*, visitors to Rachel may have expected to find a garrulous organizer and

---

* Mahood himself got the group's attention by describing a UFO he'd seen the night before: A weird pair of lights had pierced the sky near Queen City Summit north of Rachel, where he and Jeri had been camping. When Tom plotted their path on a map, the origin seemed to be Groom Lake, a fact that fascinated the collected interceptors. Later, however, driving into Vegas at night, Mahood saw the same lasers coming from the rooftop of the Rio Hotel Casino—pointing, sure enough, in the distant direction of Rachel. In between the two points was Area 51. More than anything, this seemed to bear out Campbell's observation that "UFOs and Las Vegas go together naturally."

savvy outdoorsman. Instead they encountered a curt computer nerd, simultaneously demonstrative and reserved, reliant in his rough excursions on Wal-Mart hiking boots and Mountain Dew. Living in a trailer in the desert with no discernible human ties, Campbell's personal orientation soon became a matter of considerable curiosity, as did the underlying motivations for his eccentric lifestyle. In light of the skepticism expressed in the *Viewer's Guide*, he was sometimes accused by ufologists of being a government disinformation agent[*]; inwardly, however, he was fascinated by UFOs. "It's almost like there are two Glenn Campbells," Peter Merlin observed. Or, as Eric Beckjord put it, "He's sort of into it and not into it at the same time."

"Glenn's mind is a major enigma," Stuart Brown agreed. "I have no real sense of contact with him, nor does anyone else I know. Is he gay? Is he straight? A skeptic? A believer? I have no idea. He really is the virtual person, much more four-dimensional on paper than in real life."

The on-paper persona soon essayed to expand its circulation. Under the "front" of the Secrecy Oversight Council, Campbell already had a mail-order catalogue in which he offered, in addition to the *Viewer's Guide*, books and maps and collectibles such as his Dreamland patch, Goodall's Groom Lake panorama, and an "Area 51 Visitors Permit" bumper sticker. Immediately after the opening of the Freedom Ridge Expressway, he began publishing a pithy newsletter called *The Groom Lake Desert Rat*. Dedicated to "The Naked Truth from Open Sources," it was offered free on the Internet, where it was declared to have been "written, published, copyrighted, and totally disavowed by Psychospy," Campbell's on-line alter ego. The first issue updated the status of Freedom Ridge and identified a distant pair of Groom Lake viewpoints (Tikaboo and Badger Peaks) that would remain unaffected by the pending land closure. It also described the aviation field trip (boasting that "25 of us law-abiding citizens resulted in canceled vacations and untold overtime for what appeared to be about 50 security dudes") and reported the recent arrest of seven tourists for mistakenly crossing the Area 51 border on Groom Lake Road.

Here Campbell began to unveil Psychospy's sarcastic and subversive

---

[*]A typical e-mail message read: "Glenn, you are spreading disinformation freely. You are a pawn of the aliens or a secret government agency, something many have suspected for some time. Your purpose is to keep people from finding out too much about UFOs, the government, and the aliens, while appearing to be interested in finding out the truth."

character—portraying the trespassers' arrest, for example, as a farce conducted by "bored" guards with a "limited emotional repertoire." His dander was apparently raised by the fact that, after following the paddy wagon to the county jail, he'd been made to wait outside in the cold (it was January) until he fell asleep in his car.

"Doctor, help me," Psychospy pleaded. "Ever since spending the night in the parking lot of the Lincoln County Detention Center, I have been afflicted by the uncontrollable urge to do violent damage to both the anonymous cammo dudes and the Lincoln County Sheriff's Department. I don't mean to bomb, shoot, dismember or otherwise physically harm these noble defenders of the law; I want to utterly destroy them at the very core of their being. I WANT TO CUT THEIR FUNDING."

Where Campbell had once recommended politeness with respect to local law enforcement, he now began to assume a more confrontational stance. This grew partly out of an incident concerning the hidden motion detectors on Groom Lake Road. Since the off-limits Groom Range already served as a buffer zone for the base, Glenn believed that vehicle sensors on public land created an unauthorized "buffer zone for the buffer zone." Hence, in *Desert Rat* #3, he included a how-to article entitled "Fun With Sensors." Exposing their radio-transmitter frequency to be 496.25 MHz, he described how to find the devices with a frequency counter and dismantle them long enough to pass undetected. He also said he'd given a map of the sensors' whereabouts to the local office of the Bureau of Land Management, which was none too pleased that the Air Force had installed them outside its own jurisdiction. "Bad Air Force," Psychospy admonished the celestial guardians, ending with the dutiful explanation that "Somebody has to keep an eye on Big Brother!"

Sometime after that, Campbell received a visit from Big Brother himself. A pair of Lincoln County sheriff's deputies came to his trailer and told him they were looking for eight missing sensors. When they asked Glenn if he had any in his possession, he said no—that is, none other than a broken one he'd found along the highway, which was sitting beside them in plain sight on a table. Informing him that this simple device, which Glenn surmised could be reproduced with twenty dollars' worth of parts from Radio Shack, was worth thousands of dollars, the deputies confiscated it and asked if they could search the rest of the trailer. When Campbell declined, they told him they planned to question everyone in Rachel, but if he gave them the names of suspects, he'd remain immune from prosecution. Again

Campbell declined, saying he didn't know any suspects and hadn't committed any crime. "Psychospy does not 'roll over,'" he wrote in *Desert Rat #17*. "We remain pure of heart and honest and honorable in all of our actions, so if we are accused of anything, we will stand trial and exercise every one of the legal rights available to us."

Eventually Glenn would come to see exactly how numerous those weren't, but in the meantime, he undertook some financial research at the county courthouse. There he came across an invoice showing that the Air Force paid the county sheriff $50,000 per year to patrol the boundary of the Nellis Range and provide "special assistance to the applicable on-site security force"—i.e., the Cammo Dudes. This was also where Campbell discovered that in the 1993–94 tax year, the Air Force had paid Lincoln County $65,517 on self-assessed property worth $2.5 million.

"We never went to tax assessor school and have only a vague idea of how much industrial property is worth," Psychospy wrote, "but it seems to us that $2.5 million wouldn't buy a LATRINE at a facility like Groom Lake. . . . [which], unacknowledged by the Air Force, hardly exists in the Lincoln County economy. The bulk of the jobs and contracts for the base are sucked up by wealthy Las Vegas, 90 miles to the south."

Such points threatened to gain weight at the end of January 1994, as public hearings commenced on the proposal to withdraw four thousand more acres from public entry in the Groom Range.° The first hearing, chaired by Curtis Tucker, area manager for the BLM, was held at a VFW hall in Caliente, eighty miles east of Rachel. The Air Force was represented by Nellis Range Squadron Commander Colonel "Bud" Bennett, who cited a nonspecific need "to ensure the public safety and the safe and secure operation of activities in the Nellis Air Force Range Complex." He was followed by nine civilians opposing the withdrawal, including a Native American representative of the Shoshone Nation, which still held legal title to the land from a nineteenth-century treaty, having declined to cede control to the U.S. government in the first place.

The most impassioned speakers represented a more recent "home-rule" movement, holding that the federal government lacked the authority to manage public lands within the state of Nevada. These neo-Sagebrush Rebels focused their ire on the BLM, which controls 99 percent of the

---

° According to the Engle Act of 1958, congressional approval is required only for withdrawals of five thousand acres or more.

land in Lincoln County. Among them were county commissioner Eve "Mad as Hell" Culverwell, who complained that the county had been the last agency to learn that a withdrawal had even been proposed, and Nye County rancher/commissioner Dick Carver, who demanded (and got) extra speaking time, ultimately landing on the cover of *Time* for aiming a bulldozer at a U.S. forest ranger.°

The second hearing, held in Las Vegas in early March, was a humdinger. Two hundred people and four TV news crews showed up at the Cashman Field Center, where a clutch of Air Force officers were seen beforehand chuckling over a huge map of the Groom Lake area that had been posted by Glenn Campbell, highlighting the sensor locations, a "dioxin dump," and Area 51 itself (accompanied by the notation *"Doesn't Exist"*). Queried as to its accuracy, one of the officers said: "No one has ever confirmed or denied [the base's] existence." Colonel Bennett subsequently got up and gave his spiel, explaining that "continually increasing visits" to the area by the public interfered with Air Force activities, details of which he naturally declined to describe.

A parade of protesters then proceeded to the microphone, each limited in his or her comments to three minutes. They included:

- Campbell, who argued that if the Air Force was allowed to withdraw four thousand acres of public land around a "nonexistent" base for such vague reasons, it would "be able to take all of Nevada in little-bitty pieces";
- Steve Hofer, a public-interest lawyer from Indianapolis, who said that since the land in question had been earmarked for multiple use and the Air Force hadn't provided a plan for higher use—or proven, for that matter, that its operations were currently "unsafe" or "insecure"—the proposal "should be rejected as a matter of law";

° In the *Desert Rat* that followed the hearing, Psychospy likened the anti-fed movement to that faction of feminists "who would just as soon eliminate the male gender altogether." Acknowledging that men, similar to the BLM, are "aggressive, suppressive, insensitive and demand too much," he nevertheless pointed out that Sagebrush Rebels, similar to females, "march into battle with high idealistic hopes but a few years later usually find [themselves] living with the bums anyway." He suggested that, "Instead of expending all our resources in an attempt to totally annihilate the enemy, we could take the time to understand him, learn his fears and vulnerabilities and the kind of leverage we have over him, then take him by the balls and turn him into our slave.

"No, wait, never mind," Psychospy suddenly corrected himself. "BAD example."

- UFO conference cohost Norio Hayakawa, who called for a class-action suit to find out "what our money is being spent for";
- Steve McKelvey of Las Vegas, who pointed out that, according to the Uniform Commercial Code, "lack of full disclosure is cause for fraud in any contract";
- a local Nevadan named Wayne Pierson, who recalled a time when he was "coming home from the girlie ranch and *wham!* The Air Force set the whole range on fire";
- Ed Presley, representing CAREE (County Alliance to Restore the Economy and Environment), who declared that "the land belongs to Nevada and Lincoln County, not the United States. . . . You have to come to us and ask if you can *purchase* this land";
- Mark Farmer, who, spreading his arms horizontally, displayed an eight-foot-wide print of the picture he'd taken of the Groom Lake base;
- a Lincoln County resident named Robert O'Connor, who predicted that his home would soon have no stockmen or miners, only military personnel and Congressmen. "This ain't America," O'Connor announced. "I was here when America was here, and it's gone. . . . We don't need this [base]; it's top secret because if you found out what was going on, you'd stop it. We ought to decide who the enemy is, blow 'em to hell, and forget all this shit."

The Air Force found support in only two speakers, both of whom were heckled by the crowd, and one of whom equated surveillance of secret programs with treason. Despite the recent dissolution of the USSR, he opined that Agent X was planning to sell his Area 51 photo to the Soviets. His cosupporter, identifying himself as a 1956 graduate of West Point ("classmate of Schwartzkopf"), warned: "If you think the Cold War stopped, you're mistaken. . . . I've had more experience investigating and looking into these things than ninety-some percent of you people out there, and I think, frankly, you're screwing yourselves."

Amid such histrionics, the two most dramatic speakers were a Middle Eastern man named Moe and Anthony Hilder, a tall, dark, fiftyish radio talk-show host from Anchorage, Alaska, who wore a red banded-collar shirt beneath a black double-breasted suit with a red handkerchief in the chest pocket. He was accompanied by a considerably younger (though similarly red-and-black-clad) but even darker and more dangerous-looking female.

"This is the withdrawal of freedom," Hilder told the crowd. "Not just Freedom Ridge—*freedom*. This colonel behind me is a representative of the New World Order. They are concerned about 'security'—not for you, not for your nation, not for your interests, not for your children. They are concerned about the security of those who wish to surrender the sovereignty of the United States and establish a One World Government.

"If you do not take a stand now," Hilder went on, "surely you will fall. God knows what they're testing out there. Do they have *genetic engineering programs*? Do they have *bacteriological warfare programs*? Did they not, in fact, create a thing called *AIDS*? Do they want to reduce the population of the planet by *twenty-five percent by the year 2000*? . . . There are missing children, a hundred thousand–plus across this nation. Where are they being taken to? Are they being used for medical experiments? Are there antigravitational discs being flown over there that were first developed under *Adolf Hitler*? Yes . . . yes . . . and yes. . . . You cannot allow them to take your property. This is *your* land. It is *not* their spread. . . . You cannot—you *must* not—allow it."

Moe was an urgent young man with dark, close-cropped hair, who carried a big green book up the center aisle. When he arrived at the microphone, he began shouting:

"*IN THE NAME OF GOD, MY NAME IS MOE! I am a permanent resident who's been living in Las Vegas for over six years. BELIEVE IN YOUR GOD!*"

Moe held up his book.

"*This is the last Holy Book of God, Koran, which has one hundred fifteen chapters,*" he yelled. "*Question: What is the number of the Area where the secret base is located? FIFTY-ONE. Let's see what God said in CHAPTER FIFTY-ONE.*"

Members of the panel and the audience exchanged looks. Moe opened up his book of scripture.

"*Chapter Fifty-One of Koran,*" he read. "*BELIEVE IN YOUR GOD! Promise in the winds which blow in holy directions. Promise in the clouds that carry heavy rains. Promise to the angels who perform the orders of God. Promise to all corners that whatever you say is true.*

"God say to Mohammed: 'Have you ever heard about the ester of alcohol and angels? Have you ever heard about that?'"

"The answer Mohammed told them: 'You are very strange people.'"

Moe paused.

"ALIENS!" he yelled.

Now it was coming together.

"Abraham said to the aliens: 'What is your duty here?' The answer: 'WE ARE HERE TO DESTROY THE BAD CRIME!'

Moe pointed at the BLM representatives. *"THE TERRIBLE TRUTH!"* he screamed at the top of his lungs. *"THE STONE RING OF STONE! THE STONE IS YOUR SUFFERING TO GOD! AND THERE'S A SPECIAL PART IN THERE FOR CRIMINALS! ALL ALIENS! ALL ALIENS! THE WORD OF GOD FIVE THOUSAND YEARS AGO! WE WANT TO SEE THE FREEDOM OF THOSE CAPTURED ALIENS, BECAUSE WE ARE HERE TO SAVE THE GOOD FROM THE BAD ONE MORE TIME.*

"FREEDOM! FREEDOM OF CAPTURED ALIENS! WE ARE HERE TO SAVE THE GOOD FROM BAD!"

With one more incriminating gesture toward the quaking BLM, Moe bellowed, *"FEAR IN YOUR GOD!"* and stormed back down the aisle, leaving widespread relief in his wake.

"Now that you know which side God is on," Psychospy would subsequently advise the BLM, "we want you to think about this decision very, very carefully. Remember what happened to Salman Rushdie."

Such events, along with the automotive accessibility of Freedom Ridge, irrigated a fresh bloom of media interest in Area 51. Immediately before the Las Vegas hearing, Stuart Brown's cover story in the March 1994 *Popular Science* ("Searching for the Secrets of Groom Lake") hit the stands; immediately thereafter, CNN visited the area, guided by Agent X. They were followed within a month by the *New York Times Magazine* and *ABC World News Tonight*, both in the company of Campbell.

The *Times* reporter and photographer received the not uncommon, but still privileged, helicopter-and-film-grab treatment. During the ABC excursion, however, an unprecedented move was made in the escalating match between the base and the media. Acting on a search-and-seizure warrant obtained over the radio, a pair of Lincoln County sheriff's deputies confiscated $65,000 worth of equipment from the news crew, including a video camera, a tape recorder, sound mixing equipment, a tripod, microphones, walkie-talkies, batteries, cables, and tapes. They immediately turned it all over to the attending Cammo Dudes, who said they'd seen the TV camera pointing toward the base—a charge denied by the journalists. Campbell was also relieved of his radio and scanner, which, when returned (along with ABC's equipment) by the sheriff six days later, had apparently been tampered with in order to find out the frequencies stored inside.

"They now know what we know, and since we know they know what we know, why shouldn't everyone know?" Psychospy wrote in *Desert Rat #8*. "Groom Lake perimeter security patrols (Cammo Dudes) broadcast primarily on 418.05, 142.2 and 170.5 MHz." Since not all of the frequencies had been "compromised," however, he threatened to publish even more of them in the future, seeing as how the guards "still don't know what we know they don't know, how much we know about what they know we know or what we will do now that we know what they know we know. No?" Since the ABC videotape proved, as promised, to contain no pictures of the base, Psychospy went on to wonder about the "probable cause" for the seizure, especially since the complainants (i.e., the security guards) remained anonymous and thus immune to reprisals for filing a false claim.

This appeared to open the door for further frivolous searches. The one that got Glenn's ass in a sling, however, wasn't even accompanied by a warrant. An account of the incident appeared in the *Las Vegas Sun* on July 21, 1994:

TV CREW'S GUIDE TO SECRET SITE
IS ARRESTED

A self-styled government oversight activist who takes people to view a top-secret base near the Nevada Test Site has been arrested after trying to stop authorities from seizing videotape.

Glenn Campbell, not the singer, was arrested Tuesday by Lincoln County sheriff's deputies after accompanying a Los Angeles television crew to Area 51, an Air Force installation where top-secret aircraft have been tested, including the stealth fighter.

Tuesday, about two hours after Campbell and a KNBC-TV

news crew from Los Angeles arrived on Freedom Ridge, 12 miles from Area 51, Lincoln County Sheriffs Sgt. Doug Lamoreaux and Deputy Kelly Bryant said security patrols had seen the camera pointed at the classified base.

Campbell said Lamoreaux asked KNBC's reporter Chuck Henry and camera operator Julie Yellen to turn over their five videotapes for inspection by the Air Force, but Henry refused to relinquish the tapes. He did, however, offer a view through the camera's viewfinder to assure the secret base wasn't on the film, Campbell said.

Campbell said Lamoreaux replied that he could not view the tapes because he did not have the required security clearance and authority to do so. Only the Air Force could.

A sudden rainstorm and the threat of a flash flood interrupted the incident, Campbell said. As the sergeant followed them, Campbell and crew were directed to drive from Freedom Ridge to the Groom Lake Road and then step out of their vehicle.

Again Lamoreaux asked for the videotapes. When Henry refused, the sergeant and Bryant moved toward the four-wheel drive vehicle.

Campbell said he reached over to push the locks down.

"You're under arrest," Lamoreaux told Campbell and hand-cuffed him. He was taken to the sheriff's substation in Alamo and charged with obstructing a public officer. After posting $600 bail, he was released.

Campbell said he had expected the deputies to produce a warrant to take the tapes, as they had done during another incident.

The deputy claimed that a Supreme Court ruling (later identified as *Ross* v. *U.S.*) empowered him to seize "contraband" without a search warrant. Under Nevada state law, obstruction of a police officer was a misdemeanor with penalty of a fine and/or six months in jail; the county district attorney said he would ask for only fifty dollars if Campbell pled no contest, but Glenn turned the offer down. Instead he requested a jury trial, which, if granted, would be the first one held in Lincoln County in seven years. Further, he announced that he intended to represent himself in court.

In attracting so much attention to the base and its abuse of government authority, Campbell was getting his wish. However, he gradually came to regret being caught in what he termed an "M.F.F."—i.e., a Media Feeding Frenzy, that "rare confluence of public scandal, tawdry human interest, unresolved legal charges and sufficient prior publicity that renders a story self-perpetuating and turns respectable reporters into back-stabbing bastards." In *Rat #10*, Psychospy offered a course called Media Communications 101, in which he shared his observations on the strengths, failings, and idiosyncrasies of print media, talk radio, and television coverage, the latter receiving the most space by virtue of its vast power, as opposed to its sound-bite and reenactment flair for superficiality. Still, that didn't prevent Campbell from continuing to entertain the overtures of ethically challenged TV shows. As a subsidiary to Agent X, he appeared in a July 1994 episode of *Encounters*; and a couple of months later, he agreed to be a guest on *The Montel Williams Show*.

Williams, the flamboyant, shaved-headed host of what Psychospy termed a "human conflict" daytime talk show, had fulfilled a promise to his viewers by visiting Freedom Ridge that summer. When he subsequently asked Campbell to come to New York for a studio taping, Glenn declined—until he learned that Sean David Morton would also appear on the show. Campbell considered Morton—the self-proclaimed "World's Foremost UFO Authority," who charged people $99 to watch flying saucers that were actually Boeing 737s—a criminally depraved con artist.

"As we rode down in the Humvee from Freedom Ridge with Montel and the producer, the reality to us became crystal clear," Psychospy wrote in *Desert Rat #15*. "If we did not appear on the Montel Williams Show, then Sean would have the stage all to himself and could continue to spread any sort of nonsense about Area 51. We felt that we had no choice. Either we did battle with this guy now, before he grew bigger, or we would be cleaning up his mess for many months to come."

Glenn wouldn't be paid for his appearance, but the producers agreed to fly him to New York and put him up in a hotel. He knew he'd be hard-pressed to outduel a demagogue in the free-for-all atmosphere of a "human conflict" TV show, and his trepidation began to be fulfilled from the moment he set foot in Manhattan, when, in trying (as directed by Williams's staff) to check into the Embassy Suites, he learned that he'd been relocated to a more downscale place fifteen blocks away. The next morning, not at all confident that the producers would pick him up, he took a subway to Times Square and reported to the TV studio, where he was escorted into one of many waiting rooms for guests—most of whom were carefully kept separate, as one of the show's trademark techniques involved springing surprise guests on unsuspecting other guests. The floor plan of the place reminded Glenn "of a miniature Roman Coliseum before a big gladiatorial battle": The arena-like studio was surrounded by an audience "warm-up" chamber and several soundproof waiting rooms similar to his own, each containing a green carpet, a TV set, and a selection of Pepperidge Farm cookies. Security conditions recalled Lazar's incarceration at S-4: No guest was allowed to leave the green room (not even to go to the bathroom) unless accompanied by a radio-equipped guard. Moreover, Glenn was asked to sign a release saying he wouldn't sue the producers, then to confirm for a video camera that he'd agreed to these conditions.

The first two guests were women who claimed to have been abducted by aliens. The older of the two said she'd been kidnapped repeatedly by all kinds of extraterrestrials, several of whom she'd killed in self-defense. On more than one occasion, she'd been implanted with alien fetuses, which were removed after they'd had time to develop. Following a commercial break, other guests appeared, this time claiming (similar to Ambassador Merlyn Merlin II) that they were aliens in human form. They published a journal called *Unicus*—"the magazine for earthbound extraterrestrials."

Halfway through the show, not a word had been said about Area 51. Even after Sean Morton came on—having been alerted, at Campbell's own urging, to the fact that Glenn was on the program—he kept mum on the topic, choosing instead to recycle some timeworn material about UFOs and Roswell. Williams then showed the tape of his visit to Rachel, after which Morton announced that it was he who had found Freedom Ridge.

"He had never even been to Freedom Ridge, let alone discovered it," Psychospy later wrote in the *Desert Rat #16*. "We wanted to shout, 'Liar!' but unfortunately we had not yet been introduced and did not exist as far as the camera was concerned."

Glenn was escorted into the studio when the show was almost over. He came on with Las Vegas TV reporter George Knapp, who, having traveled to New York expecting to discuss the biggest story of his career (Bob Lazar), had only enough time to complain that charlatans were taking over the UFO field. Glenn barely managed to relate the fact that, although he'd

originally been attracted to Rachel by Morton's claim that one could see
flying saucers there on a "timetable" basis, all he'd ever seen himself were
military maneuvers.

"Unfortunately, Glenn arrived too late," Morton countered, quickly
regaining the attention of the camera and the crowd.

When the time came for questions, only the abductee appeared to hold
interest for the audience. When someone asked what she'd done with the
bodies of aliens she'd killed, she said they'd disintegrated instantly; when
asked how she'd managed to do them in, she answered: "With a crystal
pistol."

Campbell returned dejectedly to the green room, only to discover a
new pair of guests—a white man and a black woman, awaiting the afternoon taping of another *Montel Williams Show*, this one entitled "Inter-
racial Couples Who Haven't Told Their Parents." In a nearby room,
reportedly, was the man's conservative mother, who, not having seen her
son in three years, believed that she was to appear on a show about "Parents Reunited with Their Children."

A few weeks later, Glenn appeared in a more serious vein as one of
four panelists on a Larry King TV special: "UFO Cover-Up: Live from
Area 51." The show took place on an outdoor set across Highway 375 from
the Little A-Le-Inn, so the mountains in the background, beyond which
purportedly lay the secret base, concealed only innocuous public land.
Amid the company of sober, suit-and-tie-wearing ufologists—Dr. Steven
Greer, founder of the Center for the Search of Extraterrestrial Intelligence
(CSETI); physicist Stanton Friedman, author of *Crash at Corona* and *Top
Secret Majic*; USAF Captain Kevin Randle, coauthor of *The Truth About
the UFO Crash at Roswell*—the blue-jeaned, philosophical Campbell
seemed out of place. Affecting a sanguine, non-paranoid posture, he pooh-
poohed the idea of a government conspiracy and sounded his familiar
refrain that, even if extraterrestrial life existed, human beings would still
have to get along on their own. In the context of the program, his bemused
and noncommittal attitude implied that not only did he not know if UFOs
were real, neither did he especially care or consider the question important. Uninitiated observers and habitual talk-show watchers were left won-
dering why Campbell was even there.

"The show is off the air ten minutes and I am left with the feeling that
Glenn Campbell works for the government," a viewer immediately

declared on an Internet newsgroup. "[He] seemed to soft-peddle [*sic*] the entire affair in a much too uncomfortable way for me to give him any credibility."

For the rest of the fall, Glenn readied himself for his trial on charges of obstructing a police officer. Acting on the advice of various "scumbag lawyer" acquaintances, in November he filed pretrial motions asking for documentation on the confiscated KNBC videotapes and requesting a ruling on the admissibility of various strategies he planned to use in his defense. He received no response until the day before the deadline for issuing subpoenas, at which time Justice of the Peace Nola Holton—who had been elected by Lincoln County voters but lacked a law degree—informed him that his motions were unacceptable because they hadn't been submitted on legal paper with numbered lines. She went on to announce that all rulings would be made on the day of the trial, forcing Campbell to pursue every potential avenue, witness, and piece of evidence without knowing if any of them would be allowed in court.

Holton shared an Alamo office suite with Campbell's arresting officer Doug Lamoreaux, who also happened to be the court bailiff. Holton was the person who'd authorized a warrant for the seizure of ABC News's equipment; who in 1988 had convicted four activists for trespassing when they tried to "work" a mining claim in the Groom Mountains (later overturned by a higher court); and who had recently fined a pair of Area 51 trespassers $500 each when they pled no contest, despite the D.A.'s plea-bargain offer of only $100. Others would soon receive similar treatment, including a couple who testified that Groom Lake guards had transported them *into* the restricted zone from public land. Though no Cammo Dudes appeared in court to refute this claim, Holton convicted the two of trespassing anyway.

Happily for Campbell, Holton and the D.A. soon decided to excuse themselves from his case. Apparently owing to "conflicts" arising from Glenn's political activity (in addition to his work on Area 51, he had recently been campaigning in print against the reelection of Sheriff Dahl Bradfield, referring to local deputies as Air Force "rent-a-cops"), he got a new justice of the peace as well as a special prosecutor from the town of Ely, a hundred miles away. "Who do you know who gets a special prosecutor?" Psychospy asked in *Desert Rat #20*. "Richard Nixon, Ollie North, maybe Clinton if he is lucky. Campbell feels similarly honored."

As the day of the trial approached, Glenn set about educating himself in the Clark County law library, choosing to ignore the adage that "He who represents himself in court has a fool for a client." "The field of law is not as intimidating as it seems," Psychospy wrote in *Desert Rat #21*. "The law is, above all, a logical enterprise where everything is written down and all the rules and procedures are easily decoded if you know a few simple rules about where to look." Proceeding from that piece of wisdom, he went on to lecture his readers on both the letter and spirit of the law, with expansive instructions on how to pinpoint and cite chapter and verse— which he proceeded to do in his own case, recounting every detail and development of the pretrial proceedings, down to the text of some of his motions reprinted in their entirety. While these newsletters might have been interesting to Glenn's most dedicated followers, for casual readers they were more likely to conjure images of comedian Lenny Bruce, belaboring hapless audiences with obsessive haranges on his trial for obscenity.[*]

Moreover, as he continued to receive rude treatment from county officials, Campbell's condescension toward them became more and more plain. "In our two years in Rachel we have been very patient with the local District Attorney and Sheriff," he sighed in *Desert Rat #21*, characterizing Nevada as an "ideal kindergarten in which to learn the law." In light of Lincoln County's relationship with the federal government, he compared its citizenry to "a wife who is beaten up regularly by her brutish husband yet who continues to rush to his defense for whatever mess he has gotten himself into. The military has cheated the county out of millions of dollars of taxes over the years, dumped hazardous fumes into the local air, doused residents with deadly radiation and returned only trivial economic benefits to the community. Yet, for a tiny fee and junior membership in the secrets club, the Sheriff and D.A. seem willing to sacrifice any amount of personal and professional dignity to defend the invisible military. It takes simple rewards to satisfy small minds." Inarguable as these points may have been, one is still struck by the writer's apparent tendency (especially in context of his comments about the Travises) to view most of his neighbors as an

---

[*] To his credit, Campbell now advises readers of back issues to skip this one as "boring."

extended, retarded, disfunctional family, stumbling blindly over the surface of Sol Three.

The trial finally took place in early March 1994. Glenn's request for a
jury was turned down; as Psychospy reported in *Desert Rat #23*:

> To no one's great surprise, Glenn Campbell was convicted at his
> trial on March 3 on misdemeanor obstruction charges. He was sen-
> tenced to a $315 fine plus five days community service at the
> Rachel Senior Center. Campbell's neighbor Miss Edith, the Senior
> Center director and its only active member, was tickled when she
> heard the news. She plans to put Campbell to work painting the
> Senior Center building, which doubles as a thrift store and commu-
> nity center. Alas, Campbell has now initiated an appeal, so the work
> probably won't get done for at least a year, if at all.

Exhibiting the same kind of symmetry that attended Campbell's arrival
in Rachel, at approximately the time of his trial, Joe and Pat Travis began
selling their own Area 51 patch at the Little A-Le-Inn. Designed by Chuck
Clark, an amateur astronomer who apparently aspired to fill Glenn's shoes
at the saloon, it showed an airplane taking off from a playa amid the words
Groom Lake Nevada, *Dreamland USA*, and *S4 Area 51*. Except for the
color and insertion of a flying saucer, it was practically identical to the
patch that Glenn had designed and manufactured with Jim Goodall (now
reportedly selling like hotcakes at "Fort America," the Pentagon's gift
shop). An outraged Campbell immediately withdrew his *Area 51 Viewer's
Guide* from sale at the Inn, electing to offer it only at his trailer/Research
Center and the Quik Pik convenience store next door. Moreover, he finally
saw fit to publish an account of his ejection by the drunken Joe Travis from
the A-Le-Inn, along with such other observations as the advice that "The
Inn is generally not the place to pick up reliable information. . . . Some
visitors, following Joe's instructions, have wandered across the military
border and been arrested."

Shortly thereafter, Glenn was invited to dine at the saloon by some
Japanese film producers. As he entered and was preparing to sit down, he
was instead escorted outside by Pat Travis, who told him he was no longer
welcome in any capacity. Since she wouldn't allow him back inside, the
Japanese visitors didn't know where he'd gone until they were clued in by

Sharon Singer, a Rachel resident who worked at the Research Center. "Campbell wonders now whether there would be a desert location closer to L.A. that would be better for filming," Psychospy wrote in *Rat #24*.°

The closing of Campbell's Rachel period was completed a month later, when on April 10, 1995, the Federal Register published an announcement by the Department of the Interior that 3,972.04 acres of public land in Lincoln County, Nevada, were being withdrawn "from surface entry, mining, and mineral leasing until November 6, 2001, for the United States Air Force to provide a safety and security buffer between public land administered by the Bureau of Land Management and withdrawn land under the jurisdiction of the Nellis Air Force Range." That same day, new KEEP OUT signs and orange markers appeared along the redrawn border, barring the public and media from White Sides Mountain and Freedom Ridge.

"The significance of Freedom Ridge was mostly political," Psychospy declared in an editorial entitled "End of an Era," in *Rat #25*. "The journey from application to the final closure may have been unstoppable, but some high-quality publicity and a legitimate policy debate was generated in the interim—all of it fueled by the apparent evasiveness of the Air Force. Had the applicant stated the real purpose of the withdrawal—to keep eyes off Groom Lake—and maybe given some journalists a tour of the base cafeteria, there would have been not nearly so much hoopla. The American public is still patriotic enough that it will usually support national defense when offered at least a plausible explanation, but the absurd nonexistence of the Groom base, mitigated only by vague AF press releases about possible 'facilities' in that vicinity, made the taxpayer feel he was being ripped off and gave rise to endless perceived conspiracies.

"The closure of Freedom Ridge may discourage casual tourists, but it won't defuse the hard-core fanatics who are rapidly hacking away at the secrets of the 'Test Site,'" he predicted. Nor would it prevent the toxic-waste lawsuit, spearheaded by Jonathan Turley of George Washington University, from proceeding in federal court.

It would, however, remove most of the reason for Campbell to remain

---

° A cumulative effect of the above events was Psychospy's decision to compile an "enemies list." It appeared in *Rat #23*, ranked with the perpetrator of "greatest evil first": 1. Sean Morton. 2. Gary Schultz. 3. Pat & Joe Travis. 4. Erik Beckjord. 5. Michael Hesemann (German producer of the video documentary *Secrets of the Black World*). 6. District Attorney Thomas Dill. 7. Sheriff Dahl Bradfield. 8. Chuck Clark. 9. Radio talk show host Billy Goodman ("who invited Campbell on his show only to abuse him"). 10. mp%mpa15c@mpa15ab.mvoc. unisys.com ("a nasty on-line dude").

in Rachel. Thus, in *Rat* #26, Psychospy announced a "reorganization" of the Area 51 Research Center. While the administration would continue to be headquartered in Rachel, other operations would be relocated to "the cultural center of modern human civilization as we know it": Las Vegas. This would afford the newly appointed Regional Director (Campbell) "access to cheap communications, public libraries, a well-connected airport, fresh produce, video rentals, all-you-can-eat buffets and 24-hour Wal-Marts" (not to mention "the possibility of decent pizza delivered fresh within 30 minutes").

When Campbell moved into his Las Vegas "annex," several Groom Lake Interceptors—Agent X, Tom and Jeri Mahood, and Stuart Brown (now known to his fellow operatives as the "Minister of Words")—were there to attend the housewarming. As fate had it, entertainment was provided by some of the same forces that had furnished them so much diversion on Freedom Ridge. It just so happened that Glenn's new apartment was located next door to the Las Vegas airport. By an amazing coincidence, his office window looked out at the terminal where Boeing 737s arrived and departed, ferrying workers to and from Area 51.

FIVE

Their Elders

Glenn Campbell had originally been spurred to move to Rachel by a chance meeting with John Andrews and Jim Goodall, the reputable pair of aircraft watchers who surprised him by saying that they believed Bob Lazar. Among the Interceptors, Goodall was known—somewhat sarcastically, I gathered—as "The Great One." He was responsible for the panoramic Groom Lake photo on the wall of the Little A-Le-Inn and had published a number of books with Bill Sweetman, including one on the *Lockheed F-117A*. Andrews was the well-known designer for the Testor model-toy company who in 1986 had created a stir by releasing a plastic scale-model Stealth fighter (the "F-19") three years before the Pentagon had acknowledged the existence of the aircraft. In its first eighteen months on the market, seven hundred thousand units of Andrews's kit had been sold. One unhappy customer was the House Energy and Commerce Committee, which summoned the model to a hearing on security leaks before its subcommittee on oversight and investigations. "It's bizarre," mused Representative Roy Wyden (D-Oregon), regarding Andrews's foot-long F-19. "What I, as a member of Congress, am not even allowed to see is ending up in model packages." Andrews himself ended up in *People* magazine, pictured with his plastic airplane alongside a satellite photo of Groom Lake.

"John Andrews has an interesting worldview that I don't fully understand," Stuart Brown had told me. "He loves spyplanes, but he hates spooks. Goodall is a roly-poly redneck comedian. He's a barrel of laughs and also a master bullshitter. He has a personal religion based around the Skunk Works—he's a huge admirer of theirs. As the unit historian for the Minnesota Air National Guard, he has a medium top-secret clearance. He somehow managed to get an A-12 Blackbird from the Air Force for a museum display, then conned the New York Air National Guard into giving him a C-5 transport, cut the A-12 into three pieces, loaded it onto the C-5, got in the cockpit, and rode it all the way from Palmdale to Minneapolis. So now he holds all kinds of records for speed, altitude, and duration of 'unpowered indoor flight.'

"I was with Goodall one time out at Groom Lake when a plane went over," Brown recalled. He said, 'That's a Russian plane.' I'm nearsighted; I need glasses for driving, but Goodall whipped out his four-hundred-millimeter lens and said, 'Looks like a Sukhoi 23'—*click click click*. 'Maybe the *D* model'—*click click click*. 'Think I got it.' I said to myself: 'This guy's blowing hard.' Two days later he called me and said, 'Those pictures weren't too bad. I'll send you a contact sheet.' Sure enough, it was a Sukhoi 23. We used one of the shots in my *Popular Science* story. The Lockheed guys think he's a loose cannon and a national hero at the same time. After all, he's preserving their heritage."

Though Goodall lived in Minnesota and Andrews in San Diego, the two were old friends. When I learned that Goodall was coming to Southern California on business, I flew down to meet them both. We convened at Andrews's office in a San Diego business park—a spacious, well-lit corporate environment whose conference-room walls were covered with racks of tiny paint jars and tubes of glue. Displayed throughout the office were various Testor products; most of the company's model kits were cars, but there was also a space shuttle, a hypothetical Aurora, and Bob Lazar's "Sport Model," shown hovering in Omicron mode on the cover of its cardboard box.

Andrews was a handsome, soft-spoken sixty-four-year-old with white hair and a square jaw, impressively hale and healthy-looking for someone who was battling cancer and recovering from a stroke. Occasionally, as a result of the latter, he broke into a slight stutter as he talked; when this happened, he'd pause for a moment, close his eyes, and say, "I have to slow down." His trademark expression was a pursed grin in tandem with twinkling eyes. Goodall wasn't so subtle, or sly; with thick moist lips, dark shining eyes, and a pot belly above his belt, he exuded a restless, expectant animal energy.

I started by asking Andrews how he managed to design aircraft models before the government had revealed their existence.

"The F-19 was the only model we ever did that was really ahead of anything," Andrews said. "It wasn't *exactly* like the F-117, though it did have an armament bay on the bottom, two F-104 jet engines, and two tails angled in instead of out. It wasn't all straight surfaces, but it did have some faceting. It came within three percent of the actual size of the F-117, and the wing-sweep angle was very close.

"When the model first came out, we were accused of spying, of buying secrets—the press was calling and we were on television, but nobody was interested in the true story: that I read a number of books, heard some anecdotes, went to air bases where things were supposed to be flying, did research in trade magazines on theories of Stealth and how radar was reacting to it, then just put all of that together and designed it. I did have to *think* a little bit. Most people don't take the time or make the effort to do that; they'd rather listen to some politician or military guy instead of trusting their own mind. I try to put myself in the same position as the people in Washington. What kind of weapon would I want to have? Right now I'd like to have a satellite that I could stealth, and I'd like to launch it from top of another plane in the air, far away, instead of from Kennedy on the East Coast or Vandenberg on the West Coast. That way the enemy would have no idea where it was launched from, so there wouldn't be picket ships with radar to get an initial track on where the orbit was going. I'd also like to have the ability to sense radioactive material from a remote satellite, look down from the sky and know the locations where it's being stored. I mentioned something like that once at an aviation and space writers meeting; an Air Force general from Washington looked at me and his eyes rolled up in his head. He said, 'Where do you get these ideas? Don't you ever ask us about anything like this!' Apparently I had stumbled onto something—I could tell I'd hit a nerve.

"So that's what you do: Build these little scenarios, run them up the flagpole, and see who comes along and salutes them or shoots them down or whose eyes roll up in their head as you're talking to them. Just for the fun of it. It's like a jigsaw puzzle—you get a little piece here and a little piece there and, in time, if you gather enough, something may fit together. This piece over here might not fit that one over there, but I don't want to throw any of them out."

"I see myself as a hobbyist and an investigative journalist," said Goodall. "I've been at this for twenty-five years. But John's been at it fifteen years longer than I have."

"During my first two years of junior college, I was employed in the summers by the Hawk Model Company in Chicago," Andrews explained. "The Korean War was going on at that time. I got 98.2 out of a possible 100 on the armed forces qualification test, and the Army Security Agency and Naval Intelligence wanted me to enlist. But I didn't want to go in for the full four years, so they drafted me. As a sergeant and NCO squad leader in the Army infantry, I had the highest rated squads; I became E-5 in twenty months. They wanted me to re-up, but Army flight school wasn't open when the war ended. So I said goodbye. I came back and studied engineering at Northwestern, then switched to business. I also do art and photography and electronics and writing, which, mixed together, makes me a bad guy—if you wanted someone with the background to be a spy, I'd be perfect.

"During college I needed extra money, so I kept doing freelance design for Hawk. In 1959, I was working on a model of the U-2. The airplane had been seen coming and going from England, from Germany, from Japan; I'd gotten a few photographs of it, and I was asking a lot of questions. I'd written to Lockheed, whose PR man, Bill Wood, requested that we not do the model. It was no secret anymore, but we were still supposed to treat it as a secret. After a while, my neighbors told me that two guys had been around asking about me; the next morning I called the FBI, told them I was an aviation historian, and offered to come down to their office and talk with them directly. That was the last I heard from them. Later I found out that they'd checked on me and found I was a flag-waving veteran.

"In the meantime, though, I had a meeting in a dark car with a friend of a friend who was flying support missions for the U-2. He said, 'You mustn't ever admit you had a conversation with me,' but he told me that the U-2 was overflying the Soviet Union. The Russians had known about it from the very first flight; they just couldn't shoot it down. Yet the American people didn't know *anything* about it, even though they were paying for it. When I later suggested this to some people, they told me I was crazy. They said I was a traitor to even talk about it; we'd *never* do a thing like that!

"In May 1960, Francis Gray Powers was knocked out of the sky. And a lot of people, those who are familiar with the structure of the airplane and the damage to its engine, contended that it was put down intentionally. That's when I said to myself that something was going on in this country that was beyond secrecy."

"The reason Powers's U-2 went down was because the airplane was sabotaged," Goodall confirmed. "They'd had 'problems' with it earlier in the day; the rules were that, if you had a problem with the airplane and they fixed it, they'd put in the backup pilot. Powers was the backup pilot."

"I wanted to talk to Powers, but he got bumped off," said Andrews. "After he was released by the Soviets and came back home, he ran out of fuel while working as a helicopter pilot for a Los Angeles TV station, and crashed near Van Nuys. I have friends who say he was an excellent pilot and would never run out of fuel. One week before his U-2 was knocked down, *Aviation Week* had run photos of the airplane; when I asked the editor if it was just a coincidence, he'd answer every question but that one. Another photo editor I know told me that a Time-Life photographer was called out to Edwards six months in advance to photograph a U-2, but was told to hold his negatives. I tried to contact him, but he never admitted it. Later I met Fletch Prouty, who wrote *The Secret Team* and *The CIA, Vietnam, and the Plot to Assassinate JFK*; he was the man called 'X' in Oliver Stone's movie. Fletch was the handler for the U-2—the point officer between the Air Force, the CIA, and Congress. And he agreed that the U-2 was never shot down."

"The Russians were embarrassed by the fact that Americans were being allowed to overfly the Soviet Union at will," Goodall explained. "Andrei Gromyko was yelling and screaming at John Foster Dulles in closed sessions at the U.N., saying, 'Stop the overflights!' Dulles said, 'If you don't like what we're doing, that's too goddamned bad—go get the best you got and try to shoot us down.' The U-2 cost two billion dollars in 1958, and the few Congressmen who knew about Oxcart, or the Blackbird program, were saying: 'Why are we funding *this* program when the reconnaissance platform in current operation is working just fine? If it ain't broke, don't fix it.' So by allowing Powers to get shot down—or whomever it was, he just happened to be the pilot that day—it (1) gave the Russians a false sense of security to think that they could shoot down one of our U-2s, (2) allowed them to save face in the world community, and (3) ensured the production of Oxcart, or the A-12."

I asked Goodall about his own relationship with the A-12. "The Blackbird was what started all this for me," he said. "I've had a love affair with the airplane ever since I saw my first two YF-12s on March 10, 1964. The first thing I did was write to Lockheed, the Air Force, the CIA, the DOD, and the audiovisual depository at Bolling Air Force Base, saying I would like photographs, in the air or on the ground, of the following SR-71s. I was willing to pay the established rate: nine dollars for color, four-fifty for black and white. The photographs were not classified. But I was told the official policy was 'not to cooperate.'

"Now, I don't care if you're a taxpayer or not; regardless of how legitimate the request was, *this was not classified information*. So I started digging into it by myself—making phone calls, tracking people down. And the more I learned, the deeper I dug. Now, when it comes to the history, operations, and capability of the Blackbird—the A-12, the YF-12, the D-21, and the SR-71—I am the world's leading expert. I have my own A-12, a 2,390-mile-per-hour Blackbird, sitting in Minneapolis. I restored it; I've painted it twice by myself. The cockpit is all there. It looks like you could put the key in the ignition and fly away."

"How did you lay your hands on it?"

"I had balls. I asked for it. I had to prove to the Air Force that our little museum was an honorable place for a multimillion-dollar CIA spyplane. And I was able to justify it, much to the surprise of all the generals who thought I'd never pull it off. I just said: 'Give me the chance to fail.' I wrote all the letters, raised the money, scrounged two C-5 transports to move it from Palmdale, and put a team together to help dismantle it. It took two and a half days to take it apart and, in the spring of the following year, three and a half months to put it back together. I don't fly—my ex-wife wouldn't allow it—but because of what I've done with the A-12, I've become a member of the Roadrunners, a group of men who operated out of Groom Lake from 1954 to 1968, flying or working on U-2s or A-12s. Bill Park, Jim Eastham, Mel Vojvodich, operational CIA guys who flew that airplane for the first time over North Vietnam to ninety thousand feet at Mach 3.3 It's an incredible honor to rub elbows with those people. They make Tom Wolfe's guys in *The Right Stuff* look like a bunch of amateurs."

"When did you first find out about Groom Lake?" I asked.

"I heard about it from John Lear," said Andrews. "In the late seventies, when I started working for Testor and came out here, he was an SR-71 researcher just like Jim. I knew there was a site for top-secret aircraft, but people in the industry wouldn't talk about it—except for Tony LeVier. Ben Rich would always tell him, 'Tony, you can't be saying that!'—thereby confirming that it was the place."

"I've known about Groom Lake forever," said Goodall. "I've interviewed people who have been there continuously since 1954—pilots, flight-test people, technical people. I have the names of some of the commanders; most of them have been civilians, but there have been some military ones—Skip Anderson, Pete Jackson. Area 51 is the most highly classified military facility you'll find in this country; if you're in any branch of the Department of Defense, you cannot refer to Groom Lake, Area 51, Dreamland, or anything, period. It doesn't exist. It's a no-man's-land. The AWACs,* who fly out from Red Flag, refer to it as Elvis's House—as in *'Elvis is not home.'*

"Anyone in Red Flag knows that if you fly into the Box, you're in deep shit. Especially if you do it on purpose. I heard about one EF-111 pilot—a full colonel, commander of the 390th Tactical Fighter Squadron out of Mountain Home, Idaho—who decided he was going to take a shortcut while he was leading a Red Flag exercise. He purposely cut the corner of the Box, and before he landed at Mountain Home Air Force Base—which wasn't that far away in flying time—he was fired and his Air Force career was down the shitter. Another time, an F-105 pilot who'd lost an engine decided that, rather than eject from a two-and-a-half-million-dollar airplane, he'd land on the runway at Groom Lake. Before the aircraft came to a stop, he was surrounded by vehicles and guards with their guns drawn. They put him in a van with no windows, put a bag over his head, drove him to a building, closed the door behind him, and debriefed and interrogated the guy for five or six hours. After they were assured that (1) he didn't see anything, and (2) they'd put the fear of God into the poor son of a bitch, they put him in another van with a bag over his head and drove him up

*Boeing 707s in the Airborne Warning and Control program.

through the Test Site—he could tell because it was a paved road, and that's the only paved road out of there—to U.S. 95 and Nellis, where he was interrogated and debriefed for three days. Another friend of mine who's a hell of a pilot was flying a B-52 in a Red Flag exercise, and to avoid a midair collision with a Canadian CF-18 Hornet, he had to veer off to the north. He knew he came close to the southeast corner of Area 51, but he didn't think he'd penetrated the airspace. When he landed at Nellis, two staff cars and two vans were waiting for him; under direct order from the base commander, he went in one vehicle and his copilot in another, and they were briefed and debriefed for four hours. They asked him, 'Did you know that you cut the corner of the Box?' He said he'd thought he was still a half-mile out, and made those maneuvers to avoid a midair collision. They said, 'Our laser rangefinder had you five hundred to six hundred yards inside the Box.' He didn't get in trouble, but he got his butt chewed.

"Area 51 is so sensitive—they want to protect the security of the place so strongly—that an operational unit could not effectively operate out of there. As soon as any airplane is out of its initial flight test phase and declared an operational asset, it moves over to the Tonopah Test Range. That's what they did with the F-117: It was first flown and flight-tested at Area 51, then when it started being turned over to the Air Force, they moved the operational squadrons to the TTR. It wasn't even until the early eighties that they got an 800 telephone number at Groom Lake; I know the guy who was responsible for putting the phones in. They change it on a regular basis, but in an emergency, the only way your family could get hold of you is to call this unpublished number. It's called the 'Hello' phone because when it rings, all the person on the other end says is 'Hello.'

"One time, a lieutenant colonel at Edwards Air Force Base called this number without knowing what it was; he had it on a piece of paper or something. The guy at the other end said, 'Hello.' The colonel said, 'Who is this?' The guy said, 'Who would you like to speak to?' 'This is Colonel so-and-so. I want to know why you aren't identifying yourself.' 'Sir, you made the telephone call. Who do you want to speak to? I will put you in contact with that person.' 'I want to know who you are.' 'Sir, I'm hanging up.' The colonel called back right away and demanded the guy's name, rank, serial number, and name of his organization. The guy hung up again. Fifteen minutes later, someone from OSI* was in that colonel's office saying,

*The Air Force Office of Special Investigations.

'Colonel, you're coming with me. You called a number you had no autho-
rization to call.' "

"To this day, people won't tell you what they did when they were in that
service or working for that company," said Andrews. "They never even told
their families what they did when they were gone for three or six months
on a project. The base is not a full-fledged modern facility with everything
you'd want; it has a bowling alley and swimming pool and those things, but
it doesn't compare to a standard Air Force base. You can't even go into
other areas where you don't have little squares on your tag. Sometimes you
work really late hours in the middle of the night, then in daytime you're
not doing anything. Everything is a little bit unusual there because of the
secrecy. So I think if somebody gets something really good there, it's okay.
If somebody got some good beef or seafood, that's okay."

"During the development of the U-2 and A-12 at Groom Lake, you
had a group of dedicated engineers who couldn't talk to their wives or their
kids and could be gone as long as two or three months at a time without
any communication with the outside world, working twelve or eighteen
hours a day, seven days a week, exposing themselves to nuclear fallout—all
in the name of national security," Goodall reiterated. "Sometimes, when
the A-12 program was behind, they worked literally twenty-four hours a
day, seven days a week, in two shifts. Temperatures could be a hundred
and ten degrees or zero. They were living in shit-hole World War Two surplus barracks, four to ten guys to a four-bedroom billet, with one guy
sleeping in the kitchen and one in the living room. Grown men would be
crying that they had to get home to see their families, saying their son just
graduated from high school or their baby just had its first tooth. The only
luxury they had there was extravagant food—the best that money could
buy. If you wanted a two-inch-thick USDA prime porterhouse steak, it was
there for you. It's a common thing for duty in remote sites like Alaska, the
northeast cape, Crimea or Kotzebue, where it's eighty-five below zero and
you haven't seen a woman for six months. The only way to keep your
morale up—the only way Lockheed or the CIA or the government
could show appreciation for what these people were doing for national
security—was to feed them well. And they deserved it. They don't have to
apologize to anybody for it. The American taxpayers have gotten more
than their money's worth out of the people I've interviewed from out
there. The people associated with Skunk Works and Lockheed are by
far the most wonderful, honorable, delightful people I've ever had the

pleasure of dealing with—and I've dealt with all of them, from the very very top on down."

"Skunk Works was always on time and under budget," said Andrews. "I've got Lockheed drawings and U-2 parts, and they're just drawn on rolls of tracing paper with no borders. Really basic—just what you need to get the job done and get the damn thing out. Kelly Johnson set the tone for Skunk Works, but Ben Rich had more of a sense of humor—he could talk with people a little bit better. Ben was a friend of mine; I could talk to him because he knew I'd understand him. He'd call me once a month and I'd ask him questions. With some, he'd say, 'You know I can't answer that.' With some others, he said, 'If you repeat this, I'll absolutely deny it.' He was very secretive, but at the same time, if he admired you and saw that you were going down the wrong path, he wouldn't tell you where to look, he wouldn't say what or why, but he'd say, 'You're looking in the wrong place.' He enjoyed our conversations, I think; we'd talk about the testing of models, air foils and things with self-stabilizing surfaces. I wrote him once saying that if you put a balsa-wood airplane underwater in a bathtub and turned it upside down, the buoyancy of the fluid provided the same effect as gravity but lifted the model up instead of down. Ben told me that they did the same thing at Skunk Works. One time I told him, 'When you guys fly a secret airplane, you ought to make a secret chase plane.' When I take a photograph of them, the chase plane gives me the size reference I need; if you use a telephoto lens with a foreshortening effect and you have two airplanes flying maybe fifty feet from each other and you recognize one as a T-38, then you get the exact size of this other airplane that isn't supposed to have any dimensions. I'd say, 'Ben—do it right!' He invited Jim and me into his office one time, locked the door, and we had an hour-and-a-half conversation about some of the things he had to do when he built the F-117. He said, 'The thing that worries us about you two guys is that you've been watching the Skunk Works for so long that you know more about the way we operate than some Air Force majors or young guys who have clearances.' But he knew we were on his side. When the last F-117 rolled out of the factory, all the security guys wanted to shake my hand; they knew everything about me. I said, 'I'm not an ogre!' They said, 'Come on, we know that! It's good to meet you!'

"Ben told me before he died that he no longer had the same kind of people as when they did the U-2 or the A-12—the generation that grew up with World War Two and could still remember ladies down the street with flags in their windows showing that they'd lost a son in the war. That generation had an innate patriotism deep inside them. Sometimes, after twenty years, they might not believe something should still be kept secret, but they'd keep it anyway. Nowadays, people don't believe in keeping quiet till their death. It's a complex change throughout our entire society; there are no secrets in anyone's life anymore. Everything is out in the open. People are more influenced now by tabloid communications. There isn't the same degree of goodness on the part of the press, where they wouldn't talk about the private aspect of things, so even the demigods in government aren't as pure as they're supposed to be now. It's hard to find a young guy just getting started in the program who has that same induced feeling of patriotism."

I felt compelled to point out that both Andrews and Goodall seemed to have done their share of shedding light on secrets. I asked how that squared with their dedication to national security.

"I figure that, if I can do it, a potential enemy can surely do it better," said Andrews.

Goodall's explanation was more elaborate. "I see myself as a patriotic taxpayer who has the right to know what my government is doing," he said. "I don't ask for classified information, though I've probably been a repository for it; I don't want to get anybody in trouble, but more importantly, I don't want to get *me* in trouble. But if it's *not* classified information, I say, 'Please tell me.' People feel comfortable talking with me on that basis."

"When I was inquiring about Stealth airplanes way back in 1977," said Andrews, "the Air Force wrote me a letter saying that it would be in both our interests if I got a visit from one of their people. It turned out to be a Colonel Leo Olsen of AFOSI, who is now dead. He said, 'We ask that you have patience. When the time comes, you'll be on top of the list to receive information.' I said, 'That's fine.' But then he went on to tell me not to correspond with Ben Rich. Well, I didn't say a word, but I continued to correspond with Ben anyway. Nobody in the Air Force has any business telling me who I should write to."

"I once spent two and a half hours in the office of Pete Eames, the Air Force OSI deputy director for program security," said Goodall. "I was trying to find out why my security clearance had a flag on it. Their statement was: 'We don't like the questions you're asking.' My response was: 'That's too goddamned bad, because as an American citizen and a taxpayer in a free country, I can ask all the questions I want of my government.' This is a government of the people, by the people, and for the people, and there isn't anybody in the Pentagon or Washington, D.C., who can intimidate me into not asking questions. You can put a bullet in me, poison me, or give me a heart attack, but as long as I'm breathing and standing on my own two feet, I will ask questions and challenge the government and go out in the desert and spend my time on public lands overlooking anything I want to look at. If you want to try and intimidate me, fine. But you're really pissing into the wind if you do, because this isn't the KGB or Nazi Germany.

"What they told me when I sat down in that office was: 'Jim, when we read your manuscript on the F-117, we wanted to put you on active duty, file charges for espionage, and send you to Leavenworth for twenty years.' I was in uniform; I stood up and said: 'I *am* on active duty. Here's Exhibit One.' I threw a copy of my book on the table and said, 'Charge me.' They said it wasn't in 'the best interests of the program.' I said, 'You can kiss my ass, because I've never signed any letter saying I wouldn't divulge classified information. More importantly, I haven't had the need to know, nor have I knowingly had access to, classified information. If I want to make assumptions based on *non*classified information, that's my business.' He said, 'You can take thirty or forty facts that are unclassified, put them together in a document, and they can become classified.' I said, 'Bullshit. Air Force security regulations say that no document can be classified higher than any single item within that document.' If you have one page that's secret, you can classify the whole document as secret; but if you have a hundred and fifty reports on Blackbird crashes and incidents, and they give times and dates and places, and they're all unclassified, then that document is unclassified.

"Finally I said, 'I'm getting up and leaving.' I looked Pete Eames right square in the eye—he's a short guy, and I'm in his territory—and I said: 'You know what really pisses you off about me? *I'm not afraid of you!*' I thumbed my nose, turned around, and walked out. Well, Pete turned beet red, and he went home about fifteen minutes later because his blood pressure went through the ceiling. The word was out through the whole Pentagon the next day. And by the time I walked from the fifth floor of the D ring down to the third floor of the C ring, the flag that was on my clearance mysteriously disappeared."

"Jim and I were out on the fence line at the Tonopah Test Range about eight months before the Air Force released any information on the F-117," said Andrews. "We saw it coming and going, and photographed it in flight. Pretty soon some guards and armed cars and sheriff's police came out with their guns and radios. One guy said, 'You don't belong here.' But we had a map, and we were on public land. We said, 'This is our side of the fence and that's your side.' We had every right to be there. We were not going to move. We gave them the names of our friends at the Air Force and Lockheed and said, 'Call these people.' And they did; it took them about an hour and a half. Finally the sheriff's police agreed that we were doing nothing wrong.'

"The Air Force doesn't own a single airplane," Goodall said. "It's all owned by the American taxpayer."

"They are caretakers and operators," Andrews agreed. "But we paid for it, and we own it. The Air Force also destroys records. Records that belong to the citizens of the United States."

"Ninety percent of what goes on in the classified world has no reason to be classified," said Goodall. "It's classified for administrative purposes, or because they screwed up and didn't want anyone to know it, or because they wanted to hide the funding from the bean counters."

"Some highly placed people in the aviation industry are pretty upset about the level of security," said Andrews. By way of corroboration, he went to his desk and pulled out an excerpt from a *Popular Science* interview that Stuart Brown had done with Ben Rich. *"The secrecy business is a bureaucracy,"* Rich declared. *"The use security (first) to protect their jobs. Second, to protect budgets—and that's wrong. . . . if you become too loose with it, you make everything secret. And that's bad. It's an abuse of power."*

"The whole secrecy business bothered Ben," Andrews said. "It's a hell of a way to build things; it costs a lot of money and it slows things up, but the Air Force was one of his clients. There's a need to have good weapons systems being developed at all times, but unfortunately, as Colonel Leo Olsen said, 'We have to keep these programs out of sight of Congress, because there are people in Congress who would kill them immediately if they knew about them.' We elect Congresspeople to guard our money, but the military says we need to hide these things from them."

"Thirteen to fifteen billions of dollars of research money per year is being controlled by a handful of people who are not accountable to anybody for Black Budget line items that you and I and ninety-nine percent of

Congress will never see," said Goodall. "Bill Sweetman figured that fifteen to eighteen billion dollars was for the Air Force, not counting *other* Black programs. Now, if you are a full colonel, or GS-14, and you control the purse strings to fifteen billion dollars' worth of research and development technology and manufacturing capabilities, and you're not accountable to anybody, you're a real powerful person. You have almost as much power and prestige as Bill Gates."

"Sometimes I think we have two governments," said Andrews. "The democratic one, and the sub rosa one where things really get done. I admit that I'm skeptical about our government; I have a distrust. I mean, who goofed up on White Sides Mountain? All through the Cold War, Soviet spies could climb up it, or drive to within four miles of Groom Lake. Why should it now suddenly be off-limits? I have an aerial photo of the base that was taken in 1968. I paid twenty dollars for it. Now it's off the list; you can't buy it. It really bugs me. If it was once available and isn't now, doesn't that rewrite history? The horse had already left the barn. What's their thinking? Is it just 'We're the big guys—we spent your money to get this photograph and now you can't have it'?"

"In that photo, you can seen smoke coming from the burn pits," said Goodall. "It's a smoking gun [for the allegations about toxic waste]. I think the environmental issue there is like Al Capone—they couldn't get him for murder, so instead they got him for tax evasion. You can't get the Air Force to admit Area 51 exists, so instead get the environmental Nazis down their throat. You know, when they started these pits in 1955, it wasn't a sin. America and the government and Lockheed and people at Area 51 didn't have the environmental conscience they have today. That's one of the bad things about some of these environmental fanatics. There's a statute of limitations on everything but murder, but even if [an environmental crime] happened twenty-five years ago* when the rules, terms, and conditions were different, you still get some of these do-gooders going after it as if it happened today. When an airplane program came to an end there, they had no way to keep the assets; they didn't *want* the assets. If you don't have the funding to store the stuff or maintain security on it, your best bet is to destroy it. So you dig a big pit, throw the stuff in there, fill it with JP-4, and throw a match on it—tools, paperwork, copy machines, files, everything.

*The crimes in question at Groom Lake are alleged to have happened ten years ago.

Who's gonna know? You're at a facility that doesn't exist, downwind of fall-out from plutonium bombs. Who gives a shit? That's what they've done there for forty years, and tradition is hard to break."

"A lot of the things we're talking about were done in violation of inter-national law," said Andrews. "Like flying the U-2 over the Soviet Union—we shouldn't have done that, but we did it. Pete Eames told me in a phone conversation once: 'Not everyone has to go by the law. We don't.' "

"That's the thing that bothers me about Area 51," said Goodall. "A camouflage dude in a white Jeep Cherokee can come up to you, shoot you in cold blood, drag your butt a quarter of a mile inside the perimeter of the base, and throw it out where the buzzards can get to you, and there isn't a government agency or law-enforcement agency in this country that has the authority to go in there and get your body. Even if they could, there's no one who can be held accountable, because the place doesn't officially exist. You might as well be on Mars. Even though they came out with an official statement a year and a half ago that there's an 'operating facility in the vicin-ity of Groom Lake,' they still won't put it in writing. It's the 'Burn before Reading' syndrome. It's a bunch of crap. The whole world knows about this place; my photographs have been viewed by millions of people. Under the Open Skies Treaty, twenty-four countries, including our former enemies China and Russia, have the ability, once a year, to overfly any military facility owned by the U.S. government, including Area 51. We even provide the airplane—they use an old OC-135-B stationed at Offutt Air Force Base in Omaha, Nebraska. But can the American taxpayer go along for the ride, or get a photograph taken by that airplane? Hell, no. We own the facility, yet we have no access to it because they won't admit that it exists."

"There are people within our government, such as the Secretary of the Air Force or the Secretary of Defense, who seem very afraid to talk about Area 51," said Andrews. "At a time when we're talking about decreasing the military and getting those funds under control, something's very wrong about that."

"In the eighties, the number of buildings at Groom Lake almost dou-bled," said Goodall. "Meanwhile, the central security facility was upgraded from a World War Two building to a state-of-the-art control center. Secu-rity became more of an issue when the Air Force took the place over from the Department of Energy of 1984, at the time of the first land grab.[*]

_____

[*] According to other sources, the Air Force took over from the CIA in the mid-1970s.

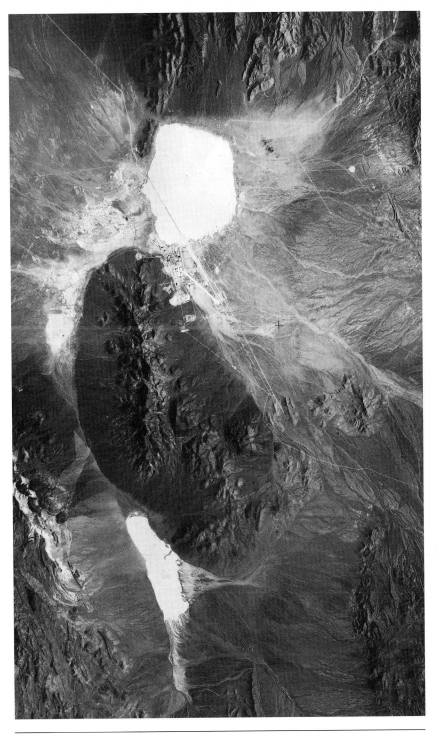

Russian satellite photograph of Area 51 from 1988, showing Groom Lake in the north and Papoose Lake in the south. (© *CNES/SPOT Image*)

U.S. high-altitude aerial photograph of Groom Lake and Area 51 from 1968. Arrow shows smoke coming from burn pits. (*U.S. Geological Survey, EROS Data Center*)

The Black Mailbox on Nevada Highway 375, traditional gathering place for UFO watchers. (*David Darlington*)

Kelly Johnson, chief of Skunk Works. (*Lockheed Martin*)

(LEFT): The A12SR-71 Blackbird—"a twenty-first-century performer delivered in the early 1960s." (*Lockheed Martin*)

(RIGHT): Bob Lazar at the Ultimate UFO Seminar, May 1993. (*Dennis Stacy*)

(ABOVE): The base at Area 51 as seen from Freedom Ridge. (*Mark Farmer*)

(LEFT): Bob Lazar's "Sport Model" flying saucer, as portrayed on the cover of the Testor model kit. (*Testor Corporation*)

Glenn Campbell. (*David Darlington*)

The Little A-Le-Inn, Rachel, Nevada. (*David Darlington*)

Joe Travis. (*Glenn Campbell*)

Pat Travis and mysterious beam of light. (*Mark Farmer*)

Ambassador Merlyn Merlin II.
(*Mark Farmer*)

Agent X. (*David Darlington*)

An unmarked Janet Boeing 737 takes off for Area 51, in front of the Luxor casino on the Las Vegas Strip. (*Maria Stenzel/National Geographic Image Collection*)

When they built the A-12 in the early sixties, there were about twenty-five security people responsible for the whole program, and twenty-five hundred people involved in every aspect of production, including subcontractors. During production and flight testing of the F-117 in the late seventies and early eighties, they had twenty-five hundred *security* people. Meanwhile, the main runway went from fifteen thousand feet to twenty-seven thousand feet. A friend of mine who was in charge of flight tests told me a runway that long would be necessary for an aircraft with a real sharp leading edge that doesn't have much wing to it. It may not even take off until it reaches three hundred and fifty knots, and it may need nine thousand feet to do that. In a worst-case situation, if you have to abort a takeoff, it takes twice that distance to stop; nine thousand plus eighteen thousand equals twenty-seven thousand. We believe it all has to do with a hypersonic vehicle known as the Aurora."

"Jim and I heard the Aurora two days in a row," said Andrews. "You can almost feel it beating against your chest more than you actually hear it—you feel the pulsation on your body. It's like one of the lowest notes on a pipe organ, about thirty-two cycles per second. The first time we heard it was at night, on the ground outside the Little A-Le-Inn. It sounded like it was being chased by a couple of F-15s above the cloud deck. There was no glow, like from a rocket launch or anything. The next day, we went up in the mountains to tape the sound, but it went away as soon as I stepped out of the car door and hit the recorder button. Once you've heard it, you'll never forget it. It's very low and"—he narrowed his eyes and shook his head—"*very, very* loud. If you had it at the regional airport in San Diego, it would wake up the whole city."

"I called Ben Rich just before he died," said Goodall. "He told me he was disappointed in John's XR-7 Aurora model 'because a Mach twelve aircraft fueled by liquid methane with the same physical size as the Testor model, if it took off from Groom Lake, would be out of fuel by the time it went over Pasadena.' He said it would have to have at least four times the physical volume represented by the scale model. So what Ben told me—and this is the way Ben did things—is that the actual airplane is a Mach twelve aircraft fueled by liquid methane, four times the physical volume of the Testor XR-7. There *has* been an eight-thousand-mile-per-hour, Mach twelve airplane tracked out of a radar control center in Oakland since 1986; it was picked up on a magnetic heading and went off the coast around Coos Bay and up and over the North Pole. If you put a straight line where they tracked it and follow it down to the Nevada desert, it goes to Groom Lake. An aircraft flying at Mach twelve wouldn't be able to pick up any electronic signals because of the ionization; same thing with a photographic optical-reconnaissance platform—you wouldn't be able to see through the ionized air. But if it had a sensor that can locate and detect fissionable material, track the movement of the stuff on the ground—that *could* be detected through a layer of ionized air. The Russians have been bragging for twenty-five or thirty years that they have this ability to detect fissionable materials at a distance. That is, if a ship goes through a strait or a narrow passage, and they're on shore, they say they can look at that aircraft carrier or destroyer or battleship and say, 'They've got eight hundred pounds of uranium 235 or 238 on board, which breaks down into so many megatons of explosive capability.' A guy who worked for the NSA and NRO told me the U.S. Navy has had a system like that on P-3s since 1975.

"If this is the mission for the Aurora—if its purpose is to track the location of fissionable materials in the former Soviet Union—you'd want to come up over the Pole. That way you're high enough so you can look at Ukraine and Belarus, Iran and Iraq. It might be partially funded by the Russians, or fully funded by the Middle Eastern countries. If the Middle Eastern oil producers wanted to keep track of Iran and Iraq, as well as the breakaway republics from the former Soviet Union, they could have funded the whole thing. To build three mother airplanes and five or six Auroras would cost ten or twelve billion dollars—say a billion a year over twelve years. To OPEC, that isn't a whole hell of a lot of money, especially if we operate it for them, manage it and maintain it and launch it out of Groom Lake on a mother aircraft, or sometimes by itself. Have you seen in the news lately where Congress is thinking of reactivating the SR-71? Well, a friend of John's and mine—as good a source as they come, a guy who's intimately familiar with the SR-71 and Skunk Works and Area 51—told us that one reason they're thinking of reactivating it is that 'They're having reliability problems on the propulsion system of its replacement.' And he asked us, 'Who do you know who has manned lifting-body reentry vehicle experience?' *Rockwell.* They have a close working relationship with Lockheed, and they bid on the B-2 and several other advanced-technology fighter and tactical attack aircraft in the 1980s. So word had it that Rockwell was the prime contractor for the Aurora, but that it was *managed* by Skunk Works. General Dynamics also had some involvement in a project referred to as 'Program 100.' If you were in their cafeteria and mentioned it, it was like someone hit the mute switch; everything suddenly got real quiet, and then you were told to leave. That could have been a competitor to Aurora."

"Bob Lazar said he saw the back end of the Aurora," said Andrews. "He was on a bus with opaque windows when he heard the sound.* Years later, the day after Jim and I heard it, we went to Bob's place and said, 'We heard it!' He said, 'I told you guys! I *told* you!' "

This mention afforded the opportunity to ask what Andrews and Goodall thought of Lazar.

"Bob is an eccentric, weird duck," said Goodall, "but he's an incredibly brilliant guy. I'm a pretty good of judge of character; I've interviewed a lot of people involved in Black programs, and from sitting down and shooting the shit with Bob Lazar, having a cup of coffee, I don't get the impression that what he's said to me is fabricated. His story has never changed; he's never embellished it or added anything to it. So when anybody asks me if I think Bob Lazar is legitimate, my answer is yes.

"I talked to a guy once who worked on cruise missiles, and another guy who was a master sergeant in the original F-117 acceptance program [at Area 51]. They told me they were bored one day and were driving around Papoose Mountain, and as they were coming down the dirt road toward Papoose Lake, all of a sudden from nowhere they were surrounded by security people. Their badges and IDs were taken; they were held for thirty or forty minutes, and then they were told to get the hell out of there and don't come back."

"I always thought UFOs were possible," said Andrews. "There have been lots of reports from good people in the military; the stories have been circulating for years. Personally, I don't want to close off my life to any ideas. Some people want their lives to be closed so nothing can get in, but they also have bad stuff that can't get out. I like my life to have a little bit of a gap so I can let the bad stuff out and let new interests in."

Andrews showed me a letter he'd written to Ben Rich in 1986 asking his opinion about UFOs. *"I am a believer,"* Rich had responded, and *"so is Kelly Johnson."* When Andrews asked for clarification—e.g., was Rich referring to man-made or extraterrestrial UFOs?—Rich replied: *"I'm a*

---

* Lazar said that his supervisor, Dennis Mariani, pointed out the Aurora to him and that the plane's engine made it sound like "the sky is tearing."

believer in both categories. I feel everything is possible. Many of our man-made UFO's are <u>Un</u> <u>F</u>unded <u>O</u>pportunities. In both categories, there are a lot of kooks and charlatans—be cautious."

"Ben Rich told me twice before he died: 'We have things at Area 51 that you and the best minds in the world won't even be able to conceive that we have for thirty or forty years, and won't be made public for another fifty,'" said Goodall. "A friend of mine at Lockheed told me, 'We have things in the Nevada desert that are alien to your way of thinking—far beyond anything you see on *Star Trek*.' One time, I interviewed a retired senior master sergeant who had been at Groom Lake three different times as an Air Force safety specialist; I got his name through a mutual friend, met him at Nellis, and then we went off base. At first he was real nervous, but when he warmed up he told me, 'We have things in the Nevada desert that are literally out of this world. Things that would make George Lucas envious.' I know one retired guy who worked at Lockheed for thirty years, most of the time at Area 51; he's very proud of what he's done, and he wants the story of the place to be told so that his grandchildren will have some idea of what he was involved in. In the summer of '86, I asked him if he believes in UFOs; he said, 'They absolutely, positively do exist.' I said, 'Can you expand on that?' And he said, 'No, I've said too much as it is.'"

"I've never seen a UFO near Groom Lake," said Andrews. "I've looked; I've seen lights and flares and things like that, but nothing I couldn't identify. Still, when Lazar's story came out, I thought: Good—let's listen to it. I don't know if he's telling the truth, but I found him to be an interesting guy. And as Jim says, his story has not changed in all these years. I sent Lazar's W-2 to a Navy captain who said he'd be happy to verify it, but then he never answered me. He could have either verified the W-2 or said Bob Lazar was a liar, but they won't do that. That's what happens with these people; if you get too close, it just dries up.

"I took Lazar's W-2 form to the Office of Naval Intelligence in the Pentagon," said Goodall. "The guy at the front desk looked at it and took it into his admiral's office. A second later the admiral came out and told me, 'I don't know where you got this, but I don't ever want to see it again—and I'm ordering you to leave this office right now.'"

Andrews pulled out another file of correspondence. On a Department of the Navy letterhead ("Headquarters, Naval Investigative Service Command"), a Captain R. A. Jones agreed in January 1991 to confirm the

authenticity of Lazar's "Employer's Identification Number of 46-1007639."
Two months later (after some further prompting from Andrews), Jones
reported that his inspector general had found that the Naval Intelligence
Command had not issued the W-2 in question.

"Nonsense, Captain," Andrews shot back. "A damn stonewall and
bureaucratic bullshit." In his own caustic letter, Andrews speculated about
the response Jones must have received when he presented a copy of
Lazar's W-2 to his inspector general: *"We have nothing to say about Bob
Lazar . . . Don't you get involved with the Bob Lazar thing . . . You are not
to say anything about Bob Lazar . . . do you understand?!!!"* Going on to
condemn the captain for breaking his promise, Andrews reissued his
demand to "confirm the authenticity" of the W-2, opining that "someone
within NISC" must be cleared to comb the Navy's classified records.

"And indeed, Counselor," he concluded, "who has the right to classify
cosmic scientific evidence?"

Confronted with this outburst, Captain Jones responded, "Within the
Department of the Navy, the Naval Investigative Service Command is
solely responsible for investigating actual, suspected or alleged major
criminal offenses committed against a person, the United States Government or its property, or private property, including attempts or conspiracies to commit such offenses." Andrews fired off a final letter, in which he
concluded from the official silence that "Robert Scott Lazar did indeed
work on recovered UFOs," and that "UFOs ARE real and our planet is
being visited and we can't do a damn thing about it."

This seemed slightly more than what Andrews had described as "a little
bit of a gap" in his point of view toward flying saucers. In fact, he sounded
suspiciously like a type of UFO fanatic that he himself had derided in his
1986 letter to Ben Rich—a class of crusader that Andrews described as
"tenacious, prolific, *wanting* to believe something is there and somewhat
prone to make macro jumps in logic and having a tendency to bombard
with writing/documentation the person he should be asking but instead his
effort becomes, by default, an effort of *convincing* the person he should be
asking and it is overkill."

As it turned out, the epistolary exchange with Captain Jones had been
preceded by a couple of others Andrews had had with the Internal Revenue Service, and with the secretary of Dr. Edward Teller.

In December 1990, Andrews filed a Freedom of Information Act request with the IRS seeking "a yes or no answer that [Employee Identification Number] 46-1007639 is a match for the U.S. Department of Naval Intelligence, Washington DC 20038." Eight months later (after an appeal and letter of complaint to Senator Alan Cranston, President George Bush, and Vice President Dan Quayle), Andrews received the response that "there is no taxpayer, agency, or other employer with this EIN [and] no practical method of determining whether the United States Department of Naval Intelligence or other employer once had this EIN." In reply, Andrews pointed out that individuals are asked to keep personal tax records for five years, and that the IRS's national computer database should have been able to verify an employee ID number within seconds unless the number was classified. "Someone is lying," Andrews had declared. "Plain and simple. The question is who and not if. And I already know the why."

As for Teller, Andrews had begun writing to him in February 1988, more than a year before Bob Lazar appeared on the public horizon. After describing himself as a longtime fan of Teller's and declaring his support of continued defense spending, Andrews eventually got around to asking if the Strategic Defense Initiative was really designed to thwart the Russians as opposed to some other "outside threat." "Dr. Teller, you spend time at the Test Site," Andrews wrote. "Is there something you should be telling us about UFOs? Are you a current member of MJ-12?"

When he received no response, Andrews wrote again to thank Teller for silently confirming that he was indeed a member of MJ-12. This prompted a response from the physicist's secretary, Patricia W. French, who reported that the ailing Dr. Teller had been incapacitated by recent surgery and would be unable to answer letters "for a long, long time." Andrews duly expressed his sympathy, but two years later, when he noticed that Teller would soon be speaking at a conference in New Orleans, he resubmitted all of his previous correspondence. By this time, Bob Lazar had come along, so Andrews also asked in passing if Teller was familiar with Element 115.

In time, Andrews conveyed all of Lazar's claims about having met and been referred for his job at S-4 by the physicist, repeatedly asking Teller to confirm or deny the allegations. When Andrews called French on the phone, she went so far as to tell him that Teller "disagrees with your thesis," but when Andrews asked for a signed statement that "Everything Bob Lazar claims regarding his connection with Dr. Teller is untrue," he remained unanswered. Interestingly enough, when Andrews asked French about another rumor—that Teller had been present at the Bush-Gorbachev Malta summit in late 1990—she denied it within a week. But neither she nor Teller ever directly addressed Andrews's question about Bob Lazar.

"Usually, when somebody fabricates something outrageous, there's an ulterior motive—money or prestige or publicity," said Goodall. "But Bob Lazar doesn't want publicity, and if he ever had a security clearance, it's now long dead. So it would serve no purpose whatsoever for him to fabricate a story about going out to S-4, especially when, in the first twenty minutes I knew him, one-on-one, he said John Lear was out of his mind for believing in UFOs."

"What do you mean?" I asked.

"When I first met Bob, in November 1988," Goodall said, "I'd just photographed the Tonopah Test Range with John Lear. I wanted to get the film processed, and Bob was over at John's house. He'd just moved out from Los—uh, Albuquerque, in New Mexico. He said he had a C-41 processor at home, so we jumped in his 280ZX and drove across town. While we were going over there, he told me: 'You know, I'm a nuclear physicist. If I can't prove it mathematically or put my hands on it, it doesn't exist. I like John Lear, but the poor guy's really full of shit. He believes in UFOs! Give me a break! How can a man that intelligent—with that background, from such a famous aviation family—believe in flying saucers?' "

"I introduced Jim to John Lear," Andrews revealed. "In fact, I'm the guy who turned John Lear on to UFOs. I remember talking to him about it on the phone when I lived in Ventura. He said, 'That's all bullshit,' but after I told him to read the literature and talk to his contacts in the military, he did a hundred-and-eighty-degree turn and became a real believer."

"Do you think he's sane?" I asked.

"John has a different way of thinking, but I think he's sane," said Andrews. "I want someone to give me a good way of determining who's sane and who's insane. Edison and the Wright brothers might have been insane. After all, if Man was meant to fly, he'd have a propellor on his forehead."

"I think there are times when John Lear pulls your leg and you don't even know it," said Goodall. "Among other things, John is a prankster. But the man lost a hundred-and-fifty-thousand-dollar-a-year job because he wouldn't back down on UFOs. Back when he was an L-1011 pilot, he gave a talk in Houston on UFOs. Some reporter called the president of John's company and said, 'You have a senior captain touting the fact that UFOs are real. Either you tell him to back off, or I'm gonna spread the word that you have mentally unstable people flying your airplanes.' The president called John into his office and said, 'Tell me face-to-face that this UFO stuff is a bunch of shit, and you can walk out of here and go back to work. If you don't, I gotta fire ya.' John said, 'I can't because it's real and I believe it.' How many guys do you know who'd give up a job like that for a belief they don't believe in?"

"I don't often agree with John," said Andrews, "but if I needed a friend, I would pick him because he's honest."

Actually, it was apparent from Andrews's letters to Teller that, by early 1988, the model designer had adopted at least some of Lear's cosmology. In his first letter to Teller on February 13, 1988—the one in which Andrews asked the physicist if he was a member of MJ-12, written ten months before Lazar claims he was sent to Papoose Lake (written, in fact, before either Lear or Andrews had even met Lazar)—Andrews mentioned that he had some friends "who have worked, or currently work, at . . . Groom Lake and S4." Television reporter George Knapp, trying to bolster Lazar's credibility, had said that "There are many things Lazar knows that he couldn't have known if he didn't work there. For one, how many people had ever heard of S-4 at all before Lazar went public?" Ufologist Bill Moore, for one, claimed that *he* had previously known about S-4 and told John Lear about it. Lear denied this, but Andrews's first letter to Teller seemed to indicate that Lear had mentioned the term "S-4" to Andrews before either man met Lazar, establishing the possibility that Bob found out about it not on the "job" but from John Lear himself. When I put this to Andrews, he acknowledged that it could be true.

It was getting late; Goodall said he had to get up early to catch a plane the next morning. As we stood up to shake hands, I asked the two what they would do now that the Air Force had succeeded in closing the nearest vantage points on Area 51.

"Just because they took away White Sides and Freedom Ridge doesn't mean you can't still see what flies out of that place," Goodall divulged. "I have a vantage point now, in the mountains on public land, where I can see two hundred and seventy degrees all the way around to the north end of the twenty-seven-thousand-foot runway. It's the same place where they looked for me and Glenn Campbell for four hours and couldn't find us. They overflew us with a helicopter and later confiscated our film because it had incriminating evidence that an Air Force helicopter was in direct violation of Air Force safety regulation 60-15, which says they cannot operate within five hundred feet of a civilian's person, vehicle, vessel, or premise within a military operating area, unless it's a rescue."

We got our coats as Andrews started turning out lights. "There's something very, very special about Area 51," he said as we made our way toward the door. "Something out of the ordinary. It's not because of the hardware; there's something else going on. I don't understand it, unless there's subterfuge at work and they're trying to make Groom Lake seem like the big thing when it's really far away. One Air Force guy, a friend of ours, told us to 'look to the north.' I think he might have meant Canada."

As Andrews flicked off the last light, Goodall turned away from the automobile models he'd been perusing on Andrews's office walls.

"Cars," he commented as he went out the door toward the elevator. "Yuck."

SIX

The Other Hand

Within a few months of the Ultimate UFO Seminar, Glenn Campbell had checked into some of the claims that Bob Lazar made about his educational background. During the conference's question-and-answer session, Lazar had repeated the assertion that he received master's degrees in physics from MIT (where he remembered a professor named Hohsfield) and electronic technology from CalTech (where he recalled a "Doctor Duxler"). Reporter George Knapp and ufologist Stanton Friedman had called MIT and been told there was no alumni record for Robert S. Lazar. But Campbell reasoned that, even if Lazar's records had been expunged as he claimed, it would apply only to computer files and not to such printed matter as yearbooks and telephone directories, which were widely distributed and retroactively uncontrollable. Hence, Glenn—a Boston native— decided to visit the MIT Institute Archives in Cambridge, Massachusetts, which has open shelves of student directories, commencement lists, and phone directories for faculty and staff dating back to the earliest years of the university.

Campbell found no Robert S. Lazar in any such volume issued between 1978 and 1990. (He located several Lazaruses, but the only Lazars were named Stephen and Howard.) Neither did he find a Professor Hohsfield in the MIT physics department—or, for that matter, in the *Faculty Directory of Higher Education, American Men and Women of Science,* or the *National Faculty Directory.* He did come across a William Duxler in the latter volume, the only problem being that Duxler was employed at Los Angeles Pierce College, the sole institute of higher learning that Lazar has ever been verified as attending. As far as CalTech was concerned, Southern Californian Tom Mahood followed Campbell's lead, going to the campus and looking through old yearbooks and directories. Not only did he fail to find any Robert S. Lazar, he learned that CalTech doesn't even offer the course of study that Bob said he had pursued there. (It has a department of "electrical engineering," but not "electronic technology.") For Mahood, however, this proved to be only the beginning of an obsessive inquiry into Bob Lazar's background. In 1994, he put out the first fruit of his investigative husbandry: a five-page, single-spaced timeline chronicling Bob's verifiable exploits, from his birth in 1959 until 1993.

In 1995, I paid Tom a visit to talk about what he'd found.

Mahood is a lean, athletic, raw-boned, square-jawed, blue-eyed, soft-spoken guy in his forties. He lives in Orange County, where he had worked as a road and traffic engineer for seventeen years. In the mid-eighties, however, after a six-week trip to Antarctica, he and his wife Jeri decided to save up their money and retire early, then go traveling and perhaps enter the Peace Corps. In between, though, Tom discovered the Internet—and having been interested in UFOs since childhood, he began spending time in such online newsgroups as alt.alien.visitors, where he soon found out about Area 51.

In November 1993, on their way home from Thanksgiving in Utah's Zion National Park (and two months before the opening of the Freedom Ridge Expressway), Tom and Jeri decided to take a detour through Rachel. They picked up a copy of Campbell's *Area 51 Viewer's Guide*, and found, to their pleasant surprise, that it "didn't say there were UFOs behind every Joshua tree." They followed its directions to the border and hiked up to look at the base, an experience that Tom likened to "peering over the Berlin wall and being watched by the Soviets on the other side." On the way, they noticed a Jeep Cherokee in their rearview mirror. "Until it happens to you in the U.S.A., it's hard to know what that feels like," Tom said. "We were scared, mad, and creeped out, all at the same time."

On the question of Bob Lazar, Mahood at first found himself positively disposed. "The way he talked rang true to me," Tom said, sitting in the spotless living room of the small clean house in the planned community where he and Jeri lived. "It was just a gut reaction; I know a lot of technically oriented people, and Lazar seemed like a typical science and engineering nerd. I was impressed by the fact that, whereas bullshit artists will answer all your questions, Lazar didn't hesitate to say, 'I don't know.' He struck me as a solid, legitimate guy.

"I became a Lazar believer—but I'd still wake up at night worrying about it. After all, if he was right, then my view of reality was wrong. So I started looking around for things to disprove his story, and started finding all this stuff on somebody who had supposedly been made into a nonperson."

One of Tom's Net contacts told him that, for a nominal fee, he could view the public records of Lazar's 1986 bankruptcy proceedings in Las Vegas. Mahood made his way up Interstate 15 to Clark County, Nevada, where a clerk duly presented him with what Tom now describes as "a hundred and twenty pages portraying an absolute flake bordering on a con man."

The report, which amounted to a financial history for Lazar in the early 1980s, revealed that Lazar had

- borrowed $15,000 from his father, Albert, repaying only $1,000 by the date of the filing;
- borrowed $4,000 from his mother, Phyllis, repaying only $300;
- borrowed $60,000 from Los Alamos National Bank (secured by a $7,900 1984 Honda), repaying only $1,300;
- bought a 1984 Corvette for $19,000, repaying only $550 (and having it repossessed as a result);
- bought a 1985 Honda CRX for $9,000, repaying only $300 (ditto);
- borrowed $2,000 from a friend named John Horne for a down payment on a jet car, repaying nothing.

At the time of the bankruptcy filing, Lazar had declared his monthly expenses to be $2,360, *in addition to* a monthly debt of $13,150 for something he refused to name, despite being required to identify it. Though the report referred repeatedly to his photo-processing business, it made no mention of any employment at Los Alamos National Laboratory. As Mahood put it in the timeline, "When asked if he had been in a partnership with anyone or engaged in any business within the preceding six years, RL stated 'No.' Within the preceding two years, RL stated the amount of income he received from his trade was 'Unknown,' that he had received no other income from other sources and had not filed tax returns for the period."

Such revelations whetted Mahood's appetite for more. He next obtained the presentencing report on Lazar's pandering conviction—which referred, among other things, to a certified copy of Bob's "missing" birth certificate, identifying him (despite his claim that he'd been adopted) as the natural-born son of Albert and Phyllis Lazar. Though George Knapp had tried and failed to obtain a hospital copy of the certificate from Florida, Mahood found out that a 1987 state law had declared birth certificates confidential there. As Tom said, "It's illegal for the state or the counties to give out copies of certificates, or to even verify the existence of a certificate, to anyone other than the birth registrant, the registrant's parents or legal guardians, or the birth registrant's legal representative."

Continuing to pore through public records, Mahood made yet more amazing discoveries. For example, when Lazar married his second wife, Tracy (at the We've Only Just Begun Wedding Chapel in Las Vegas on April 19, 1986), he apparently hadn't yet divorced his first wife, Carol—and two days after his wedding to Tracy, Carol committed suicide.

Though no autopsy was performed by the Clark County coroner, according to her death certificate, Carol's demise was caused by carbon-monoxide poisoning from vehicle exhaust at the Lazars' home on Ann Greta Drive in Las Vegas. An obituary in the *Las Vegas Review-Journal* described her as "a self-employed film processor . . . survived by her husband Robert"—who, in the wake of his first wife's death, continued to occupy their house on Ann Greta (presumably with his other wife). Two months after Carol died, Lazar declared bankruptcy, listing among his reasons for financial hardship "loss of spouse" and "loss of business." Nevertheless, he continued making photo deliveries in his jet-powered Honda.

Two years later, a default notice was issued for delinquent payments on the Ann Greta house. It was eventually sold at auction, by which time Tracy had bought her own place under the name Jackie Evans, which she had used when she married Bob a *second* time at the Chapel of Love in Las Vegas, six months after their first wedding. When Bob and Tracy/Jackie were divorced in 1990, their settlement stipulated that Bob would receive this house and any equipment and/or revenue from his own business.° Tracy/Jackie, however, would retain the name Tracy Lazar.

Five months after the divorce, the IRS placed a $4,897 lien on Bob for back taxes.

"**T**o say that I was stunned is an understatement," Mahood told me. "I thought, 'I've been had. This guy is a complete fraud.' But on the other hand, Lazar knew a lot of stuff about Groom Lake—supposedly he could describe details of the place to George Knapp. I was sure by now that his CalTech and MIT stories were phony, but I couldn't figure out why he would pick the top two engineering schools in the country for his fake degrees. I went from being a true believer to a true skeptic to something in the middle. I thought maybe he was at Groom, but not necessarily where he claims to have been."

In March 1995, when Gene Huff released his *Lazar Synopsis*, the fascinated Mahood sent Huff an appreciative e-mail. Tom got a relatively polite response, but was still put off by Huff's approach, which typically belittled a questioner's importance while cussing him or her out in the bargain. "He said he had no problem with anyone declaring Lazar to be a liar—*if* the person had looked fully into the story and knew the whole picture," Tom recalled. "But when I or others did so, he immediately started hurling invective."

By way of explaining himself, Huff declared on the alt.conspiracy. area51 newsgroup: "Generally in exchanges you teach and learn. Here I only teach, of course with pauses to clarify the misinformation, disinformation, and lack of information passed on by the typical moron who feigns authority here." For example, when someone named Nick Humphries posted the belief that Lazar's current girlfriend was named Linda (admittedly in context of surmising that Bob's first wife's suicide was "one way of

---

°The names of these businesses—Jet Processing, United Nuclear, and Red Light Racing— neatly summed up several of Lazar's enthusiasms.

getting a divorce"), Huff responded: "I think not dickless, you poor perverted dick for brains. . . . you don't know what you're talking about and you are the last cock sucker on earth that should be trying to offer that information. You are one sorry sack of shit."[*]

"One day it just got to me," said Tom. "So I sat down and put together six or seven flaws in Lazar's story—stuff that couldn't be explained away." The resulting document—*The Lazar Flaws*—is a meticulous analysis of the fine points in Lazar's story; ignoring the personal and financial questions that he had uncovered, Mahood dispassionately examines a half-dozen technical issues that poke holes in Lazar's case, closing with a range of theories, from sympathetic to incriminating, as to how such contradictions might occur. He points out, for example, that where Lazar had said at first that the "Sport Model" used all three of its amplifiers in the "Omicron" mode, he later said that it used only one, and still later said that the other two folded up out of the way. Mahood illustrates that the amount of time Lazar said he worked at S-4—six or seven hours a day, for a total of six or seven days, between December 1988 and April 1989—would seem to indicate that "he's on the job for the equivalent of about a week, and on top of all the other things he's claimed to have seen or done ('getting up to speed,' the medical exam, the security briefing, reading the various reports, watching the test flight, etc.) he 'discovers' just what the magic material is that does all this [Element 115]. If true, it would seem Lazar had one of the better first work weeks in the history of mankind!" Further, citing his own research at the Department of Energy and U.S. Geological Survey, Tom divulges that, where Bob claimed that his predecessors at S-4 had cut into an antimatter reactor and been killed by a resulting twenty-kiloton blast (later passed off as an unannounced nuclear test), the only such impacts recorded by the USGS during that time period were *previously announced* nuclear tests. Lastly, Mahood expands on his and Campbell's findings about Lazar's academic background, showing that—according to information on Bob's whereabouts contained in his bankruptcy file and the *Los Alamos Monitor* article about him and his jet

[*]Would-be connoisseurs can treat themselves to "The Wit and Wisdom of Gene Huff" at http://www.serve.com/ZERO/huff/wisdom.html. The compiler of this website, akazero, has assembled a hit list of Huff's favorite curse words, including individual word counts of twenty apiece for "ass" and "asshole," five for "bitch," three for "cock," two for "cunt," four for "dick," sixteen for "fuck," one each for "fucked" and "fucker," five for "pussy," one for "twat," and forty-one for "shit."

car—it would have been physically impossible for him to have completed graduate courses of study at CalTech and MIT.

The only place where Lazar had mentioned an *undergraduate* degree was in his presentencing report, where he claimed to have a diploma from a "correspondence" college called Pacifica University. Mahood was unable to locate this institution in any college directory, including the *McMillan Guide to Correspondence Study* and the *State of California Department of Education's Council for Private, Post-Secondary and Vocational Education*. Later, however, he learned that it had turned up on TV in 1978 (when Lazar was nineteen years old) in an investigation of diploma mills on *Sixty Minutes*. Pacifica was an operation run by an ex-con who sold bachelor's degrees for $1,400.

When Mahood put out the *Flaws*, he also published Gene Huff's rebuttal, in which the loyal gatekeeper explained some of his master's contradictions by divulging that, "if Bob Lazar doesn't find that you have a need to know any of his personal business, even some things others would find trivial or irrelevant, he doesn't share it or blows you off in the most convenient manner. He is truly the one single judge of who he should share information with and he judges only a very small group of people to be worthy of responses regarding his personal dealings." In particular, Huff pointed out, Bob's bankruptcy trustee and probation officer were deemed undeserving of accurate information; hence, any conclusions drawn from such records were based on "variables" as opposed to "constants" and were hence unreliable. It seems patently obvious, though, that if Huff believed such an explanation would enhance the integrity of his friend's testimony about flying saucers from outer space, Gene was as wacky as Bob.

"I like the idea that Lazar was a patsy," Mahood admitted as we ascended the stairs to his study. "Maybe he was set up; maybe the whole thing at S-4 was staged. After all, when he rode the bus by himself to Papoose Lake, where was everybody else—already at work? Then again, he might *still* be on their payroll, saying what they want him to say for reasons we don't know. For example, maybe there *was* no Element 115, but some other scenario entirely. There are lots of theories about what might have happened: Lazar had his mind mucked with; he repeated a story he heard from someone else; he and his friends dreamed the whole thing up in order to make money. But they all have flaws. There's no one unifying Theory of Bob. Lazar himself is one of the great mysteries of Area 51."

Mahood hadn't stopped at Lazar, however. In scrutinizing maps of the Nellis Range, for example, his attention had been caught by a place called Area 19. "It was added to the Test Site in 1962 to accommodate underground testing. Press tours can get almost anywhere, but not there. If you wanted to pinpoint the most remote area of the Test Site, that's pretty much it—it's right in the middle of the Nellis Complex. But if you look at maps, there's a power line from Highway 95 that ends at a double ring of roads in Area 19."

As Mahood pulled out a map of the Test Site, he told me that Glenn Campbell had introduced him to an airline pilot who used to fly the commercial route between Las Vegas and Salt Lake City. "This guy was a scanner buff, and he had friends who piloted Janet 737s into Groom Lake and the Tonopah Test Range. But they told him they also flew 'somewhere else' in the Nellis Range that had an 'invisible' eight-thousand-foot runway. I call it the 'Cheshire Runway'—it was disguised to look like the desert, but at the last minute they'd turn on sprinklers and wet it so that you could see it. Before going in, they had to get clearance to make sure no Soviet satellites were overhead. When they landed they couldn't linger, but they saw people going into buildings that were disguised to look like hills.

"When I asked this guy where the runway was on the Las Vegas sectional map, he pointed to where that power line ends in Area 19. Mark Farmer has a friend who worked at the Test Site; when we asked him about Area 19, he just smiled and wouldn't say a word. I've talked to other people who were driving up there and got stopped by guards, but apparently even the Test Site doesn't know what's going on there. Paul McGinniss, who runs an antisecrecy Web page, did a Freedom of Information Act request and found out that Area 19 is controlled by the Defense Nuclear Agency; the Test Site doesn't even know what classified programs are there. On the jurisdictional map, though, Area 19 is controlled by Los Alamos—and a number of people, including Ben Rich, have said that Los Alamos is the place that would handle UFOs.

"This is where we start getting into some pretty wild stuff," Tom said. "I have a contact from the Net who used to be a contract engineer for the CIA. He was also in Vietnam and the Reagan White House; he's a spook, basically. Well, he decided he wanted to build an electromagnetic radiation detector for UFOs, but to do it, he needed to find out the correct frequencies. He got in touch with a woman who'd spoken on the radio about that exact topic; and when he had lunch with her, he found out that she was a remote viewer."

"Remote viewing" is a form of extrasensory perception that was extensively researched by the CIA in the 1970s. At the direction of the agency, the Stanford Research Institute conducted experiments with people who were reportedly able to transport themselves mentally to distant spots and report what they saw with surprising accuracy. Sometimes referred to as "psychic warfare," the practice has been written up in such respected scientific publications as the British journal *Nature*.

"This woman said she'd been hired as a consultant by a certain aerospace firm," said Mahood. "They gave her a couple of geographical coordinates, and when she 'went' there, she saw this gleaming underground lab. Then a door opened and out came a gray alien. The thing that *really* disturbed her, though, was that the alien could see *her*. It went back through the door, then some more aliens came out and stared at her. In all her remote-viewing experience, she said no subject had ever been able to detect her before.

"She decided to get out of there, but when she did, she said they were apparently able to track her—she started having computer break-ins and all this other weird stuff happen. The best part is, when she reported what she'd seen to the company that hired her, they said: 'Yes, that's just what we expected. Thank you very much.' "

Mahood and his contact decided to see what this woman found out if they gave her the coordinates for Area 19. First, however, they "calibrated" her: "We asked a friend in Virginia to arrange some stuff—whatever he chose, we didn't know what—in his house. Then we told this woman his address. She said she saw a pile of rags with a yellow toy on top of it. As it turned out, the guy had put a towel in the middle of his living room and placed a yellow chainsaw on it. So that wasn't too bad.

"When we gave her the coordinates for Area 19, she rattled off a *lot* of detailed description. She said that at the end of the power line, within the ring of roads, there had once been a 'pumped photon apparatus'—which corresponds to the description of SDI laser technology. She said that an explosion had destroyed the facility, but later an underground building was constructed, with a louvered retractable roof and a circular bay for a thirty-foot disc. She said that the saucer, which had been cobbled together from a couple of others, was powered by capacitors—a very crude system, like running an airplane with a steam engine. The disc was remotely controlled on very short flights without any passengers. She also saw antiaircraft emplacements and a lot of military and security guards to the south. No aliens, though. And when we gave her the coordinates for Papoose Lake, all she saw were empty hangars."

As far as that spot was concerned, Mahood had studied an enlargement of a 1988 Soviet satellite photo and found no evidence of any structures or land disturbances at Papoose Lake. "You can see all the roads and turn-arounds very clearly, right down to the four-wheel-drive level," he said. "The road that runs down the west side of the Papoose Range is very poor."

As we went over this material, Tom's wife, Jeri—a sturdy, friendly, apple-cheeked blonde—appeared at the door with a tray of coffee and cookies. This was a homey accompaniment to her husband's more cosmopolitan pursuits. Soon I learned that she was also an expert quilter; she'd recently completed a couple of bedspreads decorated with what appeared to be Navajo patterns. On closer inspection, however, these turned out to be B-2 stealth bombers.

As for Tom, he had digested much of his research into his own Internet Web page. It was called *Blue Fire*,* named for a security condition reportedly imposed at Area 51 during the first UFO conference in Rachel. In addition to such features as the Bob Lazar Corner and Papoose Lake Primer ("Everything you ever wanted to know . . . but had the good sense not to ask, because other people would think you were nuts"), *Blue Fire* explores such hot topics as Los Alamos, the Tonopah Test Range, radiation gauges of southern Nevada, and radar-cross-section facilities of the Mojave Desert ("Underground bases or something neat but mundane? You decide"). Mahood's curiosity clearly extended beyond the boundaries of Area 51 to encompass the entire nuclear/defense landscape of the American Southwest. To hear Tom tell it, though, that was necessary when confronting the craftiness of Black Budget puppeteers.

"When I watch a magician, you know, I always look at his other hand—the one that's not supposed to be doing anything," he said. "There's 'secret,' and then there's *really* secret. If you study the Manhattan Project, you learn that these guys are really clever about hiding things. The *really* secret facility could be fifty miles away on the other side of Groom Lake. There might be stuff so Black that it's not even at Area 51."

*www.serve.com/mahood/bluefire.htm

SEVEN

A Higher Form of Hungarian

When Freedom Ridge and White Sides Mountain were closed to the public, Glenn Campbell predicted that the move would not "defuse the hard-core fanatics who are rapidly hacking away at the secrets of the 'Test Site.' " In fact, Campbell himself had already begun publishing something called "Tales of the Test Site" in *The Groom Lake Desert Rat*. Whereas, up until then, he had concerned himself mainly with issues of government accountability, he now began to address the local UFO stories (*other* than those espoused by Bob Lazar). Reiterating that he didn't care whether extraterrestrials existed, Campbell still stressed that the vicinity of Area 51 was "the place to understand how people deal with with UFOs, real or imagined, teaching us what we can trust about human witnesses."

That said, Glenn revealed that two years of experience in and around Rachel had changed his mind about one thing: Where he'd once believed that a secret as big as alien contact could not be kept hidden for half a century, he now admitted that, in the vicinity of Groom Lake, it could. In this vast desert of sheltering mountains and enclosed valleys, sealed off by security for atomic testing and military training, inhabited since World

War II by some of the best scientific minds in the world, it stood to reason that, if UFO crashes *had* occurred, the materials would eventually have found their way to Nevada and the Nellis Range.° Accepting this basic possibility, Campbell commenced collecting "folklore" that supported such a scenario—although, true to his passive intellectual stance, he remained ostensibly unconcerned about proving its truth or falsehood. As he explained in *Rat #22*:

> The truth holds together over time, while lies and misperceptions fall apart on their own. The truth, even if a government secret, is supported by a million connections to the outside world, and over time many of these connections are bound to emerge just by our being open to them. A lie or fantasy is supported only by the inventiveness and brain capacity of the person telling it. No person's mind, no matter how brilliant or twisted, can reproduce all the rich interconnections of reality. A liar may be able to generate a story that sounds good on the surface, but closer inspection will eventually reveal glaring internal flaws and probably an irate and defensive storyteller.

Or, in *Rat # 29:*

> To call a story "folklore" does not mean it is a fabrication: In most cases people are telling the story honestly as they have interpreted it, but their perception, memory and sense of human [*sic?!*] inevitably idealize and simplifies the facts. Any time a remembered narrative is re-told by a human, it becomes distorted, but this does not mean the story is worthless. There is data in folklore, maybe not the data the speaker intended, but usually some ancient basis in a worldly event.

The first talespinner that Campbell produced was a man who had contacted him after reading Glenn's first *Rats*. "Alfred,"† as he called himself, had grown up in Farmington, New Mexico, which in 1949 had been the

---

° Conversely, it's been suggested that any area so thoroughly overseen and heavily instrumented would be a terrible place to conduct secret flight tests of alien craft.
† This man later went on to talk to George Knapp and to appear on *Encounters*.

scene of several UFO sightings, including a purported crash near the neighboring town of Aztec, reported by the local newspaper but dismissed as a hoax the following day. Alfred himself had seen a formation of airborne discs from his school playground and later been questioned about it by the Air Force. After he grew up, he went to work at the Nevada Test Site as a technical photographer; awarded a "high Q" clearance, he said he was assigned to German physicist Otto Krause, who had come to the United States after World War II to work in the atomic testing program.*

Sometimes, while waiting for a shot to go off, Otto and Alfred would sit in a trailer at the Test Site, playing cards and talking to pass the time. Eventually Alfred brought up the UFO stories from his childhood. To his surprise, Krause—who said he had been stationed at New Mexico's White Sands Missile Range at that time—confirmed that one disc had crashed at Aztec and another at Roswell. Both contained alien beings, one of which survived. The debris was first brought to White Sands; the EBE was eventually moved to the Nevada Test Site. After a lengthy period of study, human scientists figured out that the craft moved by magnetics, which enabled it to leave its mother ship and negotiate the atmosphere of Earth. Oddly, the saucer itself was never declared top secret, though its propulsion system was "more classified than the atomic bomb."

While working at the Test Site, Alfred occasionally saw discs operating above Yucca or Groom Lakes, usually at night. Appearing in groups of two or three, they could ascend so quickly that they'd be out of sight in a few seconds. In the early sixties, he said, a three-man device developed on these principles was tested over West Texas; its magnetic energy dimmed the headlights of cars and knocked out the power of two small towns. Eventually, however, engineers succeeded at duplicating the craft for the purpose of delivering nuclear weapons, which it could do more effectively than any missile or bomber. This to Krause was the most beautifully kept secret of them all: that the rockets sitting in silos around the country were unnecessary for strategic defense. They were actually intended for outer space, since—not understanding the operating system of the alien mother ship—we still didn't have a better way to leave the atmosphere of Earth. But to guarantee that rocket research would continue to be funded by Congress, the public had to be convinced that we needed them for war.

*This would be consistent with Operation Paper Clip, which brought top German scientists to America to work on advanced rocketry and atomic weapons.

Alfred said that Area 51, "back in those days, was kind of something you didn't discuss. If you had to go over there, you went over there. Other than that, it was like a different world." After retiring from his job at the Test Site, he wasn't allowed to leave the country for ten years; he'd kept his disc sightings and talks with Krause secret for decades, but was finally spurred to speak out by the TV show *UFO Cover-up Live*, where he'd heard the information corroborated by informants "Falcon" and "Condor."

"We don't expect anyone to believe Alfred's tale," Campbell disclaimed in *Rat #23*. However, he observed, "What we get from Alfred's testimony are certain elements of the story which emerge again and again in the folklore." For example, the allegation of multiple disc crashes in the late forties and early fifties; the rumor that a live alien was recovered from the wreckage; the idea that the craft had been studied and flown around Area 51. Alfred's story disputed Lazar's in the craft's adherence to magnetic principles as opposed to gravity waves, and in its assertion that humans had duplicated the craft by the early 1960s, whereas Lazar maintained that the program was still groping blindly about in 1989. But in Campbell's mind, that very metaphor might be employed to explain the contradictions.

"The story of the blind men and the elephant applies," Psychospy wrote. "One of them grasps the trunk and says the elephant is like a snake; the other feels the leg and say it is like a tree." Noting that yet another theory of UFO propulsion involved microwaves and plasma fields, Campbell suggested that "all three systems could be employed in your modern flying saucer, just like in a modern car where it takes more than just the engine to make the vehicle go. Perhaps gravity waves levitate the craft; microwaves eliminate friction and magnetic fields move the craft around."

"**I** think you've gone nuts!" one of Glenn's readers opined when he started publishing such stuff. "First, the Cammo Dudes successfully distracted your attention from doing real reporting of the Groom area. Second, somebody has turned you into today's version of the 1950s Contactee with all this crap about UFOs and aliens. In the beginning you did excellent work . . . but you seem to have lost your way."

Campbell remained undeterred, however. He next unveiled his biggest find—his own personal program insider and top-secret informant. "Jarod" (pronounced "Jay-rod," and thusly pseudonymed for reasons that will be revealed presently) claimed to have worked for thirty years in the secret saucer-duplication program. A retired, seventy-year-old mechanical engineer, he said he'd been employed in the design of flight simulators used to train human pilots to operate extraterrestrial-inspired craft. This project was called FOGET, for Fundamentals of Gravity Envelope Technology. Its purpose was to duplicate an alien disc recovered in a crash near Kingman, Arizona, in May 1953. Jarod said he was speaking to Glenn and small UFO groups on his own initiative but under the scrutiny of his former employers, who had granted their permission for unknown reasons. Although he was now officially retired, he still received regular visits from a security officer, and could lose his pension if he stepped out of line.

Jarod said he'd spent most of his career at an unnamed location ("Facility X," surmised by Campbell to be Los Alamos), where he'd worked in a design office as part of an engineering team for the flight simulator. He had no involvement with the operational craft, whose team he wasn't allowed to contact. He couldn't confer with anyone outside his own group, so if he had a question about some feature of the actual disc (as opposed to the simulator), he had to pose it to his boss, who passed it along to his counterpart in the other group. Delays in the exchange of information, materiél, and paperwork led Jarod to believe that the operational craft was housed elsewhere (perhaps at Nellis). The simulator, however, was in a nearby building where, on occasional visits, Jarod came into contact with an actual EBE. He described this being (who was assisting the program as a technical adviser, and whose name was also Jarod—hence our engineer's nom de guerre) as a hairless Gray alien with four fingers and large, dark, wraparound eyes that became clearer in subdued light. Jarod 1 (the ET) wore conventional human clothing, if only to put his associates at ease; Jarod 2 (the engineer) said that being in the company of this entity was ultimately no more disconcerting than, say, encountering an African pygmy. He did, however, report the rather exotic fact that when such a being addresses you, "You hear in it your own voice." Apparently similar (in Campbell's view) to a schoolteacher withholding the solution to a math problem, the visitors were willing to go only so far in helping us understand their highly foreign systems; the alien discs were impossible for our pilots to fly, so the program's aim was to reproduce their avionics using our own technology. The simulator was intended to familiarize a human pilot with the experience before embarking on an actual flight in the operational saucer.

The craft that Jarod described was very similar to the one portrayed by Bob Lazar. Made of a light, strong, dull-metallic boron composite, it was divided into three horizontal sections, the largest of which had a reactor in the middle with a vertical pipe running straight up through the center of the craft. The lower level contained three hanging cylinders (corresponding to Lazar's gravity amplifiers), while the uppermost chamber (which Lazar wasn't allowed to enter) contained, as Bob surmised, a navigation compartment. Jarod believed that the floors and walls were not merely structural but constituted a complex power system, a "collapsing grid" capable of storing and releasing an electrical charge. The reactor was flanked by six capacitors, three on each side, while the disc's outer perimeter was embedded with forty-eight anodes that generated an electrical field around the craft, enabling it to move without friction through space (and giving rise to the glow reported by witnesses). The craft itself was almost tantamount to a tiny planet, with its own magnetic, electrical, and gravitational fields. Artificially generated gravity kept the operator seated without restraint, even when the saucer attained its maximum pitch of sixty-five degrees. Jarod 2, who had often ridden in the device, said that when it first powers up, "You may think you're paralyzed, but you're not." He described the sensation as being akin to moving underwater, even though one's actions were not in fact impeded. (Campbell noted a parallel with the Travis Walton story, dramatized in the film *Fire in the Sky*, in which a UFO abductee felt oddly paralyzed.)

Glenn described Jarod as a down-to-earth engineer with a nuts-and-bolts knack for technical detail but a number of rough human edges—for example, a tendency to ramble and a reactionary political viewpoint (which Campbell attributed to an overdeveloped relationship with talk radio). Essentially, though, Glenn found his informant to be a straightforward and trustworthy person with "no signs of any clinical pathology." Campbell had been introduced to him by members of Jarod's family, who confirmed that the man had spent much of his career in classified defense work, partly at Cape Canaveral and partly in the NERVA nuclear rocket program (he even had a photo of himself proving this latter employment). His brother, an aircraft mechanic, and his son, a radiographer, considered him honest but decidedly mysterious; after all, for a period of over twenty years, his brother hadn't even known where he was. Most of this time, Jarod its subcommittee on oversight and investigations. "It's bizarre," mused Representative Roy Wyden (D-Oregon), regarding Andrews's foot-long F-19. "What I, as a member of Congress, am not even allowed to see is ending up in model packages." Andrews himself ended up in *People* magazine, pictured with his plastic airplane alongside a satellite photo of Groom Lake.

"John Andrews has an interesting worldview that I don't fully understand," Stuart Brown had told me. "He loves spyplanes, but he hates spooks. Goodall is a roly-poly redneck comedian. He's a barrel of laughs and also a master bullshitter. He has a personal religion based around the Skunk Works—he's a huge admirer of theirs. As the unit historian for the Minnesota Air National Guard, he has a medium top-secret clearance. He somehow managed to get an A-12 Blackbird from the Air Force for a museum display, then conned the New York Air National Guard into giving him a C-5 transport, cut the A-12 into three pieces, loaded it onto the C-5, got in the cockpit, and rode it all the way from Palmdale to Minneapolis. So now he holds all kinds of records for speed, altitude, and duration of 'unpowered indoor flight.'

"I was with Goodall one time out at Groom Lake when a plane went over," Brown recalled. He said, 'That's a Russian plane.' I'm nearsighted; I need glasses for driving, but Goodall whipped out his four-hundred-millimeter lens and said, 'Looks like a Sukhoi 23'—*click click click*. 'Maybe the *D* model'—*click click click*. 'Think I got it.' I said to myself: 'This guy's blowing hard.' Two days later he called me and said, 'Those pictures weren't too bad. I'll send you a contact sheet.' Sure enough, it was a Sukhoi 23. We used one of the shots in my *Popular Science* story. The Lockheed guys think he's a loose cannon and a national hero at the same time. After all, he's preserving their heritage."

Though Goodall lived in Minnesota and Andrews in San Diego, the two were old friends. When I learned that Goodall was coming to Southern California on business, I flew down to meet them both. We convened at Andrews's office in a San Diego business park—a spacious, well-lit corporate environment whose conference-room walls were covered with racks of tiny paint jars and tubes of glue. Displayed throughout the office were various Testor products; most of the company's model kits were cars, but there was also a space shuttle, a hypothetical Aurora, and Bob Lazar's "Sport Model," shown hovering in Omicron mode on the cover of its cardboard box.

It was not decided until the Eisenhower administration in the early part of 1953. A group was formed by the President, and the chairman of the group was Vice President Richard M. Nixon. Around June of 1953, the final decision was made to set up a "satellite government." This separate government would interface with the U.S. Government for support only. Personnel involved in any part of disc retrieval, including first hand knowledge, were reassigned as satellite government entities. Additionally, new security requirements were established and new clearances assigned. . . . Normally, clearances take two to three years for any responsible positions connected with disc design. (Bob Lazar was an unusual case due to his recommendation by Teller. This gave him an edge without going through a long clearance process. Teller is high up in the satellite government organization.) The rule for disclosure of information is fifteen years after retirement in cases like mine. . . . Here is a list of what is classified under their rules: technical data, drawings, photos, sketches, illustrations, procedures, all documents relating to personnel, companies, related associate military groups, code names, types of classifications, names of people, etc. Yes, I have dropped a few names, but only with permission. During my tenure at Facility X, Nixon and another former president made visits. We even got a handshake. What was amusing to us in the group was that most other visitors to our facility did not shake our hands nor did we know their names; they were familiar to us by face only.

The background as told to my group had some very interesting twists regarding craft retrieval and the first visitor encounter. Little did the government know that retrieval operations were monitored by the visitors. They, the visitors, were well aware of the mishap of one of their vessels; however, the military got to the crash site first. No details were provided to us on how contact was made to set up the initial meeting. The reason for contact almost six years after the Roswell incident was recalled as follows: The vessel that fell in Arizona in 1953 contained four entities; two were disabled and two were reasonably well but somewhat confused. (The visitors monitoring the retrieval activities noted with much pleasure the humane treatment provided to those involved.) All entities were later taken to Facility X for medical treatment and tests. Additionally, before leaving the scene, the two that were standing upright were allowed to reenter the vessel. They entered the craft and disappeared from view. Some time had passed before exiting; it was later assumed that they were communicating with the monitoring craft.

A bizarre situation was encountered at the retrieval site. With the entities removed from the area, work proceeded: clean up and loading of the vessel on a trailer used to haul Sherman tanks. While preparations for this were being made, an entry crew was formed. They were dressed in clean-room clothing with medical surgical masks. The size of the crew was not mentioned to us. Communications was set up prior to entry. What happened when the entry crew went inside the vessel was noted as follows: Communications failed. After one hour inside, the crew emerged from the craft confused and with upset stomachs. They removed their masks and threw up. What was astonishing, they could not remember any of the inside details of the craft. The craft was sealed, camouflaged, loaded and shipped to an undisclosed Nevada test facility. The entry crew was sent to Facility X to undergo medical examinations. Results of the tests were not explained to us.

The vessel was exactly ten meters in diameter and loading it on the tank retriever was simple. However, the overhang raised some concern due to road width. Since the pneuma-grips were still in place, it was decided to raise one end of the vessel to reduce the width. To the astonishment of retrieval crew, the crane located on the tank retriever was unable to raise the vessel. Horizontally raising or lowering was simple with no effort by the crane. Finally, it was decided to use the house-moving method with road blocks secured by military vehicles. Upon arrival in Nevada, two conditions annoyed our best intelligence support: (1) the problem with reentry and (2) a strange low frequency humming sound still emitting from the lower part of the hull.

A particular item came to light as an anecdote: A member of the initial entry crew happened to be a fighter pilot. When asked if he would like to be part of the crew on the second attempt at reentry, without much hesitation he said, "I would rather take a rocket ship to Hell than go back inside that craft." So it was a major item that had to be considered in the plan. It became paramount what the first item was: Establish a communications link with the boys. The boys had their own agenda: They were busily doing their own analysis of items provided in the quarantine area. This included food, facilities and us. It began to appear that we were the captees and they were the captors.

The entities, referred to now as the "boys," were secured in a medical facility that was manned by doctors, bioastronautic physicists, chemists and linguist. Initially, communications were limited to basic sign language. The first significant communication was between the bioastronautic engineer and the tallest entity of the four, who was dubbed "Smiling Eyes." This happening pleased the people in charge, but what ensued created a dilemma: The boys wanted to return to their vessel. After much deliberation, it was agreed to take them to the Nevada Test Site where the vessel was now located. They, the boys, were pleased upon inspection of the vessel's condition. The hatch was reopened for their entry. The four filed in. After a few minutes, the hum was silenced. "Smiling Eyes" came out and went directly to the bioastronautic engineer requesting his presence in the craft. The team leader gave the okay and the two entered. After some time passed, both made their exit. The engineer looked well and smiling. The final outcome of this process was good news for the management. A request was made by the leader of the boys that they be housed at the Test Site, and they made additional requests for material, equipment and literature. So began a new era.

Before proceeding any further, one item has to be understood. All of the information presented here was provided to our group over a number of years, generally in technical briefings, design differences and discussions of classified requirements. The fact that we were young nuts-and-bolts type engineers made us quite skeptical of most information. After each session there was a lot of chuckles and further discussion within the group. Little did we know at the time that we were being monitored. Our comments were aired in following sessions in a very subtle manner; it did take some time to catch on. This made a big difference as time went on as our joking diminished with only serious discussions by the group after meetings.

To provide an illustration on how the structure of the program was decided on, one only has to look at the existing government. Think about what you would do to maintain a level of secrecy of something inherently totally bizarre in nature. Nixon did it right by establishing the satellite government. This provided cover for the visitors plus a totally new concept for protecting all information relating to this subject. The most complicated provisions of this pact was meeting the demands of the boys.

Selection of personnel in the organization was directed by the visitors. The leader was named to be the bioastronomical engineer who first made contact; his name cannot be told at this time. You cannot imagine the situation this caused. It was like putting a private in charge of the generals. Nearly all appointments were selected from the science field. All of the direction did not come from those boys picked up in the Arizona scenario: There is a chain of command. What they asked for is not completely known but some of the items included materials. One item was boron. We use this material for many things such as metals and nuclear processes. Some discord between us and the boys was identified but it was not necessarily a problem that could not be dealt with.

What is surprising to me after reading many of the UFO books and listening to various speakers on this subject is that they almost have it right. But the information they are looking for is not in the known governmental chain of agencies but only in the exacto facto organization described above. It is believed that release of further information will come from the visitors themselves, but it will be accomplished a piece at a time. If you have understood any of the above it should give one clue. Impatience is not a virtue of the visitors. To shed some light on how it will proceed the example is a recent episode going on in New Mexico. [Reference to the recent Midway sightings by a family in New Mexico.] Of course, this is where most all activity began. From what I know, the exacto facto government is again scrambling for a solution; the probable reason is distrust, not us of them, but them of us. These displays are one way for them to show disfavor. From my experience, the boys are very conservative with some emotions and occasionally show a sense of humor. Hard to get used to but nonetheless amusing. Whatever way they decide, I am sure it will be beneficial to mankind. For me, the sooner the better, some weights will be removed. No, I am not radical, just a practical engineer.

In that and other issues of the *Desert Rat*, Campbell went on to reveal more esoteric details of Jarod's framework. Two elements in particular would attain immortality in Interceptor lore. In one of his talks about the visitors, Jarod said in passing: "All I know is they sure take a lot of boron." Upon being questioned about this, he mentioned that boron was useful for preserving human bodies, but said that he didn't really know what the visitors needed it for. Still, he felt that the aliens had been harvesting boron from Earth for centuries, having only recently been forced by the spread of human civilization into direct contact with *Homo sapiens*.

"Boron is a fascinating element, important to many chemical reactions and as an ingredient in some high-strength fiber composites," Campbell revealed in *Rat #24*. "As a water softener in laundry detergent, boron helps get clothes 'whiter than white'—which may be important if you are a Gray. Boron is among the hardest substances on earth, second only to diamond. . . . Another interesting property of boron, according to a colleague who has done some research, is that it soaks up neutrons like a sponge, which may be useful in shielding or controlling nuclear reactions."

Yet another *Rat* reader revealed that boron was a common component in control rods for fission reactors, and that during the Manhattan Project, denizens of Los Alamos were forbidden to wash their clothes in boron bleach. Campbell learned from an encyclopedia that the majority of the world's boron comes from the United States "and most of that is extracted from a big hole in the ground at—you guessed it—Boron, California, which happens to be adjacent to the most secret part of Edwards Air Force Base. The second largest producer is Searles Dry Lake at Trona, California, which happens to be adjacent to the highly restricted China Lake Naval Weapons Center. The other boron mines in the U.S. are in those military/UFO hotbeds, Nevada and New Mexico. Are we beginning to detect a BORON CONSPIRACY??? In any case, our recommendation to investors is BUY."

Another intriguing tidbit had to do with the visitors' language. Psychospy related that, at a small meeting of UFO buffs, Jarod had asked his audience: "What is the most difficult language on Earth to learn?"

" 'Hungarian' said someone in the back.

"Jarod was impressed. 'Who said that? Right, Hungarian. They speak a higher form of Hungarian.' Jarod said this is what his supervisor had told him and his supervisor had never lied. Jarod then moved on to other topics in his talk without us having a chance to grill him.

"Oooo-la-la!" Psychospy remarked. "This is something we never expected. The aliens can talk to Zsa Zsa Gabor! But it's a HIGHER FORM of Hungarian, so maybe they can talk to Eva Gabor now that she has passed on.

"With all due respect, THAT'S THE STUPIDEST THING WE'VE EVER HEARD. We can't think of any reason extraterrestrials arriving on Earth would step off the ship speaking Hungarian, but we can imagine the headline in the *Weekly World News*: 'Zsa Zsa Consults with Space Aliens.' If the aliens were to speak an Earth language, you'd think it would be English, the dominant tongue of the boron trade, or maybe Esperanto, a highly rational language invented by academics and rejected by the rest of humanity. . . .

"[May] we suggest ambitious college students consider the bene-fits of Hungarian," Psychospy concluded. "Take a few introductory classes, and when the aliens reveal themselves, you'll be way ahead of every-one else."

Psychospy joked, but a little background research revealed some intriguing facts about Hungarian. Not only was Magyar (the dominant language and people of Hungary) difficult to learn, it was surprisingly disconnected from any neighboring linguistic tradition, having more in common with Finnish and even Mongolian than with the Indo-European–derived tongues surrounding it. Magyar-like archaeological artifacts have even been found in the Xinjiang Province of China, dating from the ninth and tenth centuries.

Moreover, a millennium after that—as William Broad writes in his book *Teller's War*—a clutch of brilliant Hungarian scientists

> were to have a remarkable impact on science in the United States and were universally seen as visionaries. Szilard, Wigner and Teller played important roles in the push for the atom bomb. Von Neumann was a mathematical genius who helped build giant computers used for H-bomb calculations. Fermi, the Italian physicist, once mused over the number of stars in the universe and its age, saying that if aliens existed they should have visited Earth. Indeed, Szilard joked, "They call themselves Hungarians." Teller also delighted in this notion, applying it to himself with relish. Late in

life, after getting to know someone he liked,* he would sometimes give the person permission to call him "E.T."

John McPhee elaborated on this theme in his book *The Curve of Binding Energy*:

> Not all Los Alamos theories could be tested. Long popular within the Theoretical Division was, for example, a theory that the people of Hungary are Martians. The reasoning went like this: The Martians left their own planet several aeons ago and came to Earth; they landed in what is now Hungary; the tribes of Europe were so primitive and barbarian that it was necessary for the Martians to conceal their evolutionary difference or be hacked to pieces. Through the years, the concealment had on the whole been successful, but the Martians had three characteristics too strong to hide: their wanderlust, which found its outlet in the Hungarian gypsy; their language (Hungarian is not related to any of the languages spoken in surrounding countries); and their unearthly intelligence. One had only to look around to see the evidence: Teller, Wigner, Szilard, von Neumann—Hungarians all.

The connections weren't limited to Los Alamos. Looking through *Scientific American* magazine one day, Campbell came across an IBM ad describing the science-fiction concept of quantum teleportation (the disappearance of an object in one place as a replica of it appears in another place), accompanied by the apparent non sequitur of a recommendation on how to learn more about—Hungarian goulash!

As far as folklore was concerned, Campbell was to have a field day with the idea of Hungarian aliens. Trying to imagine how such a story could have gotten started (but assuming that Jarod was sincere), Glenn posited that perhaps the program linguists, after gaining some exposure to the visitors' language, had concluded that it was *similar* to Hungarian—albeit with refinements or eccentricities that called to the academic mind a "higher form" of a Magyar-like structure. Then again, aliens or no aliens, it was entirely conceivable that, in the late forties and early fifties, the Hungarian faction at Los Alamos, feeling homesick and out of place, puckishly

* E.g., Robert Lazar?

adopted the moniker of "ETs" in response not only to their own alienation but to then-rampant headlines about flying saucers. In a sheerly strategic capacity, Magyar speakers at Los Alamos might have modeled themselves on the Navajo Code Talkers of World War II, cultivating an impenetrable means of communication among the cognoscenti (modified into a "higher form" to thwart translation and accommodate jargon), whether in regard to atomic secrets or alien contact or both. If the government *was* involved with extraterrestrials, it stood to reason that (as Skunk Works chief Ben Rich had opined to Stuart Brown) Los Alamos—home to the nation's preeminent brain trust besides being situated near so many secret facilities (not to mention saucer crashes)—would have functioned as program headquarters. To deal with the pressure involved in containing such an explosive secret, Campbell surmised, "A patently ridiculous folklore about Martians, inspired by the truth but far enough from it to not violate security oaths, might have been a way for participants to express themselves and reinforce camaraderie in public without getting in trouble."

Among attendees at Nevada UFO meetings, the source of these stories was not known as Jarod. It was a tall and crusty redneck named Bill Uhouse—a heavy smoker with a gravelly voice and white muttonchop sideburns. Under the aegis of "EBE Enterprises," he marketed alien posters and playing cards out of his house and at UFO conventions. To the Interceptors he was something of an enigma, but a far less polished and more accessible one than Bob Lazar.

"He has workman's hands, not pianist's hands," Stuart Brown observed. "He's definitely spent a lot of time building things. He may be lying or crazy, but he's not an actor." Former engineer Tom Mahood reported that he "used to work with guys who were just like Jarod. He's dead-on for that type of elderly engineer." Of course, Mahood had said something similar about Bob Lazar—but, Tom testified, "Uhouse's leads go somewhere. Lazar's lead to dead ends."

Uhouse told Mahood and Campbell that he'd been born in the town of Johnnie, northwest of Las Vegas between Death Valley and the Nevada Test Site. He claimed to have been a pilot in World War II and Korea, and to have a degree in mechanical engineering from Cornell University. He'd originally been recruited for the secret program while working at Wright-Patterson Air Force Base on early jet engines. Obtaining the requisite security clearance for briefings had taken four and a half years, during which time he'd been confused by the strange technology, since he didn't understand what he was working on. Gradually, though, he'd come to the conclusion that it was "science from someplace else." He said that the control panel of the craft had palmlike insets for alien hands, which have only four fingers; though Campbell never publicized this, the same feature was later reflected in the alleged alien-autopsy film shown on the Fox network, but the movie showed six finger positions instead of only four. Jarod explained this difference by comparing Zeta Reticuli to a city of racially divided neighborhoods, with each planet's denizens differing slightly from the next in the way that Europeans differ from Asians or Africans.

Eventually Uhouse revealed that, at least for a while, he had worked at Papoose Lake, which was connected to Groom by—what else?—an underground tunnel. He also disclosed that the major player in the secret government was the Bechtel Corporation, which was not only involved in drilling technology but had helped start the Stanford Research Institute and worked with the CIA. Eight months before it actually occurred in late 1995, Uhouse predicted that Bechtel would replace EG&G as the main contractor at the Nevada Test Site.

After Campbell began publishing Jarod's disclosures in the *Desert Rat*, Uhouse said he was approached by a curious consortium about building a flying saucer. The group, reportedly financed by a wealthy New Age philanthropist named Robert Bigelow, who had also funded Bob Lazar, supposedly included John Alexander, a pioneer in nonlethal weapons technology and author of *The Warrior's Edge*, and Hal Puthoff, who'd headed the CIA-sponsored remote-viewing program at the Stanford Research Institute. Uhouse said that, at their meeting, Puthoff did most of the talking, which centered on the concept of "zero-point energy"—an area of quantum mechanics hypothesizing that a fleeting but pervasive energy field might be responsible for gravity, inertia, and the energy tricks associated with UFOs. Uhouse, for his part, felt that the others were "on the wrong track" and never met with them again.° Recently, however, he'd come into contact with a Stanford professor named Zoltan Komar who said he was working on an antigravity disc but was having trouble steering it around inside a test chamber.

° Another description of the meeting portrayed Uhouse and the others as "mutually unimpressed."

"I was interested in him because he was Hungarian," said Uhouse, who also divulged that, when Komar had first phoned him, he'd used Uhouse's real name—the native spelling of which was Juhasz, which means "shepherd" in Hungarian. Apparently even Jarod was descended from this fabled stock, which had somehow managed to establish itself as the aliens' people of preference.

Jarod's assertions would keep the Interceptors busy for some time. For his part, Tom Mahood, looking for clues to the possible formation of a secret government department after May 25, 1953 (date of the alleged Kingman saucer crash), noticed in a *Washington Post* of that period that President Eisenhower had lunch on May 27 with the Joint Chiefs of Staff immediately after a morning meeting with the National Security Council, Vice President Nixon and other members of the cabinet, CIA head Allen Dulles, Atomic Energy Committee chairman Gordon Dean, Robert Oppenheimer, and Manhattan Project bigwig (and alleged MJ-12 member) Vannevar Bush. One nuclear blast subsequently took place on June 1 at the Nevada Test Site, followed by an eighteen-month moratorium (during the period that Uhouse said the Boys and their hardware were getting situated). Looking through Nixon's appointment books for the same period at the southwestern office of the National Archives in Laguna Niguel, California, Mahood was unable to turn up anything more unusual than two canceled visits to the Test Site; Los Alamos also reported no visits from Nixon during his vice-presidential term.

Another potential mine site was the new Nixon Library and Birthplace in nearby Yorba Linda. However, in a controversial circumstance ostensibly related to the Watergate legacy, the library hadn't yet gotten around to organizing the deceased president's papers. It did, however, boast an arresting wall mural entitled "Nixon at Andau," whose inscription informed the viewer:

In the fall of 1956, the Soviet Union brutally suppressed an anti-communist revolution in Hungary. At Christmastime, President Eisenhower sent his young vice president, Richard Nixon, on a goodwill mission to build sympathy for over 100,000 refugees who had flooded into camps along the [Austrian] border with Hungary.

After official meetings and a dinner in his honor, Nixon broke away from the constraints of protocol and returned to see what conditions were really like in the camps. He stayed up all night, riding in a haywagon pulled by a tractor as he accompanied the freedom fighters on their rounds through the countryside to search for others who had escaped the Soviet crackdown.

The painting portrayed Nixon as a trenchcoat-clad shepherd of the Hungarian masses, comforting huddled, downtrodden refugees while strange lights and clouds swirled mysteriously in the sky. "What more proof do you need of a Nixon-UFO-Hungary connection?" Psychospy asked in *Rat #34*.

Apparently Campbell himself did need more, however. In November 1995 he embarked for Budapest, the better to till the earth of this fertile new field in ufology. Glenn had utterly no background in Magyar, but because of his well-honed investigatory skills, he was able to glean some interesting facts. He learned, for example, that, like Americans, contemporary Hungarians were highly interested in the paranormal. The country had a couple of successful UFO magazines, one of which (*Ufomagazin*) had distributed the recent Roswell alien-autopsy film. Even the nation's minister of defense, Gyorgy Keleti, was known to be fascinated by flying saucers. This cultural trend was attributed to a popular disenchantment with politics, which had dominated Hungarian discourse for decades if not centuries. The fall of communism had thus set the stage for one of Eastern Europe's most rapid defections to capitalist consumerism: Downtown Budapest, Psychospy noted, had the highest concentration of McDonald's restaurants he had ever seen.

Campbell's most telling observation, though, took place in the train station when he first arrived. Unsure of how to tackle Budapest, he'd gone to the nearest public telephone but couldn't figure out how it worked. Stymied, he stood there like some new arrival from Reticulum Two on Reticulum Four. But just as alienation was beginning to close in, Glenn's eye came to rest on that least assuming but most valuable of intelligence tools. He put down his bag, picked up the phone book, and, in the listings for Budapest, found 422 listings for "Lazar."

EIGHT

Loose Fur Rising

In early 1996, I received a flyer from the Little A-Le-Inn announcing the upcoming "UFO Friendship Camp-Out." Among the scheduled speakers, I noticed, was Anthony Hilder—the tall, dark, red-and-black-clad man who, at the Las Vegas land-grab hearing before the BLM, had accused U.S. Air Force Colonel "Bud" Bennett of working for the New World Order, which in turn had invented AIDS and was hiding kidnapped children at Area 51. Other speakers for the weekend included Norio Hayakawa, the funeral director and conspiracy theorist who broke with Gary Schultz after the Ultimate UFO Seminar; Chuck Clark, the astronomer who'd copied Campbell's cloth patch and issued his own Area 51 guidebook; Richard Sauder, author of *Underground Bases and Tunnels: What Is the Government Trying to Hide?*; and Bill Uhouse, the notorious Jarod himself. This, I concluded, was not an opportunity to be missed. I drove to the airport on Friday afternoon and, within a couple of hours, was speeding north in a rented car on Nevada 375, cresting Hancock and Coyote Summits, passing the Black Mailbox and Groom Lake Road, and pulling into the parking lot of the Little A-Le-Inn.

The joint was already jumping. The tables were full, with people standing in line for the buffet; there was even a French film crew documenting the festivities. A sweet little old lady named Mary, wearing what appeared to be a brunette wig, with painted red cheeks and penciled eyebrows (an unintentional vaudeville costume, not inappropriate to the circumstances) was helping out with drink orders; Pat Travis was busy in the kitchen while her husband Joe sat behind the bar, looking—with Campbell gone and the Inn full of true (and paying) believers—pleased as punch.

As I got in line for the buffet, Norio Hayakawa was speaking. Casually dressed in jeans, polo shirt, and windbreaker, the Japanese-American mortician was waxing urgent about the "paradigm shift" that would accompany the approaching millennium. "Something is happening worldwide in science, politics, and religion," he said. "I've talked to many people around the world who believe that our generation will see a one-hundred-and-eighty-degree shift in the way of thinking. The speed of change is increasing. There's a constant bombardment now; we're being conditioned for something by the news media, film industry, science and technology. With things like the release this summer of the movie *Independence Day*, slowly but surely the nation is being saturated with the idea of an alien presence."

Hayakawa took a sip from a bottle of Budweiser. "I'm not really a paranoid person," he said, "but I like things that are interesting. I noticed recently that the HAARP° system is supposed to be complete in 1998. This is meant to heat up the ionosphere for military purposes—through a virtual lens, it can create a holographic image to confuse the enemy, maybe by projecting a religious figure into the air. Nineteen-ninety-eight is the only year that, if you divide it by the number of the Trinity, you get (the Satanic number) 666. It is also fifty years since the creation of Israel in 1948. The first Mideast war was in 1947, the same year as the Roswell crash, which was also when the Air Force and the CIA were created.

"Nothing is coincidental," Hayakawa declared. "Nobody is here this weekend by their own volition. If you reflect back on your life, there will

°High-Frequency Active Aural Research, jointly managed by the Air Force and Navy to affect the Earth's ionosphere through low-frequency radio waves. Potential uses include the detection of enemy weapons and manipulation of local weather; some believe that mass mind control is also part of the agenda.

be some kind of order or design that has brought you to a certain type of worldview. *Something* has brought you here!"

With that, Hayakawa introduced some of the weekend's scheduled speakers, who presented capsule teasers on the content of their talks. A slight, mustachioed man named Shawn Atlanti, who said he specialized in "on-board abduction experiences," mentioned the fabled *Chupacabra*, the hopping, batlike "goat sucker" that had recently been sighted in Mexico and Puerto Rico.° Richard Sauder, a soft-voiced blond man with an East Coast accent, revealed that he had been inspired to pursue subterranean research when he woke up in bed one night and heard a voice in his right ear ("a North American male speaking English") telling him that "the underground bases are real." Then, as promised, there was Hilder, now wearing a checked, double-breasted blazer with his black turtleneck and red handkerchief, black boots, and black commando pants equipped with cargo pockets. His female companion had also changed form: Though still half Hilder's age, this time she was a beautiful black woman dressed in silky summer clothing, though outside the Inn it was decidedly wintry.

"We're about to be freaked out," Hilder announced to the collected listeners. "There isn't anything you have that they aren't planning to take away for all time. I'm talking about a plan to enslave *everybody*. All of our sovereignty and all of our belief systems will be destroyed if the people at this Frankenstein factory over here succeed at pulling off the Big Con.

"You have to connect all the dots to see the big picture," Hilder said. "Each of the people speaking here, just doing their program by themselves, doesn't really make a lot of sense. But all of the people who should be here are here. This is a phenomenal event."

From behind the bar, Joe Travis commandeered the attention of the crowd. "The reason people like us come together is to seek truth from chaos," he said. In that spirit, he introduced a "young man" who wanted to share something with the crowd. I recognized the ensuing speaker—an unshaven geezer in a straw cowboy hat who was missing several teeth—as someone who had once flagged me down on Highway 375. He'd had a flat tire on a bicycle that he apparently planned to ride over Queen City Summit on a hot summer day; I stopped and gave him some water, though I was

---

°Hayakawa added that this creature had also recently made its way to Tucson, Arizona, and Riverside, California.

going the other way and couldn't help him with his tire. "God bless you," he'd said in return.

"I've been living here now for almost a year," this man now announced as he took the mike, cigarette in hand. "I work in the hay fields on a tractor. What I've noticed is, every time a rainstorm comes, the planes start flying. They give off their sonic booms, and within a half hour to forty-five minutes, the clouds disperse and the rain stops. My feeling is that the government has found a way to control the weather, and they're trying to run people out of this valley because of Area 51."

Murmurs of agreement arose from the audience. "That's amazing!" said Hayakawa, reclaiming the mike. "That technology has been developed by the military. At Wright-Patterson Air Force Base, they're working on controlling planes just by thinking—it's a brain-command system, so the pilot can do it just by moving his eyeballs. Many years ago, this government had better technology than Sony, but it went into the military. Right over here in your backyard is technology you've never even dreamed of. But it's being hidden, and this is not right. A private cabal is moving Earth in a direction where the entire population can have its thoughts controlled."

As the weekend wore on, I would learn that to Hayakawa just about everything was "amazing" or "incredible" or "fantastic." And as the mini-speeches concluded, he put on a remarkable demonstration himself. Sitting at an electric piano with an organ and synthesizer alongside, he commenced to entertain the crowd with a varied country-western repertoire, crooning away with his eyes closed and shoulders hunched, twisting emotionally in his seat as he sang a song about getting out of prison.

Soon Joe Travis himself got up and, clearly in his element—wearing jeans and dirty boots, swaying to the music with his shirttail out, an unlit cigarette in one hand and a can of Old Milwaukee in the other—delivered a warm and smiling rendition of "Today I Started Loving You Again." Hayakawa's synthesizer contributed a drumbeat, along with a sound that merged a brass section and pedal steel guitar. Norio's own voice shifted uncannily from that of Waylon to Willie to Elvis, depending on whose hit he was performing at the time. After a while I began to wonder if his vocals were also somehow synthesized, or if he had somehow found a way to channel the spirits of the aforementioned singers even while most were still alive. Hayakawa assured us, however, that his technology was "low-tech compared to Area 51."

Dreamland's diabolical wire-pullers weren't making things easy for the Friendship Camp-Out. All through that night and next morning, brutal wind gusts and cloudbursts took turns battering the Sand Springs Valley, doing their best to dampen the spirits of attendees. In the three years that had passed since the Ultimate UFO Seminar, however, fortifications had been made against the nefarious next-door neighbors. A quarter of a mile from the A-Le-Inn, a steel Quonset hut had been built, so mass gatherings in Rachel were no longer relegated to a circus tent. On the other hand, popular interest seemed to have tapered off: Only about thirty people paid to attend this "phenomenal event." They huddled inside the Quonset hut in heavy coats and jackets, since, despite the rudimentary shelter, the structure had no heat.

The atmosphere was warmed up somewhat by the fact that Hilder was emcee. Though he shared the vast-conspiracy viewpoint of deposed "moderator" Gary Schultz, the host lacked his adversary's° Bible-thumping bent, replacing it with a sinister singsong throatiness spiced by clever coinage of phrase. "An oligarchy of evil plans to control this country and everyone in it totally, from erection to resurrection, from womb to tomb, by the turn of the century," Hilder told the tiny crowd. "How much time do we have? We don't have any time. There's none left. It isn't optional that we incite a revelation; it's mandatory. You are here because you are a step above, or in some cases ten or twenty steps above, the average Joe and Jane."

Hilder went on to outline the overarching plot orchestrated by the New World Order.† AIDS, he said, was developed at Fort Dieterich, Maryland, and "deliberately put into smallpox vaccine shots in Senegal, Uganda, Zaire, Haiti, and Brazil, and into hepatitis-B vaccine shots in the gay population throughout the United States through the Public Health Service." This was all part of the plan to reduce the world population by 25 percent by the turn of the century.

"In *The Impact of Science Upon Society*," said Hilder, "Dr. Bertrand Russell said that war has hitherto been unsuccessful in reducing the population, but bacteriological war may yet prove effective. If a Black Death

---

° Schultz had recently suggested that Hilder was involved in the 1968 assassination of Robert F. Kennedy at the Ambassador Hotel in Los Angeles.

† Since Hilder seemed to speak without notes, I've rearranged the order in which he presented some of his points.

spreads around the world once every generation, the survivors can procreate freely. After the Golf War, you saw babies being born—without legs, without arms—to the men who came back. Some people call it Myto-plasma Incognitas, or the 'Gulf War Syndrome.' I call it Doctor-Engineered Antipersonnel Disease—DEAD. Our guys went over there not to live or die for their country, but to die for the New World Order.

"This is not an accident. This is by design. They also plan to have race riots of black against whites. At Guantánamo, they have little bands which they now rivet to the wrists or ankles of the blacks and the browns. It's tantamount to a slave bracelet—a transponder, identifying and tracking people like dogs."

Here Hilder lapsed into his incantatory point-making style. *"It's . . . planned . . . that . . . way,"* he almost chanted. "I came across a 1991 statement by Herr Doctor Henry Kissinger where he said: 'Today Americans would be outraged if U.N. troops entered Los Angeles to restore order. Tomorrow they will be grateful.' I'm thinking: Who else in history made that statement? It sounds like Adolf Hitler! Kissinger goes on to say that 'If there were a threat from beyond, either real or promulgated'—staged, fixed, a scam—'that threatened our very existence, it is then that all the peoples of the world would plead to be delivered from this evil. The one thing every man fears is the unknown; when presented with this scenario, individual rights will be willingly relinquished.' Because we're *scared to death!* And so we have the Panic Project, and the 'UFOs.' Two of my listeners sat out here in the Tikaboo Valley three or four years ago and, for an hour and five minutes, watched what was tantamount to an invasion from space. Out of an orb came twenty-five airborne craft. But they were not from another world. *They . . . are . . . of . . . THIS . . . world.* They're *not* 'unidentified.' They're *identified.*

"You've got to understand where all of this is coming from. Go back to Nazi Germany and there's a picture of Walter Durrenberger, who was head of the Nordhausen concentration camp, with Werner Von Braun. They were involved in a project called 'Paper Clip' that brought German doctors and scientists here who had been involved in genetic engineering—creating new people or entities and antigravitational flying discs. The technology isn't new. It's old; they've been working on it for half a century. So over here at Area 51, we also have a Frankenstein factory where they have genetically engineered creatures. I don't think this thing called a *Chupacabra*, or 'goat sucker,' is from outer space at all. I don't think it can fly from Puerto Rico to Mexico, then pop up in Riverside and Oregon and Florida and Arizona. If something like this is coming down the street, gang, *you know about it*—unless it's *transported* by somebody who wants to *freak . . . you . . . out*. I call it a 'Created Reptilian Alien Vampire Engineered Species,' or CRAVES. And it's going to freak out a lot of people, especially if this is done in conjunction with the belief that we have been invaded by some alien entity from outer space.

"They're now ready to release this 'information' to you under the illusion that our best hope is the United Nations. I believe, as Norio does, that there will soon be some sort of announcement, and that this film *Independence Day* is part of that announcement. What we will be witnessing in the next few weeks and months is an advance warning of a police state. It's absolutely incredible that the State of Nevada is naming this the 'Extraterrestrial Highway'—but then, when you think that they're going to make an announcement that there's extraterrestrial life, it all makes sense. Not to frighten the hell out of us, but to put the hell *in* us. It isn't being done to educate us, but to reducate us—to indoctrinate us. To destroy our basic belief systems in God and in sovereignty. *Independence Day* is not for our independence; it's for our *dependence* on global government. If the U.N. is 'our best hope,' then we have no chance. How clear can Herr Doctor Kissinger make it? How stupid can we be if we don't believe it? We've got to take these people out. *For . . . freedom . . . to . . . live, what . . . they . . . are . . . doing . . . must . . . die*."

Hilder went on to enumerate a list ("murder after murder after murder after murder") of Clinton administration advisers who'd died unnatural deaths; to suggest that the President himself ordered the Oklahoma City bombing "to get you and I to surrender our rights to the government"; and to predict that "Colin Bowel" would replace Bob Dole as the 1996 Republican candidate. "I can't believe that anybody as dumb or as dull as Dole will be allowed to take that position," he said, "in spite of the fact that we have a one-party system. Colin Powell is a member of the Council on Foreign Relations—as is Bob Dole, as is Bill Clinton. *It's . . . all . . . rigged. There . . . is . . . no . . . election. It . . . is . . . a . . . selection. It . . . is . . . a . . . coronation*. And I believe it will be the last that we will see in the United States of America. In the year 2000—or just moments before—the Millennium Society will be lined up at the base of the Pyramid at Giza, waiting for something wonderful to happen. As Norio knows—and we've discussed this with Richard Hoagland*—I believe there is going to be an explosion from the forty-nine-and-a-quarter pounds of plutonium that is now traveling around the unexploded star Jupiter. When it goes off, it could be at the turn of the century—and the planet will be renamed Lucifer.

"You say, 'That's preposterous!' But the Galileo mission has already left. In Arthur C. Clarke's book *2010*, he talks about this. The last chapter is called 'Lucifer Rising.' But they forgot to mention in the film what they mention in the book: that these people have a religious agenda. A Luciferian agenda.

"You can see this at the Little A-Le-Inn. You can learn about it at this conference. You can begin to gain this understanding, this awareness, this revelation. The information that gets out here needs to get out everywhere. The television cameras will do that. Our friends the Frogs, from across the pond, will take that information to France; and tomorrow or maybe this afternoon we'll have a film crew bringing it to Germany. We've got to make people understand what's coming down, because we have a situation impending that is the most disastrous for any people anywhere at any time in the history of the world."

With that, Hilder introduced Richard Sauder, whom he described as "the ultimate researcher. He will put hard-core documentation on the table. He doesn't believe in anything that he can't see, feel, or touch. But *you . . . will be . . . amazed.*"

Sauder didn't return the compliment. The first thing he did, in fact, was apologize for Hilder's remark about "Frogs," explaining that, to the French, the term was tantamount to "nigger." "It's just not something you say," Sauder said. When someone in the audience reported that the French had reacted by leaving, Sauder said, "I feel like leaving myself." This inspired Hilder to hustle outside in search of the crew.

Sauder gamely began his slide show of aboveground features of underground installations—buildings, bunkers, air vents, et al., most of which were remote-looking facilities with barbed wire crowning chain-link fences

*Former NASA consultant and author of *The Monuments of Mars: A City on the Edge of Forever*.

and U.S. GOVERNMENT—NO TRESPASSING signs excluding would-be snoops. Sauder said that New Mexico seems to have more than its share of such features; some are adjacent to abandoned uranium mines, and some are near microwave relay stations. When he mentioned that AT&T owned underground facilities all over the country, I was reminded of the sixties film *The President's Analyst*, in which the telephone company was exposed as the nation's covert puppetmaster. Sauder said that, until it was recently taken over by Lockheed Martin (né Martin Marietta), Sandia Laboratory in New Mexico had been run by AT&T right next door to the Manzano underground base, where "workers who were digging the tunnels were transferred to different parts of the project before completion, so that no one would have the complete layout. It has a very high security level; there are four fences, one electrified, and you need a retina scan to get in. I've heard it's partly for back-engineering recovered technology, but I don't know if it's alien."

This was a topic, Sauder admitted, that he didn't much care to address. "I haven't said anything about extraterrestrials underground, and probably won't for the remainder of my talk, because I can't prove they're there— although it's my personal belief that the universe is so stupendously huge and unimaginably ancient that I would be shocked if we were the only technologically capable species of life in the universe. I'll reserve comment about the 'intelligence' of the human race until all the evidence is in. If there *are* other technologically capable species of life, it may be that one or more of them have come to the Earth, are coming, or will come. But since I personally don't know much, I don't say much. I stick to what I have evidence of."

Although he was forging on with his talk, Sauder still appeared upset by what he perceived as Hilder's faux pas. He seemed to be having trouble keeping his mind on his material; he kept interrupting himself to inquire, "Are the French coming back?" and muttering, "You just do *not* say things like that." Just when it was beginning to seem that the sensitive researcher might not be able to go on, Hilder burst back in to report that the Gallic visitors had taken the "Frogs" reference in the humorous spirit in which it was intended. "They were only offended by the perception that they'd been offended," he said. "I offend everybody, so if I haven't offended you, please let me know."

With that, a visibly relieved Sauder was finally able to marshal his concentration. He explained that the Department of Energy had built various underground bases for storing nuclear waste, and that the Federal Emergency Management Authority has a system of COG ("continuity of government") bunkers scattered around the country. "The President has at least two that are known, under the White House and under Camp David," Sauder said. "The Pentagon has several. There's also one beneath the Greenbriar Hotel in White Sulfur Springs, West Virginia, that was recently decommissioned. There's a huge underground facility in Denver between Alameda and Sixth Avenue; I took some pictures there, and when the film came back it was all washed out and fuzzy.

"Usually the justification advanced for building these facilities is 'national security.' But whose nation are they talking about? Our nation? The Native Americans' nation? Or the Pentagon's nation? The Fortune 500's nation? Security for whom, on whose terms and for what reason? In the case of underground bases, it turns out that it's usually to provide secure cover or shelter for the governing elite—the military command structure and upper echelon of the political structure, along with the support personnel needed to serve them and maintain and operate the underground facilities in the event of a nuclear war. On the East Coast, a three-hundred-mile radius of Washington, D.C., referred to as the 'Federal Arc'—clearly a play on Noah's Ark—consists of a number of underground installations. At least five or six are for political leaders in the event of nuclear war.

"Another reason I think there has been such a vast program of underground construction in the last few decades is that the Earth is facing an ecological crisis. I know it's fashionable nowadays to say that the environmental crisis is vastly overstated, but I think it's rather seriously *understated*. If we understood the full consequences of the destructive effects of this civilization—with its toxic pollution, nuclear radiation, destruction of the oceans and swamps and forests, spewing chemicals into the atmosphere—we would have stopped it not yesterday but a thousand yesterdays ago. The rate of species extinction is just tremendous, and not getting any better. And at a certain point, as the links in the ecology below us weaken—remembering that we human beings are at the top of the food chain—our own position becomes more precarious. My guess is that the plan of some of the actors and agencies involved in building these underground facilities is to provide themselves a safe haven in the event of ecological catastrophe, which is already well along, and in which case you'll see them scurrying for their holes."

Sauder paused for a drink of water. Freed from the burden of a breach in international etiquette, he was warming to his subject.

"If you look at the budget for the U.S. Government, you won't find any line item for 'secret underground installations,'" he said. "There is no regular statement and account of receipts and expenditures of money devoted to these projects. It's hidden in the budgetary shell game of the Black Budget, where up is down, left is right, black is white, right is wrong, and nothing is as it appears. If the government itself is not violating the Constitution, then the offices of the government that swear to uphold and defend the Constitution are [violating it], in that they are not acting lawfully. How can such a nation be called 'secure'? I would argue that national security is endangered by these very people. The danger is from within the government, and from within the political underground, the *real* political underground—physical, literal, and concrete—acting from within the bowels of the military-industrial complex."

Now he was really hitting his stride. "What we're dealing with here— and the pun is fully intended—is a problem of depth psychology," he said. "Psychologists like Freud, Adler, and Wilhelm Reich talk about repressed complexes—things, oftentimes connected with our sexuality, which people push down into the depths of their psyche and may not even know are there. The way a lot of this underground technology looks is frankly sexual: The tunnel boring machines, for example, are like stylized phalluses— long, cylindrical objects that penetrate into the earth. Then there are tunnels with caverns inside, where the analogy with vaginal, womblike, uterine structures is very clear. We live in a very artificial, violent, and repressed society and global system, and my feeling is that, at a deep level, it's almost as if these people are trying to work it out through their technology from the outside, rather than dealing first with what's inside and getting that right in their own lives. Instead they project it on the outside world, or, in this case, on the world 'underneath.' They're trying to *shove it down*. This is the reason that people go to psychiatrists—to bring what's been shoved down up into the open, deal with it, integrate it into their life, move on and mature as human beings. So maybe this is telling us something about ourselves as a society: that there's something wrong in our collective life, issues that we haven't dealt with as an aggregate of a quarter of a billion people or maybe as a whole planet. I think it has something to do with our sexuality. I mean, why do we kill each other in such large numbers over all kinds of little trivial nonsense issues? Chopping each other's heads off in Rwanda, or slaughtering each other in the former Yugoslavia by the tens and hundreds of thousands. Or in Central America, where the CIA has been fomenting wars for many years. Or in Haiti, where the CIA has also been very active. Or World War Two, with the gassing of the Jews. It's *awful*, the things that we do to each other, just *despicable*. *Torturing* each other, doing *unspeakable* things to each other. And now we're doing them underground—in preparation, among other things, for all-out nuclear war or ecological collapse."

On this rousing note, Sauder stepped down. Soon there was a break for lunch, during which he told me that most of his research on underground bases was carried out simply by asking questions, perusing public records, making Freedom of Information Act requests, and using his common sense. "Intelligence organizations do the same thing," he said. "They send out thousands of people and tell them to go to the library, read the newspaper, talk to people, hang around town, and see what shakes out of the bushes." For example, he said that "a guy working in a gas station" had told him about a high school field trip he'd taken to a Maryland facility with three or four underground levels. Still, in the course of his inquiries, Sauder said he'd developed a "sixth sense" about the locations of subterranean facilities.

"There's a type of architecture that doesn't quite fit," he explained. "It's not residential, but it's not military; it's nondescript in a way that looks like it's *supposed* to be nondescript. Hoover Dam, for example, is a place that looks to me like it might have an underground component. A part-Indian woman I met had a brother who worked on secret underground Navy projects, and he said that most hydroelectric projects in the West have an underground element. Given its high level of security, I'd be shocked if there weren't underground facilities at Groom Lake. The Nevada Test Site is documented to have underground tunnels, and given what I know about tunneling technology, which is very sophisticated, and the Black Budget, which is very large, I think there's an excellent chance there are tunnels there."

Okay, but wasn't it sort of silly to claim that tunnels connected Groom Lake with Edwards Air Force Base in California or Los Alamos Laboratories in New Mexico?

"Not really. Suppose you had ten machines that could tunnel five miles a year. Since World War Two, that's twenty-five hundred miles. The only limitations are funding and keeping it secret."

Good point. What do they do with all the dirt?

"There are rock quarries all over the West. You can take dirt and grind it down. When they made the interstate highways, there were years of heavy construction and nobody even thought about it. In the desert, the wind blows sixty miles per hour, scattering dirt day after day. Plus, nuclear power can melt dirt—you don't even need to carry it away."

"I've been watching them excavate at Groom Lake for two and a half years," interjected a guy sitting near us. "I see a lot of eighteen-wheelers going in and out of the back gate, bringing dumptruck loads of dirt every few minutes, and a lot of cement trucks going in west of the jet-fuel tank farm. What you see on the surface is only a small percentage of what's there. I know a guy who went underground there; one button on the elevator said '22.' If there are twenty-two levels, and each one is thirty feet, with fifty feet of bedrock in between so that they don't collapse, it would be fifteen hundred feet deep. That could be disinformation, though; they might have lots of elevator buttons for each level."

As it turned out, this was Chuck Clark—the guy who'd replaced Glenn Campbell as the A-Le-Inn's Area 51 expert. In *The Groom Lake Desert Rat*, Campbell had described Clark ("Chuckie," as Glenn called him) as "Rachel's own 'Forrest Gump' but without the charm." Clark was a tall, pale, short-haired guy with a boxy, clean-shaven face; although he was about fifty, he looked well-scrubbed and brushed in the manner of a little boy, with a neat clean polo shirt tucked into a pair of jeans that needed just a scosh more room.

To illustrate the points he made about Area 51, Clark had a packet of telephoto pictures he'd taken of the base—something like a family album, except that the snapshots were full of tanks and buildings on brown, barren hills. "Laid out on the bar, these twenty photos are nine feet long," he said. "They cover two and a half miles of the base. The big hangar there could conceal the entrance to an aircraft-carrier-type elevator; behind there is the nuclear weapons storage area. Nellis and Vandenberg have them too, but according to them, they don't have any."

Looking through the photographs—all of which had been taken in broad daylight—I asked Clark how he managed to avoid getting in trouble with the law.

"The sheriff asked me for my film one time," he said. "I said, 'Fine, if you have a warrant; otherwise I'll be on my way.' He made a radio call and finally said, 'Okay, you can go.' They never bothered me again. A lot of times they've known I was up there and run stuff anyway. Frankly, I don't think they realize what kind of lenses I'm playing with. Most semiserious amateurs have three hundred millimeters, max, but I shoot a majority of my pictures with a fifteen-hundred f24 with folded optics. It's only this long." He held his hands about nine inches apart. "I also have a twelve - thousand-millimeter that I bought at an auction at Vandenberg Air Force Base for a hundred and fifty dollars. It cost the government twenty-four thousand, but the only use for it is very long-range, narrow-field photography—you need two frames for just one hangar." He'd taken the shots in his wallet collection with a three-thousand-millimeter lens.

Clark said he had a total of between twenty-two hundred and three thousand such images. "I keep the negatives elsewhere—and no, I'm not gonna tell you where. When things get slow, I sit around and look at them under a loupe. I've found all kinds of interesting gadgets—things that pop out of the ground that are concealed near the runways, some of them fifteen feet tall. I've shown them to pilots who say they have no idea what they are."

I asked Clark where he was from and what he did for a living. He told me he'd grown up in Southern California and was self-employed building big-game fishing rods. He'd come to Rachel a year and a half earlier from Lompoc, California, where he'd been a member of an amateur astronomy club and director of operations for a local observatory.

"It was next to the Space Launch Complex at Vandenberg Air Force Base. Almost all the launches there are secret—but a launch is a hell of a show, and since we're paying the bill, I figure we might as well enjoy a little bit of free fireworks. Basically, I don't see the need for secrecy in a lot of things. When I was in the service, we were developing chemical weapons in Utah and attack helicopters in Alabama; I worked for the commanding general of the Continental Army Command in the Pentagon, responsible for all enlisted people in eleven western states. It gave me a perspective most people don't get. I kicked around two- and three-star generals, and had a high-level security clearance. But there isn't much secrecy at the higher levels of the military. It's mostly added on by lower levels of command out of paranoia that they might get their rears in hot water. So at Vanderberg I was watching everything that left the ground and sharing it with the media, since they weren't being very forthcoming at the base."

"Why did you come here?"

"I wanted to get away from state income tax and be closer to my son in

Las Vegas. For astronomy, I needed a place about a mile high to get away from lights. The skies around here are nice and dark; the base was just a bonus. I'd been aware of this place since 1970. Because of my interest in astronomy, I had lots of contacts at Lockheed and Skunk Works. I used to have a neighbor who would vanish for two or three weeks at a time; he said he was working on temporary duty at a place called Groom Lake. It didn't take a genius to figure out it was secret stuff.

"I didn't find out about the UFOs until I moved here. I'd been interested in them, though, since I was eleven years old, when I had a forty-five-minute sighting near Pasadena. My friends and I were playing baseball one day when we saw this triangle of nine airborne objects. I was familiar with aircraft technology, because my family had always lived near airports and the Pasadena area was in the flight pattern for Lockheed in Burbank. We thought we were looking up at delta-wing F-102s flying at forty thousand feet. But when two F-89 Scorpions came out to intercept them, we realized they were much lower and smaller than we thought— only two and a half to three feet across, and totally silent. When the jets were scrambled, this triangle of nine objects broke up into three triangles of three; two of the triangles placed themselves opposite each side of the tail of one of the fighters, and the other triangle circled back and got next to the tail of the other one. They stayed glued in that position no matter what the fighters did. At that point, the ballgame had stopped and we were all just standing there watching—thirty kids and five adults.

"Twenty-five minutes into this little skirmish, the jets were running low on fuel. They broke off and headed back toward Lockheed, and as soon as they set their course that way, these things only followed for a few seconds. Then they broke away and formed back into the triangle of nine. They made a few more lazy circles and headed northeast toward Mount Wilson in Sierra Madre northeast of Pasadena. They disappeared behind a thunderhead over the San Gabriel Mountains. From then on, I read everything I could get my hands on that was semiserious about UFOs. I've talked off the record to career Air Force officers—generals and colonels— and it's amazing how lightly they take this thing. They say, 'Oh sure, there are UFOs. We know all about 'em.' "

"Ever seen anything like that around here?"

"For my first eight or nine months, I didn't see anything unusual. But since moving here, three or four times I've seen amazing stuff that was absolutely unconventional: yellow or orange lights, quite bright—as big as Venus—that would appear or disappear or make a-hundred-and-twenty-degree sharp turns with no deceleration, or go from a motionless hover and then streak off at tremendous speed and then stop instantly. I saw one that covered four-point-eight miles in one to one and a half seconds. I was able to identify the start and stop points on a topo map because the thing was only a few feet above the ground, in front of the hills. Usually they're up in the sky. The government is definitely experimenting with something that doesn't fall within our general understanding of physics out there; I don't think it's necessarily extraterrestrial, though. There are three or four hundred billion stars in our galaxy alone, and less than one one-hundred-thousandth of one percent are visual to the unaided eye—yet every place people say the ETs come from is among those. Pleiades, Zeta Reticuli, Ceres, Orion, Andromeda, Coma Berenices, and Epsilon Boötes are always mentioned as origins of the aliens, and every single one is a naked-eye place. The odds are so radically against that. Plus, unlike most people, I appreciate the distances in space. The nearest star to ours is *twenty-four trillion* miles away. If you put a trillion BBs end to end, they'd go around the Earth a hundred and nine and a half times—so we're talking a long, long ways. I just think there are too many UFO sightings for that. The 'foo fighters'—balls of light that travel along with airplanes, which showed up in World War Two, Korea, Vietnam, possibly Saudi Arabia, and also over nuclear power plants and missile sites—make me think they're near rather than far. I mean, if they were monitoring us from only four light years away, it would still take four years to reach us. Bob Lazar claims they bend time and space to travel great distances almost instantaneously, but my understanding is that if you bend time/space with an immense gravitational field, you create a visual distortion that should be seen from time to time if that's what they're doing out here. I spend a lot of time looking at the sky, but I've never seen anything like that.

"I think it's just as likely, if not more so, that the source of these things is a parallel dimension right here. We know there are sounds that we don't hear and colors we don't see, like infrared and ultraviolet, even though they're all around us. We don't see every electromagnetic frequency, either—but if we had different bands of X-ray vision, we'd see things differently. By the same token, I think there may be entire civilizations coexisting among us right here on this planet. It's possible that UFOs travel between dimensions rather than between stars. That would explain why they blink on and off, just like adjusting from one frequency to another. They may be doing that without even moving."

"Are you saying that this is what's being experimented with at Area 51?"

"Whether it's extraterrestrial or interdimensional, it's there. And they're hiding it from the general public, though they changed the game about a year and a half ago. It used to be that, on Wednesday nights, if they were aware of somebody out there, they'd get the stuff down below the hills. Now they seem to be showing it to isolated groups of people. They fly things all week long, and some of the best sightings have been on holiday weekends—Memorial Day and Labor Day. They've been flying at times when people are likely to be around, which is one of the things that makes me conclude they want it to be seen. They're covertly telling us a little bit of what's going on. And I get the impression it's the people they're testing now, not the technology. They've got the technology down."

"How do people tend to react?"

"Among people watching from the road, I've seen a mix of curiosity, fascination, and terror. I've seen some people scared out of their wits. Lately, between thirty-three and fifty percent of the people have freaked. That's way too high."

"For what?"

"For it to be revealed to the general public. With their optics and sensors, they know everything you're doing out there; they've got night-vision capabilities and all kinds of other stuff—they can see a blemish at thirty miles. In fact, it would be real scary if the average citizen knew the technology they could use if they wanted to. Stuff that can hear what you're saying from fifty miles away: If you aim a laser beam at a window pane, you can use it as a microphone by measuring the vibrations that a voice indoors causes in the glass. Through synthesis in a computer, the pattern can be reconstituted as audio sound. That's old technology; it goes back to early Vietnam. And I know there are experiments on mind control using chemicals, light waves, and sound waves—subliminal stuff, like in department stores and TV commercials. I don't think it's as sinister as a lot of people make it out to be, though. They don't need to do that here; this is just an ideal place for flight testing. In summer, though, the Milky Way runs due north and south, so if you're near Groom Lake Road, it's right over the base and you can see the silhouette of anything that flies up there. Supposedly the TR-3A Black Manta doesn't exist, but I see it here all the time; it's flat black with a manta shape, a little bigger than an F-117. I even saw the Aurora take off one night—or an aircraft that matched the Aurora's reputed configuration, a sharp delta with twin tails about a hundred and thirty feet long. It taxied out of a lighted hangar at two-thirty A.M. and used a lot of runway to take off. It had one red light on top, but the minute the wheels left the runway, the light went off and that was the last I saw of it. I didn't hear it because the wind was blowing from behind me toward the base."

I asked when this had taken place.

"February 1994. Obviously they didn't think anybody was out there. It was thirty below zero—probably ninety below with the wind chill factor. I had hiked into White Sides from a different, harder way than usual, and stayed there two or three days among the rocks, under a camouflage tarp with six layers of clothes on. I had an insulated face mask and two sleeping bags, so I didn't present a heat signature. I videotaped the aircraft through a telescope with a five-hundred-millimeter f4 lens coupled via a C-ring to a high-eight digital video camera with five hundred and twenty scan lines of resolution, which is better than TV."

"Where's the tape?"

"Locked away. That's a legitimate spyplane; my purpose is not to give away legitimate national defense. When they get ready to unveil it, I'll probably release the tape. In the case of UFOs, though, the fact that they exist outweighs the security interest."

"Got any evidence of that?"

"I don't know anybody who's ever seen an alien, but I know two people who have touched a disc. The first one wasn't here, but at the Tonopah Test Range five years ago. They brought out five guys who had the highest clearance and had each one touch it. Then they were backed up about thirty feet to look at it, and it vanished right before their eyes. As soon as it disappeared, they were walked through the spot it had occupied. Then they sent them back to 51. It was a psychological experiment and they were the guinea pigs.

"Another guy touched a disc in an underground hangar out here. When I talked to him, he had no clue that I knew anything about Area 51; I met him at a shuttle landing at Edwards, and he brought it up. He was a hydraulics technician. He was looking for something in one compartment and went into a different one where he saw this disc hovering three feet off the floor, making no sound, no hum, no nothing. He said it felt like plastic, although it looked like tarnished metal. He was surprised to find that it was room temperature. He could move it back and forth with one finger, but couldn't even rock it up and down. Then he got the hell out of there and went back to where he was supposed to be. I don't think I would've even touched it, myself."

"Who did this guy work for?"

"He was a civilian contractor for Lockheed. But I don't think any one company or agency has control there; it's a cooperative effort. The Air Force has the runway, the tower operations, and the security operations; the Navy has more of the R&D. The Navy has always been involved in leading-edge technology. When you consider that three-quarters of the planet is covered by water, they need a big presence on the surface *and* in the air. I suspect that the Navy is the biggest player at Groom Lake, plus maybe some department we haven't heard of. There's a bus that comes into the base every day from Alamo; it makes two or three stops, and people park their cars at the junction of Highway 375 and 93 all day long. Also, twelve or fifteen private vehicles enter and exit the base every day. If you followed those people home, got their license number and address, you could also get their name and social security number; then, if you ran a credit report on them, you'd have their whole life history. I think most of those people are civilian contractors paid by the Navy, or companies like Bechtel—for the normal congressional programs, that is. A lot of the money there doesn't ever see Congress. I think they get most of their funds through other-than-normal channels; that's why they keep it so secret. I don't think anybody would have had trouble with it if they'd just said, 'Yes, we have a secret base—stay away because it interferes and costs us money.' But I suspect they're getting a lot of CIA money—maybe drug money—and that's why its existence is being denied."

Clark had written his own *Area 51 and S-4 Handbook* to take the place of Campbell's *Area 51 Viewer's Guide*. It was a slimmed-down, straightforward discussion of the known information, containing more photographs than Glenn's but none of Psychospy's philosophy or wit. "I'm limiting the sales just to here and the gas station to subsidize my film and expenses," said Clark. "When you're making a big chunk of change off it, people look at you as less credible. I'd guess Glenn is pulling down fifty or sixty thousand a year from his operation; after all, he hired a girl full-time here and a guy to run his computer business. I don't consider him a researcher; he's more of an entrepreneur. In my first ten months here, I was spending four or five nights a week in the desert, and I only saw him go out once. He was doing paper research, not field research.[*] I tried talking to him a couple of times, but he didn't seem interested. I guess I didn't have a big enough reputation."

I mentioned the well-known fact that Campbell didn't cotton to the similarity between his Area 51 patch and Clark's.

"He was playing games with Joe and Pat," Clark explained. "So they asked me to do something along similar lines. It's not remotely the same, though; you can't copyright Area 51, or a round patch. Lately he's been slandering me on the Internet. I've got enough stuff to sue him and win right now, so if he continues, I'll empty his wallet a little bit."

Actually, Clark had made a few uncalled-for remarks about Campbell too. When Chuck's patch first came out, he took some heat for it on the Net; Mark Farmer, for one, posted a broadside inpuging Clark's integrity. "Sorry you're so intimidated by a little healthy competition," Clark had countered. "Obviously, you and your lover, Glenn, are not going to be pleased by upcoming events that are currently in the works. You've made a healthy business for yourselves, but now it's time for you to share the stage with other viewpoints and products." (In return, Campbell had asked, "Is that sexual innuendo we detect? Both Campbell and his lover X, secure in each other's arms, eagerly await those 'upcoming events,' whatever they may be.")

"He was knocking me with no basis," Clark said. "So I decided to rattle his cage a little bit. I sent a private e-mail to Agent X, but I hoped they'd post it—and knew they would. It's easy to manipulate them; they're like little kids playing a game."

"Glenn called us gun-toting ignoramuses," interjected a lady nearby.

Now Pat Travis came out of the kitchen. A short, stout woman with an open, friendly face, she wore a loose blouse that hung from her like a smock. "Glenn made a lot of tensions for everybody," she said. "He came in with his shelf full of books and said, 'This is the way it's gonna be.' He had things in the wellhouse, the laundry room—I couldn't clean the floors because of all his boxes. He even wanted to sell big bags of popcorn as

---

[*] Campbell had been living in Rachel for a year before Clark arrived.

on very short flights without any passengers. She also saw antiaircraft emplacements and a lot of military and security guards to the south. No aliens, though. And when we gave her the coordinates for Papoose Lake, all she saw were empty hangars."

As far as that spot was concerned, Mahood had studied an enlargement of a 1988 Soviet satellite photo and found no evidence of any structures or land disturbances at Papoose Lake. "You can see all the roads and turn-arounds very clearly, right down to the four-wheel-drive level," he said. "The road that runs down the west side of the Papoose Range is very poor."

As we went over this material, Tom's wife, Jeri—a sturdy, friendly, apple-cheeked blonde—appeared at the door with a tray of coffee and cookies. This was a homey accompaniment to her husband's more cosmopolitan pursuits. Soon I learned that she was also an expert quilter; she'd recently completed a couple of bedspreads decorated with what appeared to be Navajo patterns. On closer inspection, however, these turned out to be B-2 stealth bombers.

As for Tom, he had digested much of his research into his own Internet Web page. It was called *Blue Fire*,° named for a security condition reportedly imposed at Area 51 during the first UFO conference in Rachel. In addition to such features as the Bob Lazar Corner and Papoose Lake Primer ("Everything you ever wanted to know . . . but had the good sense not to ask, because other people would think you were nuts"), *Blue Fire* explores such hot topics as Los Alamos, the Tonopah Test Range, radiation gauges of southern Nevada, and radar-cross-section facilities of the Mojave Desert ("Underground bases or something neat but mundane? You decide"). Mahood's curiosity clearly extended beyond the boundaries of Area 51 to encompass the entire nuclear/defense landscape of the American Southwest. To hear Tom tell it, though, that was necessary when confronting the craftiness of Black Budget puppeteers.

"When I watch a magician, you know, I always look at his other hand—the one that's not supposed to be doing anything," he said. "There's 'secret,' and then there's *really* secret. If you study the Manhattan Project, you learn that these guys are really clever about hiding things. The *really* secret facility could be fifty miles away on the other side of Groom Lake. There might be stuff so Black that it's not even at Area 51."

°www.serve.com/mahood/bluefire.htm

ing the night that the beings didn't want us to leave yet because our work here wasn't finished."

"A lot of people come here who feel they've been abducted," said Joe. "No one here will scoff or ridicule or laugh at 'em. I think that's a great service."

"It's an important function that we serve," said Pat. "I've always felt this was an information exchange area. People can come here and talk about anything under the sun."

"We've learned so much from being here," said Joe. "We've met so many beautiful people from all over the world. I'd never had an opportunity to meet people from other countries before, but they come here from Europe, Japan. . . ."

"Holland, Belgium, Germany, France, England, Peru, Mexico, China, Japan, the Dominican Republic," Pat recited. "Every day we meet new people from somewhere. We have a good life here; we enjoy it. I feel what happened in the end with Glenn is best for all of us. Now we can each run our own business."

I noticed that, on the wall behind the bar, Joe had a number of bumper stickers. My personal favorite—*If You're Gonna be a Turd, Go Lay in the Yard*—was unusual in failing to flog the familiar themes of the Sagebrush Rebellion. To wit: *Don't Steal—The Government Hates Competition; Our Constitution Protects Our Rights—the U.N. Charter Surrenders Them; The West Wasn't Won with a Registered Gun;* and *All in Favor of Gun Control*, featuring pictures of Adolf Hitler, Joseph Stalin, Fidel Castro, and Bill Clinton.

"I just heard that in Canada, people have to register all their guns," Joe said. "That's the first step toward world dictatorship. Any tyrannical government has to disarm the people first."

"Are you talking about the New World Order conspiracy?" I asked.

"It's not a conspiracy," said Joe. "It's a *plan* that's been carried out since day one of the United States. It was present even during the Declaration of Independence. The idea was to let people explore and settle all the resources, which *they* would then take control of. Now that everything is developed, they no longer need to let people be free."

"Who is 'they'?"

"The Federal Reserve and their cohorts—the people who own all the money and have been bleeding this country dry for any number of years.

It's a highly secretive, loose-knit organization that has been in existence since May 1, 1776. The torch on the Statue of Liberty, which came from the French Templar Masons, isn't of liberty but enlightenment. That's why they're called the 'Illuminati.' "

"Are we talking about the Founding Fathers?"

"No. The framers of the Constitution did the very best they could to make it so it wouldn't have to be translated or deciphered; it was supposed to be self-explanatory, so that the future government couldn't destroy it. But people are like sheep; they aren't capable of governing themselves. They've left it to the few, who have usurped power ever since. Look at what happened in 1863 when the North took over the South. The Civil War wasn't about slavery; it was about tariffs and trade and ownership of land. Obviously the wrong side won and took over Wall Street. As Baron Rothschild said in 1725, 'Give me a nation's capital and I care not who makes its laws.' You think you own your house or car? Look at the deed—it says 'fictional title.' You don't even own *yourself*. As long as you have a social security number, you owe everything to them.

"These globalists are the architects of all the wars," Joe revealed. "They're everywhere, but primarily in the White House. FDR, by the way, was a Satanist. Read *Behold a Pale Horse* by Milton William Cooper. Go to Las Vegas and look at the Luxor casino."

"Does this have anything to do with Area 51?" I asked.

"It might. Who knows? Who's in charge there is anybody's guess. I can tell you one thing, though: Whoever's running the show there is not connected with Washington, D.C. There's no money allocated to that area by the government. And when they do announce what they have there, it won't be used in an interplanetary war. It will be used against the people of Earth."

During the break, I noticed a quiet, fortyish guy with an Abe Lincoln beard hanging around the Inn. This turned out to be none other than Ambassador Merlyn Merlin II of Alpha Draconis (formerly David Solomon of Silver City, Nevada), who had been lobbying the state legislature to designate Route 375 the "Extraterrestrial Highway." Wearing a blue blazer, a big-collared polyester print shirt, and a broad-brimmed leather hat perched high atop his head, he confirmed that he was an alien in human form.

"I'm like a hybrid," he explained. "I have two human birth parents and a physical human body—I was born in L.A. in 1949—but I found out twenty years ago that a Seraphim angel has been in this body since birth. I was in Bible college in the early seventies, but I was also studying mystical things with a spiritual group in Carson City. I wanted to ascend to Heaven, and to do that, you go out of your body and commune with Seraphim angels. It took a while, but eventually I realized that what was going out of my body *was* a Seraphim angel."

I asked him if he was going to speak at the conference. "No," he said. "I'm not a government conspiracy wacko. These people are radical right-wing conservative Christian fundamentalist militia supporters. I'm *for* the New World Order. When the United Federation of Planets is connected to the United Nations, that will be the New World Order—a permanent golden age. At this point we've been quarantined because of our barbaric ways. People like Anthony Hilder see barbaric things because the prisoners here are running the government, but they have limited perception. They can create horrible things, like slavery, for themselves, but those following the positive energy will experience the golden age.

"I'm working with the government now to establish what we set out to do originally," Merlyn said. "There's going to be a major change soon; there will be a landing here in three years and total adoption by 2012. After that, these people will continue with their negative thoughts, but on another planet."

Just to make sure I had this straight, I asked Merlyn if a Seraphim angel was the same thing as an extraterrestrial.

"That's part of the problem," he answered. "It used to be common knowledge that experiences with supernatural beings were encounters with extraterrestrials—like Elijah ascending into Heaven in flames and a whirlwind. But in the Dark Ages, they took that out of the Bible; it doesn't talk about flying saucers, so we have a distorted picture. But really we're all part of the great God that's everywhere at every time. As well as being here, we're everywhere else. So we're all really extraterrestrials."

In the afternoon, Bill Uhouse took the stage. He was wearing a windbreaker, stylishly baggy pants, high-top leather basketball shoes, and a white "Antimatter" baseball cap cocked at an angle—a rather youthful style, really, for a seventy-year-old guy. Soon enough, though, I saw what

Campbell meant when he mentioned Uhouse's tendency to "ramble." With no introduction to who he was or what he'd supposedly done, he spoke without much direction, spicing his own sensational story with hearsay, speculation, and tall tales. In one of his weirder revelations, Uhouse divulged that, two weeks after the previous Friendship Camp-Out, he was out working in his yard when he was "hit in the left arm. The muscle was hanging out, but my neighbor helped me push it back in, pour peroxide on it, and bandage it up. I didn't know what it was that hit me; I thought maybe a turbine blade from an airplane. But a month later I went to the doctor and he told me I was shot. I didn't hear anything or see any-body; the shooter would have had to be three hundred and fifty or four hundred yards away. But ten days later, I was visited by two nice young gentlemen in their thirties—NSA guys who asked me a few questions about what I'd been doing. Later a colonel from Nellis spent three or four hours with me."

Uhouse didn't seem to think he'd been shot for something he'd said. "I worked for this group for thirty-eight years," he said. "They've made my life comfortable; I'll be in good shape till the day I die. The average person working today, with corporations downsizing, is being made into a peon."

Uhouse went on to say that he'd been recruited for the secret program while he was working at Wright-Patterson Air Force Base on early jet engines. He said it had taken sixteen years to design the disc simulator, whose frame had been built by Lockheed (the craft's propulsion system was built by Johnson Controls). He said that the alien Jarod 1 had only been around till the mid-1970s, but that six species of Grays totaling two thousand individuals were currently visiting Earth. He also opined that the reason Teller had taken a liking to Lazar was that Lazar was Hungarian. Moreover, the United States was going to have a Hungarian president by the year 2008. The satellite government was currently "standing by, wait-ing to see what happens politically before they take control; when they do, there won't be any Constitution—it'll be a dictatorship of banks and some military people." Still, Uhouse said, that would be better than what we have now.

Uhouse was followed by Shawn Atlanti, the "on-board abduction" spe-cialist who showed slides of alien images reported by human beings. Quite a diverse gallery it was, ranging from the knockout Nordics of the 1950s to the goat-sucker Reptilians of today. Whenever a descriptive discrepancy arose within a given category, Atlanti acknowledged it by explaining that "there's a variety of types"; to illustrate, he showed a drawing that pictured the whole motley menagerie in a "cosmic family portrait." Analyzing these creatures in chronological order of their reported sightings, a person—though not Atlanti—could chart earthly evolution in reverse, beginning with blond Caucasians and progressing backward through big-headed bipeds toward scaly, primordial monsters from swamps. Atlanti said he felt that the Ursula Andress–like figures of the fifties—whose "very attractive" looks he noted with no trace of irony—had naively been declared to come from Mars or Venus "because that was what our culture would accept at the time." True enough, I had to allow.

After a while, I needed some air. As I stepped outside, though, I heard Anthony Hilder discussing HAARP with Richard Sauder. "Cellular phones operate on the same frequency as the human brain," Hilder was saying.

"ELF* waves have been around since World War Two for communicating with submarines," said Sauder. "Our brains do interact with radio frequencies. It's been shown that, between one and ten Hertz,† your mood can actually vary. And at higher frequencies, the human mind is subject to psychoactive influences. When you vector together everything around us—power lines, antennas, aerials—you realize that maybe what we're dealing with is an interaction between this technology and mass consciousness. We need to understand a lot more about that. If you read Dr. Becker's book *The Body Electric*, you see that we are, among other things, bioelectronic beings."

I insinuated myself into the conversation, introducing myself to Hilder. As I was talking to him, though, he suddenly pointed to the septum of his nose. "You've got something right here," he said.

I wiped my nose; Hilder said, "Nope." As I kept probing for the unspecified substance, he continued to shake his head. "There!" he finally said. "You got it."

Having thus won my trust and obedience, Hilder volunteered to meet with me privately later that evening. We repaired after dinner to the Travises' home trailer, which felt as familiar as any living room in the USA. Hilder told me that his satellite-and-shortwave show, formerly called *Radio Free America*, had recently been renamed *Radio Free World*. When I asked why it was broadcast from Anchorage, Hilder said he'd moved to

---

*Extremely-low frequency

† Cycles per second

Alaska in order to run for the U.S. Senate, but had recently returned to California when his mother took sick.

Preliminaries aside, I asked if he could elaborate on the concept of doctor-engineered antipersonnel diseases (DEADs).

"Doctor Robert Strecher was the first major personality in the medical field to state that AIDS was genetically engineered," Hilder said. "His work was published in the London *Times* or *Express* in the late 1980s, though I found out about the AIDS program several years before that. The disease was developed by combining the bovine leukemia virus, which creates cancer in cattle, with a virus that creates brain rot in sheep. It was mixed with a voracious human cancer culture, and then this new retrovirus was injected into the black population in Senegal, Haiti, Zaire, Uganda, and Brazil through the smallpox vaccination program conducted by the World Health Organization. The Evilarchy are not only elitist but racist. They consider blacks and browns to be almost subhuman—useless eaters, not worthy of space."

"Is this related to the 'Frankenstein factories'?"

"The difference between the legendary Doctor Frankenstein, who created his monster and performed his experiments on the dead, and the modern-day Doctor Mengeles and Frankensteins is that they're creating their monsters and performing their experiments on the living. In Bill Hamilton's book *Cosmic Top Secret*, he talks about the many levels below Dulce, where they keep human body parts in vats. On the fifth or seventh level, an individual was told not to look at or talk to people who were screaming and begging for help from cages. He was told, 'They're insane—ignore them.' We have footage in our videotape *The Panic Project* that shows some sort of energy being created there. It appears to be pods—some sort of plastic or glass bottles, with lots of wires. I believe they are trying to create a hybrid species, just like Mr. Boysen used two berries to make the boysenberry—a subservient race of people or clones, some sort of robotoid, or maybe a reptilian-looking *Chupacabra*. And they plan to introduce this to the world to panic the public into accepting the New World Order. It may not come in the form of an announcement from CSETI°; it may come in the form of a mock invasion from space, like H. G. Wells."

° An aboveboard, mainstream organization called the Center for the Search for Extraterrestrial Intelligence.

"Where do the kidnapped children come in?"

"Milk carton kids? Of the million children the FBI shows missing each year, ninety percent are recovered; they wind up with their uncle, or their drunken mother, or as a sex slave in some cabin, or as prostitutes, or in a shallow grave. According to *The Franklin Coverup*—a book promoted by Ted Gunderson, a friend of mine who was the agent in charge of the Los Angeles, Memphis, and Dallas FBI offices for twenty-seven-and-a-half years—many of these children have been used as sex slaves by members of Congress. Kathy O'Brien is one of them; she has the whole story in a book called *Trance-Formation*. Still, a small percentage—though a large number—are never returned, and we believe that these Frankenstein factories may be using them for medical experiments. This is the same thing that was supposedly unheard of in Nazi Germany. At the time, people couldn't believe Hitler could be so horrible as to perform medical experiments on human beings. But that scientific work has been continued in the U.S. on American citizens, who I believe are being abducted not by aliens but for purposes of medical experimentation."

"So this goes back to the Nazis?"

"We're talking about a conspiracy that's longer than most nations," Hilder said. "The Illuminati was formed by Adam Weishap on May 1, 1776. His intention, and that of those who backed him—the Rothschilds and other very wealthy families in European banking circles—was to take over the Continent and install themselves literally as the gods of the Earth. But a courier carrying a set of papers stating their plans was struck by lightning, and they were revealed to the Bavarian government. The Illuminati were exposed to the European heads of state and forced to go underground. But they later emerged in the French Revolution, in the Jacobin Society and the Reign of Terror.

"In 1967, I produced a set of records that was heard by thirty-eight million people over the next several years. A group of actors talked against the control of Hollywood and Broadway by the oligarchy that is controlling the media and motion pictures, though they didn't identify the oligarchy by name. Joe McCarthy mistakenly called them Communists. They aren't Communists, though their goals are similar, if not identical. Communism is simply a tool of very rich men; it is not a creation of the masses to overthrow the banking establishment, but rather a creation of the banking establishment to overthrow and enslave the masses. Karl Marx was hired by the 'League of Just Men'—very wealthy men, Illuminists—to come forth with a program that would be acceptable to the stupid, to the greedy, to the downtrodden seeking justice. It was a sham, a scam, a con—and the U.N. is in the center of it. *Comm-U.N.-ism* was never run from Moscow, Beijing, Hanoi, or Mobutu. It was always run from New York, London, and Washington, D.C. When Communists celebrate May Day throughout the world, they're celebrating the order and sect of the Illuminati. It has also been the moving force behind Masonry and the Scottish Rites. The author of the Masonic Bible, General Albert Pike, was cofounder of the Ku Klux Klan. In Washington, D.C., the Masons—who laid out the configuration of the streets and put it all together—placed the Capitol building at the top, so that the eye of Lucifer goes out to the pyramid. Below the base of the pyramid is the Washington Monument, which is simply a five-hundred-fifty-foot-tall phallic symbol. Most of the buildings at that time had twenty percent of their structure below ground; twenty percent of five hundred and fifty-five is one hundred and eleven. If you add them together it's six hundred and sixty-six, the Biblical reference to the Antichrist. The name 'Illuminati' comes from 'the illumined one,' or the fallen angel Lucifer. The oligarchy has a spiritual agenda. Most people think it's simply a cartel of Cashists—a Faustian Financial Fraternity, which controls the currency by the issuance of Federal Reserve notes. It's neither federal nor reserve; it's a system totally unacceptable and abhorrent to the Constitution of the United States, in which these *banksters* create fiat funny money for less than two cents a note and lend it back to us at face value. Through the issuance of these notes—which are debt-bearing obligations at the point of origin—they are able to control the Congress and the clergy and the media and the course of the country. You'll note that Chevrolet now has the Lumina car. CBS has always had the Illuminati eye, the eye of Lucifer, which is also on the left-hand side of the dollar bill over the Great Pyramid. A pyramid is the ultimate symbol of slavery; it has nothing to do with the formation of the United States of America. Just below that, it says *Novus Ordo Seclorum*, which means 'New Order Secular' or 'New World Order.' On the right side, the Great Seal was introduced in 1934 by Franklin Roosevelt, who was an Illuminist. His vice president, Henry Wallace, was called 'the corncob mystic'—he had a shrine at the end of a hall in the White House to Madame Helena Petrovna Blavatsky, who was coeditor and publisher of *Lucifer* magazine, which later became the Lucifer Trust, which became the Luces Trust. Take a look at the U.N. literature—at the bottom, in six-point type, you'll see 'Printed by the Luces Trust.' The Great Seal was directed by the same people who financed Hitler. Joseph P. Kennedy, when he was ambassador to the Court of Saint James, was a financer of Hitler, as was George Bush's father, Senator Prescott Bush. Hitler was merely a tool of the Illuminists. His second book after *Mein Kampf* was entitled *The New World Order*—a term that George Bush introduced during the Golf War. The Illuminists financed both sides of the Second World War. My book *The Warlords of Washington* talks about how Roosevelt shipped the Japanese the metals that came back in the bodies of our boys. He said [here Hilder lapsed into a broad FDR impersonation], 'I hate war. . . . Eleanor hates war. . . . your boys will never die on foreign soil.' Well, they didn't have to! He took the U.S. Fleet, which was stationed at San Diego, and shipped it out to Pearl Harbor. He put Admiral Kimmel and General Short in charge, dismantled the radar, ignored the reports of Admiral Yamamoto coming across the Pacific, and antagonized the Japanese by telling them they had to get out of Manchuria in ninety days, which was tantamount to a declaration of war. The war was fought not to bring about freedom but slavery, a system by which this oligarchy could control the Earth. World War Two was a tremendous success for the Illuminati because it created the United Nations. There have been more wars since the creation of the U.N. than ever before in the history of the world—all fully orchestrated and financed. Wars, like bridges, are engineered; they do not come about accidentally. If there's a war between Rwanda and Burundi, where are those poor starving people getting the arms? In whose interest is it to have the Hutu wage war against the Watusi? In whose interest is it to have a weather war declared upon East Africa? They use weather modification to bring about drought and starvation. They create problems to bring about solutions; they create chaos to bring about control. On the Masonic temples it says *Ordo ab Chao*: 'Order Out of Chaos.' Hitler's motto was *Ein Volk, Ein Reich, Ein Fuhrer*: 'One Race, One World, One Ruler.' It has been the dream of many dictators to have a world government under their control. Essentially we had a world government under the Roman Empire; the guys who stood out in front of the Coliseum in their battle garb facing Caesar and said, 'We who are about to die salute you' were forerunners of a widespread attitude in the United States today. I call it 'acceptathetic.' Not ignorant but arrogant people who accept the unacceptable and tolerate the intolerable. Today there's a whole army of these IGORs—the Invisible Government's Obedient Robotons—who work in the Frankenstein factories, and for the alphabet agencies. With the E.C. and a united Europe, Hitler's dream has now come true; exactly what he planned is exactly what happened. Nobody even objected; they just put out their hands and had them banded. I advocate a world that is not united, but divided. Divided we stand, united we fall. Rather than the unification of mankind, I'm for the acceptance of independent linguistic, tribal, racial, religious, and ethnic nation-states as separate and sovereign. I'm in favor of wars of liberation. We need to have three or four thousand different nations, and no individual or group of individuals in an oligarchy controlling the currency. I'm an anarcho-capitalist. I believe in the free right of choice. Freedom is choice; choice is freedom. A world united is not free."

At this point, Hilder's friend Daphne came in, saying that she was going out to the Black Mailbox. Hilder suggested instead going north toward a place "where Jordan Maxwell saw some orange globes." I recognized this as the name of an individual I'd heard at a UFO conference near San Francisco the previous year. Admonishing the crowd that "You have to do your homework," Maxwell had narrated a slide show of "hidden" symbols in Western religious and political imagery, coming to the shocking conclusion that "It's all about sex, drugs, and rock 'n' roll." As a self-proclaimed expert on the links between "secret societies" and the world's power élites, Maxwell appeared to have exerted a strong influence on Hilder—who, for example, set considerable store by a report that when George Bush was a student at Yale, he "laid nude in a coffin and was born again into the Satanic Order of Skull and Bones as a part of their ritual initiation.

"Did you ever see the film *Brotherhood of the Bells* with Glenn Ford?" Hilder asked me. "It's about a fraternity similar to Skull and Bones, which was started in 1832 as a sort of Faustian fraternity, carrying on the tradition of the Bavarian Illuminati. You can't get into their tomb unless you break the lock." I hesitated to tell him that, with a friend who was a member, I'd once entered Skull and Bones in the wee hours of an undergraduate morning; we went in armed with another New Haven secret weapon, an onion pizza from Wooster Square, which we consumed within a ring of skulls that lined the tomb's central chamber. As I was mulling what Hilder might make of such a story, however, Joe and Pat Travis came in.

Pat, who had been on her feet all day, excused herself almost immediately and went to bed. Joe, however, went to the refrigerator and got himself a beer. Pretty soon, Bill Uhouse showed up too. He took a chair in the kitchen doorway as Joe returned to the living room.

"A guy came into the bar who's in the loop," Joe announced, sitting down and lighting a cigarette. "He said Hillary's in deep shit from Whitewater and Clinton's gonna be forced to resign. Gore's gonna take over, and then Banana Bob 'Let's Make a Deal' Dole is gonna find a reason to bow out. So it'll be Gore versus Gingrich in the election."

"There are two guys I've met who have the genuine sage wisdom about the government," said Hilder. "One is an old miner in Colorado. The other is Joe Travis."

"Bill Cooper is the one who opened my eyes," Joe revealed. "I voted for George Wallace twice in the sixties. Then suddenly it hit me between the eyes: 'This is what they're doing! They've got to destroy the country before they take it over!' Now I tell it like it is, and don't give a damn who it offends. I think things are gonna come to a head pretty soon."

"I wish they'd get it over with," said Uhouse. "I'm sick of this shit."

"It's never gonna be over, Bill," Joe said. "But we have them very nervous because they know the people won't buy what they're up to."

"We have to have our house in order," said Hilder. "We have to have gold, guns, groceries, and God."

Joe upended his beer. He looked very tired, but not especially relaxed. "This thing we're supposedly coming into—maybe it *is* an Earth change," he said. "An age of Aquarius. The problem is, I don't see love. I see evil."

"The Masonic monthly is called *The New Age*," Hilder pointed out. "The new age the Illuminati are talking about, though, is the Age of Lucifer."

"You can deal with evil," said Joe. "If you have an enemy, you can deal with him—even love him. But not a guy who has an arm around your shoulders and a knife in your back. Man, Comrade Clinton makes Fidel Castro look like a right-winger! What I want to know is, how did these people come into such prominence?"

"They have an army of IGORs," Hilder explained. "The battle is over before the engagement begins."

Joe polished off his beer and immediately went to the kitchen for another. "The people are being stepped on," he continued to fulminate on return. "It used to be that, if you needed to put a septic tank in, no problem. Now you have to file an application and a plan, then a guy has to come out and look at the ditch. For one of the most basic necessities of rural life! It's not constitutional—it's blasphemy! It's disrespectful of the people!"

"The Nazis were bureaucrats," said Hilder. "It's the bureaucrats versus the people."

"The first attempt to control the people was Prohibition under Woodrow Wilson," said Joe. "That put the G-men in action; it put the CIA in action. I don't understand how a man can say, 'Well, I have to pay more taxes; guess I better work another shift. But hey, I'm doing well—I got a boat and two cars!' It's like driving with your gas gauge on empty. You're destroying the very thing that supports you! It's like cutting up your ship and using it for firewood!"

Suddenly Joe turned toward me. "What do you think about all this?" he demanded.

I looked up from my notebook. "What do I think about it?"

"Yeah. Don't you think you're less free now than you were twenty or thirty years ago?"

I thought this over. "Um," I said. "Yeah—I guess I do."

Joe leaned back in his seat, apparently resting his case.

"The UFO community is quite diverse," Hilder put in. "Liberals, conservatives, New Agers—they're all being introduced to the conspiracy by the hard-core researchers."

"We can all live together," Joe agreed. "But we've got to find something to unite the people. No military in the world can defeat the American people."

With those words, Joe dropped his beer. He cast a distant downward glance toward the place where it was soaking into the rug, but hardly moved to pick it up; instead Daphne went into the kitchen and got a sponge.

"How can a man live without honor?" Joe asked as Daphne cleaned up his mess. "I will die on my feet before I bow on my knees to any man."

There was a knock on the door. It was a friend of Daphne's, ready to drive out to the boondocks to look for UFOs. Just as they were getting ready to leave, though, they looked outside and noticed that it was raining. They decided to abort the mission and go to bed.

Chalk up another one for the wily weather controllers.

The next morning dawned cold and gray. After the previous day, however, the lure of even an orchestrated outdoors was more enticing than the "shelter" of the Quonset hut. For one thing, Rachel seemed permeated by a certain stench; I suppose it might have been the smell of paranoia (or plutonium), but I suspected it had more to do with tobacco and red meat. I decided to skip town and drive out to the back gate of the base—not on Groom Lake Road, but on the well-graded thoroughfare that departs 375 directly behind Rachel. This was where Chuck Clark said he'd seen so many dumptrucks coming and going. Glenn Campbell had told me that the gate was ten miles from town, and that if I asked the guard what it was for, he'd "probably say something like 'the Nellis Range.'" By contrast, Clark said the distance was only seven miles, and that if the guard said anything at all, it would be monosyllabic.

After driving exactly ten miles, I came to a stop sign, a barbed-wire fence, and a white guard shack in the middle of nowhere. I didn't see anybody around, so I got out with my motor still running and approached the gate. As soon as I did, a camouflage-clad guard emerged from the shack. "What can I do for you, sir?" he asked with a southern accent.

"What's this gate for?" I inquired.

"The Nellis Bombing Range."

I looked out beyond the gate. "So it's unsafe?" I asked.

The guard chuckled. "Yes sir."

Enough tomfoolery. "Is this Area 51?" I demanded.

"No sir," the guard answered without missing a beat. "I have no idea where that is."

"Have you heard of it?"

"Yes sir, in the newspapers. But it's not here."

"How about Groom Lake?" I suggested.

"I've heard about that too, but I don't know where it is."

I pointed to the southwest. "It's over there," I said. "What about Papoose Lake?"

"I haven't even *heard* of that."

"S-4?"

"No sir."

"Okay," I said. "Thanks a lot."

I turned back toward my truck, but the surprisingly garrulous sentry seemed to be enjoying my company. "They say it's gonna snow on us," he called out.

I looked up at the sky. "Is it?" I said.

"I don't think so," he said.

I drove back to Rachel, then turned south on 375 and took the diagonal dirt cutoff from the Black Mailbox toward Freedom Ridge. The mountains to the west looked threatening, shrouded as they were in dark gray clouds and dense precipitation. When I reached Groom Lake Road, I saw a dust cloud between myself and the highway; the dust was angled away from me, so I knew the vehicle was coming toward the base. When I got near the border, I stopped my truck on the shoulder and waited.

The Cammo Dudes weren't in their usual place, a low saddle just north of the road. But when I got my binoculars and scanned the top of Freedom Ridge, there in the gray light was the outline of a Cherokee: silent, inanimate, barely perceptible where the ridge met the sky.

Pretty soon the other vehicle caught up. It wasn't a white Cherokee, but rather a beige Land Cruiser driven by a respectable-looking guy in wire-rimmed eyeglasses. Without slowing down, he continued past me toward the border of the base.

Recalling Clark's investigative advice, I pulled out and gave chase. But when the driver reached the boundary, he never even hesitated: He sped right around the bend and into Area 51. Just before he vanished, though, I braked to a halt. I steadied my binoculars against my window frame, trying to focus on the distant, disappearing license plate. My vision was admittedly obscured by murky meteorological conditions, and then there was the destabilizing influence of all I'd been fed the day before. But as I squinted through the dust and rain, I found myself, like Tom Mahood, "scared, mad, and creeped out, all at the same time."

It wasn't so much that the plate said "U.S. Government." That was pretty much to be expected. The unsettling part was the word that the bigger letters spelled out:

IGOR

NINE

The Tour de Luxor

In his explication of the evil designs of the New World Order, Joe Travis had advised me to visit Las Vegas and the Luxor casino. This megalith is the big black pyramid (fourth largest in the world) on the Strip—a provocative vision, one must acknowledge, in context of everything I'd just learned. With a xenon ray shooting from its peak and a gold Sphinx and Washington-monument-like obelisk out front, the Luxor can be seen from almost anywhere in southern Nevada. As it happened, however, it was also the closest casino to the Area 51 Research Center's Las Vegas Annex—i.e., Glenn Campbell's apartment. Considering that the Annex also overlooked the Janet 737 air terminal and its Groom Lake commuter flights, those who suspected Campbell of being a government operative—or, by extension, an agent of the New World Order—could have found ringing confirmation in this coincidence.

Actually, soon after the Luxor opened in 1993, traffic engineer Tom

Mahood had rented a room there to chart flow rates in the Janet parking lot. "It's like flood routing," Mahood explained. "If you measure the water coming into a reservoir and the water leaving the dam, you know how much water is collecting." With the help of a telescope and radio scanner, he'd calculated that 600 to 650 employees made the round trip to Groom Lake each day, with 300 bound for the Tonopah Test Range. (He found no evidence of anyone going to Area 19.)

For his part, Glenn Campbell—oddly, perhaps, for someone who doesn't drink, smoke, or gamble—is a careful student of Las Vegas casinos. "They're so illogical and insane," he explains. "All of life is irrational, but in no place is it more plainly seen than in the casinos. You can't win in Las Vegas; the more you bet, the more you'll lose. So I'm fascinated by how people keep coming here and betting and losing. Their emotions over-whelm their logic. When I interact with the common man, I have to realize that this is his way of making decisions. You just have to live with it."

Because of all this, Campbell was fond of referring to Las Vegas as the center of modern civilization—or, in his more (or less) Earthcentric moments, of the entire universe. "I've always loved Las Vegas," he told me. "It's a city created from scratch, so it's totally without airs. In Europe, everybody is weighed down by huge castles and cathedrals and ancient his-tory that has to be maintained. To a certain extent, the eastern U.S. has that too—a set of rules that have to be followed. But in Las Vegas there's nothing to live up to—all that matters is getting things done and living in the moment. It's all business. Whatever you want, you can get it in Las Vegas twenty-four hours a day."

Of course, for all the democratic rhetoric, Las Vegas casinos could be called the cathedrals of today—more and weightier all the time, in fact, as the Strip's can-you-top-this credo shows few hints of downsizing. Aside from the trademark gambling and glitz, the contemporary Vegas tradition is to reproduce exotic environments (Rome, New York, the Riviera) under climate-and-culture-controlled conditions, accompanied by cheap liquor and familiar food in all-you-can-eat buffets, the better to lure weak-willed customers past slot machines and gaming tables. For these reasons, Las Vegas has lately come to be known as Disneyland for Adults, but also—with the introduction of fun rides, magic shows, and pirate battles—as a gaming park for kids. As such, it is ironically the nation's new All-American destination—though it should be acknowledged that, as one of the weekly newsmagazines pointed out, this status can also be attributed to the fact that, in the half-century since World War II, the rest of the country has simply caught up to Vegas's once unique level of vulgarity. Away from the Strip, Las Vegas has in the last decade been the fastest-growing city in the country: Even as its water supply evaporates, five thousand new residents arrive each month in pursuit of untaxed earnings and affordable housing. While the character of its spreading civilization—a Southern California-style grid of suburban housing tracts serviced by Wal-Mart and McDonald's—has little to do with the Las Vegas of legend, the modern standing of Sin City seems to say something significant about late-twentieth-century "family values."

In any case, the Luxor is a prime component in the new vein of Vegas entertainment. Since Campbell himself had told me that its rides were one of the Strip's few worthy attractions, I asked if he would consent to guide me through its maze of wonders. Hence, I rendezvoused with him one morning at the Annex, to which he'd transplanted conditions from his trailer in Rachel: Besides his computer, there was a photocopier, a twenty-seven-inch television, two VCRs, a globe of the world on a floor stand, a vacuum cleaner (still in the box), and a folding cafeteria table holding a box of Wheat Chex and a bottle of Windex. On the walls were a three-by-five-foot aeronautical chart of southern Nevada, an Area 51 No Trespassing sign facing the front door (WARNING: USAF INSTALLATION), and a couple of posters from Los Alamos, one of which showed the fireball from the 1951 Ranger Fox nuclear explosion, part of the first series of aboveground tests ever done in Nevada. Among the many books on the shelves, I noted *Philosophical Ethics*; *Black's Law Dictionary*; *The Disorganized Personality*; *Diagnostic and Statistical Manual of Mental Disorders—IV*; *Military Monitoring*; *The Fantastic Inventions of Nikola Tesla*; *Darwin Ortiz on Casino Gambling*; *Guidebook to Central Europe*; *The Making of the Atomic Bomb*; and *Our Kind: The Evolution of Human Life and Culture*.

Leaving the apartment, we strolled up the street toward the Luxor. Along the way, we passed a house that had been burned down in a drugs-versus-cops confrontation; a block to the north was a Catholic church; in the other direction, a row of jet tailfins overhung a chainlink fence like the elms of Shady Lane, U.S.A. Away from the Strip, Las Vegas was an even weirder juxtaposition of laissez-faire non sequiturs.

Making our way through the blinding sunlight, we crossed the Strip, passed the Sphinx, and entered the maw of the Pyramid, whose exterior angles were mirrored within by walls converging toward the center of the ceiling. Actually there *was* no ceiling—only a dizzying succession of walk-ways leading to hotel rooms, each horizontal handrail higher and shorter than the next. As we rode an escalator to the mezzanine, a cruise boat passed below us, carrying passengers in an indoor canal, an apparent fac-simile of the Nile. "Just like the real thing," Campbell commented, "only not so dirty. You don't have to worry about catching diseases here. And you can't go to Egypt and gamble or buffet."

To Glenn, "buffet" is both a noun and a verb. Since relocating to Las Vegas, he'd obtained most of his daily calories in these gastronomic extrava-ganzas, gorging himself on one buffet per twenty-four-hour cycle (specifi-cally lunch, which has lower prices than dinner) while snacking on chips and diet soda the rest of his waking hours. "Did primitive man eat three squares a day?" he posited to me in his own defense. "No—he filled him-self when food was plentiful. If you don't *hate* food by the time you leave here, you aren't doing it right." (He'd also once used those last five words when I told him that I seldom get flat tires on desert roads, which he drives at speeds similar to those portrayed in television commercials.)

In the Las Vegas section of the *Area 51 Viewer's Guide*, Glenn had included a directory of casino buffets.° Holding that none of the Strip venues, being generally overpriced and mediocre, warranted trips in them-selves, he instead recommended the outlying neighborhoods, where, unbeknownst to outsiders, good-sized casinos catered to locals who demanded a bang for the buck. Glenn considered the multicultural, kiosk-laden Carnival at Rio the most spectacular spread in town ("gaudy, exces-sive, and superficial . . . stunning variety representing everything that is Vegas"), but his favorite was Boulder Station on U.S. 95 ("not as flashy but excellent quality, variety, and rotation"). A constant orgy of indulgence, efficiency, and waste, the Las Vegas buffet is indeed a metaphor for the city—and, as such, a tidy microcosm of the nation.

When the Luxor first opened, Glenn had described its buffet as "supe-rior food in a spectacular setting." To sample it, we ponied up seven dollars and, after waiting briefly in line, were directed to our table by a headset-wearing hostess. A server appeared to take our drink orders (Pepsi for Campbell, iced tea for me), which were replenished as often as desired. A receipt held our table while we were away loading up our plates.

° It has since been greatly expanded and updated on his World Wide Web site: www.ufomind.com.

Depositing a copy of the *Las Vegas Review-Journal* on his chair, Glenn turned his attention to the task at hand, striding purposefully into the interior—all business. I was somewhat more circumspect, overwhelmed as I was by the panoply of prime rib, beef stew, fried or baked chicken, shrimp, swordfish, sausage, pizza, chow mein, cheeseburgers, green beans, corn on the cob, honeydew, cantaloupe, salad, bread, rolls, and desserts including brownies, cheesecake, pie, chocolate cake, chocolate-chip cookies, and various kinds of pastry. "It's only food," Campbell informed me. "You just have to get it in."

After I'd made my first tentative pass, Glenn said that anything I didn't want would be whisked away if I got up to fetch more. Under the profligate circumstances, I regretted not having brought along a bag, but Glenn told me sternly that such pilferage was against casino rules. "A little opportunistic grabbing is okay," he allowed, "but a bag would clearly indicate premeditation." Obviously, in his role as watchdog, he felt compelled to remain above all reproach.

After an inadequate period of digestion, we embarked on the Luxor experience. Buying tickets to all three segments of the intra-pyramid show (collectively entitled "In Search of the Obelisk"), we soon found ourselves before a sign that said LUXOR ARCHAEOLOGICAL EXCAVATION SITE. Erected by MacPherson Development Enterprises, it explained that an "Ancient Pre-Egyptian Civilization" had been found 8,527 feet below the place where we were standing.

"This exposed surface of limestone buildings was first discovered in 1991 by Middle Eastern linguist Carina Wolinski, Ph.D," the sign said. "Previously owned by MacPherson Enterprises, this property is now protected under contractual agreements which are available at the site superintendent's office." I noticed that one of the "site archaeologists" was Douglas Trumbull, a Hollywood special-effects guru.

In order to visit the research site, we had to enter a "National Security Area." (Apparently, "protected under contractual agreements" meant that the government had grabbed control of the excavation project.) As we stood in line for the elevators that would carry us into the earth, a video monitor showed snippets of the Luxor story thus far. A "Dr. Reginald Osiris" was standing at a podium, upon which was written the name *Enlightened Society for Global Transformation.*

"Osiris is sort of a Sean Morton type," Glenn whispered. "He's a charlatan who's trying to take whatever happens and turn it to his own purposes."

A manly looking, middle-aged bad guy with a banded collar and receding hairline, Osiris was talking about a crystal obelisk that had been retrieved from the excavation site. "Its power is unlimited and unknown," he announced. As he did, Campbell chanted the words along with him. I gathered that, for Glenn, this would be a *Rocky Horror Picture Show*–style exercise in audience participation.

Next we saw the good young handsome hirsute guy "Mac" MacPherson and his colleague, the lovely linguist Carina Wolinski, being ushered into a conveyance to descend into the shaft. When a mustachioed paramilitary guard insisted on searching them, Mac informed him that the government had no right to his personal property.

"The government has a right to anything it wants," the quasi-Cammo Dude corrected him. "We're all expendable when it comes to national security."

"That's the key line of the story," Glenn said. "In a cultural sense, it shows society's clichés about these things—New Age types pitted against a government that's trying to suppress information. Apparently the audience is very comfortable with these concepts."

There followed many thrills and chills, mostly of the tilt-a-whirl and roller-coaster variety. The first such ride occurred in the elevator, where we learned to our shock that the cables had been cut by the evil Osiris. On a movie screen in front of us, the shaft flew upward by at breakneck speed while Mac clambered under the plunging platform, Indiana Jones-style, struggling to repair the device as we all experienced vertigo.

Amazingly, he succeeded at the very last instant. The elevator doors opened and we filed out into a gallery, past a device called a Monolev. Reportedly discovered onsite, it was able to fly by "opposing the Earth's magnetic field."

Before we entered the next set of doors, pregnant women and those with weak stomachs were advised to reconsider. Why became clear as Mac reappeared onscreen before us. He was now at the controls of a Monolev, upon which we were apparently passengers, seeing as how he kept turning around and telling us to hold on. As we took off behind him, the underground chamber opened out into a vast underground city. Someone or something was gunning for Mac, who piloted us on an aerial chase through the dizzying caverns of this subterranean world, our queasy participation ensured by a lurching platform beneath our seats. (As we survived one near miss after another, I wondered how often "MacPherson Enterprises" had to clean the place up.)

Eventually, and thankfully, the ride ended. I can't remember what happened to the obelisk, although it would resurface in Episode Three ("Theater of Time," wherein Mac and Carina triumphed over Osiris, imposing their beautiful ecological vision of the future on the villain's dark and dirty one). Meanwhile, during a break between Segments One and Two, Campbell asked if I was interested in penetrating Luxor security.

You needed a room key to reach the upper floors, so instead we went to the basement and boarded a freight elevator, which whisked us high into the Pyramid without interference. Making our way down one of the walkways, we stopped and peeked over the railing into the vast interior of the casino. We were right above the restaurant.

"We could probably spit on someone's buffet," Campbell suggested, but instead of trying, he backed away. "I'm afraid of heights," he explained. "This makes me very nervous. It's not that I can't do it, but I'd prefer not to." In that light, I wondered how he'd survived the Monolev ride.

For Segment Two, we entered a mock TV-studio waiting room, where we were scheduled to be the audience for a talk show called *Luxor Live*. "It's just like the *Montel Williams Show*," Glenn said, but he was disappointed to find that the operation had been scaled down since his last visit. Whereas, in the past, a warm-up host had met the crowd before the show began, now we were left to mill around and fend for ourselves before being ushered into the studio.

Here again, the "live" action took place on a screen, where a smarmy emcee brought Mac on to talk about the excavation. Carina was contacted on "live remote" from a location where she was awaiting a total eclipse. When it occurred, she went into a trance, which enabled her to translate symbols on an ancient tablet.

True to *Montel Williams* form, our hero Mac was soon surprised by the onstage appearance of his nemesis: the Cammo Dude, who toed the government line on the Luxor project. During the argument that ensued, flashing signs appeared by the stage, urging us to thunder *"Applause"* or to protest, *"No Way!"* The audience—Glenn included—obediently screamed its support or derision of everything that took place.

This to me was an amazing spectacle. After all, in "real" TV studios, such artificial stimulation is intended to ensure that a distant viewing audience will find the onscreen events entertaining. In this case, though, there were no viewers to convince except us, watching third-rate actors in a canned comic-book scenario that we had already seen, in one form or another, ad infinitum, all our lives. Yet this sort of exercise in directed masturbation was purportedly the prime trend in Vegas (read: American) entertainment.

Could this really be called the center of modern civilization? Did Campbell really love it as he claimed? Sure enough, he was right in there, cheering and hissing on command along with the "common man." But even as he wallowed in the tackiness of Vegas, he still somehow managed to remain detached. Once more, as Erik Beckjord had observed, he was "into it and not into it at the same time," recognizing and embracing his own alienation.

The word caused me to wonder what the ETs thought of Las Vegas. That their evolutionary experiment had perhaps gotten out of hand? Judging by the Luxor, earthly society at the end of the century was nothing more than a mass migration of oversized but pea-brained organisms, waddling about in T-shirts and shorts, pointing cameras at moronic diversions, tugging at slot machines, staring at dice, passively importuning fate while smoking tobacco, drinking alcohol, loading up on cholesterol, and throwing away their hard-earned money. Witnessing this display, the only explanation I could muster was that Americans were desperately bored; like UFO conventioneers, these creatures seemed willing to bet on anything, no matter how mindless or far-fetched, that offered escape from everyday life. For the exploitation of such ennui, the wastage in Las Vegas's Black Budget probably rivaled that of the Pentagon.

In fact, that undemocratic archetype Area 51, sitting quietly but purposefully out in the desert, seemed downright inspiring by comparison. Here at the Luxor, paragon of the republic, it was easy to see how the Powers That Be had achieved such a secret state of affairs—and how effortless it would be for the Illuminati to seize control. Joe Travis had argued that "No military in the world can defeat the American people," but military action was hardly necessary. As Richard Sauder had suggested, manipulating the masses was merely a matter of electronics. What was harder to understand was why the New World Order hadn't already taken over—but as Campbell and I went back out on the Strip, where people continued to stream into the Pyramid from all over the country and world, something occurred to me: Maybe it had.

Just as with Joe, what was happening suddenly hit me full in the face. Similar to the church and government, Las Vegas was rife with respectable images from the history of Western civilization. This was obviously window dressing for its Satanist agenda, subsidized by gambling but directed by the oligarchy. Think it over: Las Vegas had thrived throughout the Depression; modern Las Vegas, like the U.N., had gotten going in the wake of the War. The Strip, originally run by the Mob, was now controlled by corporations like MGM and ITT, whose profits were nurtured and furthered by federal manipulators. The situation was even less subtle than the city's reputation: Vegas existed to empty pockets while maintaining the illusion of optimism and hope—and more and more, it was being held up (even by Campbell!) as a model for the nation and world.

Harmless capitalist enterprise? Fruits of free enterprise run amok? No—tools! Cashist tools of the Illuminati! The sage Joe indeed had it right: The conspiracy had *created* Las Vegas—and as anyone could see from one look at the Luxor, enslavement of the American people was well under way.

TEN

Agent X

In spring of 1996, I rendezvoused in the Nevada desert with Mark Farmer—the infamous Agent X.

This was a portentous prospect. Farmer's reputation, which of course preceded him, had recently been retooled by Glenn Campbell over an alleged indiscretion/intelligence leak. The previous year, Campbell had attended Bob Lazar's annual fireworks party, "Desert Blast," whose exclusive announcement warned, *"If you don't know where it is, you're not invited."* Campbell had, however, shared the time and location with Stuart Brown—who divulged it in turn to Farmer, who reportedly passed it along to the Bureau of Alcohol, Tobacco, and Firearms.

"Agent X is a trader in information," Campbell explained. But since trust was crucial in the unwritten oath of the Interceptors, he had chosen to sever relations with the slippery Blackworld sleuth—even though Glenn admitted that "There's some irony there. After all, we want the government to give us its secrets, but we don't want to give them ours."

There were other things about X that troubled Campbell, though. A shameless self-promoter, Farmer was always eager to appear on television—and in that bargain, he seemed willing to stretch the truth by staging reenactments for the camera, going so far as to gesture toward things that weren't even in sight. Then there was his uncontrolled urge for acquisition of kitsch. One time, walking back to the Annex from the San Remo buffet, Mark and Glenn passed through the Tropicana hotel and casino, which happened to be hosting a bioengineering convention. One entrepreneur had set up a sign advertising his business—SPERM WASHING—which so enchanted Farmer that he stole it. "That sort of thing really irritated me," Campbell recalled. "After all, it was the other guy's livelihood." While most Interceptors seemed circumspect about such behavior, it was (as previously observed) important to Glenn to remain above reproach.

Forewarned, I agreed to meet Farmer in the parking lot of the Tonopah supermarket in mid-March, when he was visiting from Alaska for the annual Green Flag exercises in the Nellis Range. The weather for our engagement was glorious—calm and sunny with temperatures in the seventies, hardly sure things for Nevada in March. When Farmer showed up, he was at the wheel of a red convertible, its back seat crammed with camera and survival gear, including a semiautomatic assault rifle. On the glove box he'd taped a yellow sign that said WET in black letters—undoubtedly lifted from some cement sidewalk, but exuding ambiguous connotations away from its customary habitat. The freelance troubleshooter was attired in full-dress three-color* desert cammo: jacket, pants, and broad-brimmed bonnet tied with string beneath his chin to keep it from flying off in the wind. He was also wearing Ray Ban sunglasses, black half-fingered gloves, an olive-green V-necked undershirt, a Fu Manchu moustache, and straight, brown, jaw-length hair.

I was surprised to see that the vehicle was a Mustang. Stuart Brown had told me that Farmer's favorite rent-a-car was the Chrysler LeBaron convertible; the fellow operatives had reportedly made some lively reconnaissance runs in Humvees, Acura NSXs, and other esoteric transport that

---

*Even this was cause for controversy among the Interceptors, some of whom favor six-color, "chocolate-chip"-flecked camouflage.

Brown had scammed for purposes of "product familiarization." They'd even devised a ten-point "LeBaron Scale" to assess the impassability of desert roads, LB-0 representing a paved highway and LB-10 a field of boulders. If a route was capable of being negotiated at all, it was declared "LeBaronable"—or, Brown explained, "as the French would say, '*Luh-bear-uh-nah-bluh.*'" Upon returning a rented convertible, they cursorily hosed down the car's interior, rinsing away potato tubers and any other crops that may have sprouted in the seat cracks.

"LeBarons are no longer being made," Farmer informed me when I expressed my disappointment. "I still need a convertible, though, so that I can look up. Plus in Juneau we have three hundred days of cloud cover per year, so when I'm here, I like to get as much sun as I can." He claimed that the low-slung transmission didn't cramp his off-road style. "I grew up four-wheel-driving; give me four inches of clearance and I can negotiate anything."

Farmer told me that he'd been raised in the town of Willits in northern California—redwood country through and through. He'd gone to Alaska with the Coast Guard in 1983, and continued living there after being discharged with testicular cancer (from which he'd since recovered). He'd run for mayor of Juneau on a part-environmental platform, one plank of which was a plan to tax cruise ships as soon as they entered the city. As his campaign manager pointed out in *Snowboarder* magazine, "Alaska was once part of Russia, and if we'd stayed Soviet we'd be free now instead of being an oil reserve/petting zoo for the Lower Forty-eight." Farmer described his constituency as "the young, the old, and the disaffected mainstream." In one election he'd gotten 36 percent of the vote; upon losing, he decided to declare himself emperor anyway. Heralding a new era of honest accountability, his first act was to change the name of Juneau to "Rain."

On his weekly radio show, *Oil of Dog,* Farmer said he played everything from underground rock to Inuit throat music, Betty Crocker cooking records, Tiny Tim, and William Shatner. "William Shatner is one of my role models. He's totally bombastic and self-congratulatory, but also sort of self-deprecating—a very cheesy person. *Oil of Dog* is not easy listening. It's difficult listening—a sonic landscape that questions how our society got to the point where we'd make this kind of music. There's a lot to our culture that's eminently disposable, but I won't *let* it be thrown away."

Occurring intermittently amid all this were Farmer's trips to Nevada, which required "scamming equipment, money, time, and motor vehicles, and getting people to take care of all the stuff I should be doing while I'm in the desert. Then I just come out here and sit. Usually nothing happens; the vast majority of the time, I see absolutely nothing. But then there are moments when shit just happens. Most of the time it's Whiteworld normal stuff, but that can still be very exciting—B-1s at a hundred feet, or maximum-performance dogfights right above your head, dropping flares all around you. That's a great show, rewarding in itself. Then sometimes you see airplanes doing things they shouldn't do, or exhibiting strange modifications—C-130s with extra bumps and bulges, or stuff that doesn't belong, like a Sukhoi 27. Any time you look at an airplane and see weird bumps, it means it does something spooky: gathering intelligence, jamming, or spoofing, making the enemy believe something's happening in one place when it's actually happening somewhere else. Hearing stories, dealing with security guards—all of it's good for me. A lot of it, too, is getting out of my town—I have no privacy in Juneau. If I don't come down here for a couple of months, I start itching. I don't have a lot of control over it."

That established, we prepared to leave Tonopah. "They don't trust us here," Farmer said, referring to the fact that the Texaco required us to pay before we pumped. He proposed that we drive 150 miles southeast to Delamar Dry Lake, where Green Flag exercises were currently concentrated. "At the Ash Springs gas station this morning, I talked to a group of eight guys wearing basic woodland camouflage, which is what Air Force people wear. There were two colonels, a couple of captains, junior lieutenants, and sergeants. Two of them had Space Command patches, but the majority were Air Intelligence Service. One of them had seen a story I wrote about HAARP for *Popular Science*. I told them I was interested in doing an article about the use of unmanned tactical aircraft and the increased emphasis on intelligence-gathering capabilities—how they're able to synthesize a coherent battlespace picture. They said, 'That's the kind of stuff we're working on today at Delamar.' It's pretty easy to break the ice with military guys as long as you show you're knowledgeable about what they can do and don't ask them something classified straight off. It's a matter of filling in between the lines."

As we began driving east on U.S. 6, we were immediately engulfed by yellow-green sagebrush, dirt-brown mountains, and an enormous azure sky. I followed Farmer's convertible in my truck, but in relatively short order, he pulled over at the entrance to the Tonopah Test Range.

"I always like to see what stickers are here," he told me, peering at the baby-blue sign adjoining an upright white missile. "Here's one for 'Andre the Giant—7'4", 529 pounds.' There's 'OPTEC Threat Support Activity—El Paso, Texas.' The guys in these operations are so sophomoric; they come out and leave their trail everywhere." Looking through his binoculars further up the sign, he found the spoor of a Patriot missile operation and a wolf's head with a crown and coat of arms—"I assume a British Tornado squadron."

With regard to the looming missile, Farmer said, "This thing is sort of a mishmash. It's a hybrid of a Navy Terrier or Tartar antiaircraft missile with a V-28 hydrogen bomb on top. TTR is where they drop nukes without any physics package in them; it's Air Force administered by Sandia, though lately DOE in Las Vegas is taking over more of the responsibility."

It had also been home base to the first operational squadrons of F-117s—for five years, TTR had a secret air force of some fifty stealth fighters. According to John Lear, the base also boasted a dry lakebed with a door for alien discs—which made sense, seeing as how it was the place where (according to Chuck Clark) a group of "human guinea pigs" had been shown a disc that disappeared right before their eyes. Another little-known (but verifiable) fact was that in the 1992 internal phone book for Nevada DOE, TTR was referred to as "Area 52." The base even had its own "Site Four"; reportedly used to test Soviet radar, it had a back road leading to Rachel. When Glenn Campbell's assistant, Sharon Singer, once tried to get a job there, she was told that Site Four employees commuted by air from Las Vegas. Some suspected that this was where Lazar (via Lear) got the original idea for "S-4."

Farmer explained the command structure governing U.S. Air Force bases, classifying them by division of duty: Strategic, Combat, Mobility, Logistics, Materiel, and Space. "Nellis is Combat," he said. "Edwards is Materiel. The headquarters for Materiel is Wright-Patterson in Ohio; I suspect that Groom is an Air Force Materiel Command base, but it's also got Navy, CIA, NRO,° and DARPA.† Supposedly Groom has a museum; I'd sure love to see it. Imagine what's in it!"

° National Reconnaissance Organization

† Defense Advanced Research Projects Agency

Actually, Glenn Campbell, with the help of "astute Web surfers," was soon to uncover a direct link between Edwards and Area 51. In 1994, Glenn obtained a copy of an alleged Groom Lake security manual; entitled "DET 3 SP Job Knowledge," it directed its personnel (for example, the Cammo Dudes, who claimed to be county sheriff's deputies) to say they were assigned to a facility called Pittman Station. Going through Lincoln County files later, Campbell came upon some records of Dude deputizations; one of the presiding notaries—all of whom were affiliated with something called "DET AFFTC" (and employed by Clark, not Lincoln, County)—listed "Pittman Station, Henderson 89044" as his mailing address.

Glenn knew that "AFFTC" stood for the Air Force Flight Test Center at Edwards. A call to the Las Vegas postal center further informed him that Pittman Station was a decommissioned substation on the Boulder Highway. Feeding the words into a Web search engine, a reader of Glenn's newsletter found a 1990 NASA press release that said astronaut candidate Captain Carl Walz was employed at "Pittman Station, Nevada"; Walz's bio, scared up by yet another Net detective, said that the captain had served as flight-test program manager at "Detachment 3" of the Air Force Flight Test Center.

From all of the above, Campbell concluded that, within the military chain of command, Area 51 was Detachment 3 of the Flight Test Center at Edwards Air Force Base, and that Pittman Station was a mail drop enabling Groom-affiliated personnel to claim that it was the facility to which they had been assigned.

Farmer and I continued east into the fallout zone. When we stopped at the intersection with Highway 375 at Warm Springs, I noticed that his method of making a turn involved depressing the accelerator while rotating the wheel, thereby spinning the rear end while spewing a jetwash of dirt and gravel—sort of like a little kid on a spider bike. After investigating a fenced-off hot pool where Farmer had been known to take the odd clandestine bath, we turned south on 375 toward Rachel. East of the Reveille Mountains, however, we pulled over again.

"I saw some dust trails going in here yesterday afternoon," Farmer said. "I think it was a radar truck. They might have just been putting their equipment away for the night, but maybe the battle they're fighting is a very fluid one and they were moving stuff to simulate troop movement. From what I know of the games, they're fairly realistic; the guys in the cockpit can't tell the difference between what's being done to them and what their targets are."

Off to the west over the Nellis Range was a pair of bombers. "Hey!" said Agent X. "B-52s! I love B-52s. They're America: big, robust, ostentatious, and over-engineered. They look like they belong on the hood of a Chrysler Imperial. Actually they're the most versatile airplane we have— they can drop nukes, fire cruise missiles or anti-shipping missiles, drop iron bombs or cluster bombs or mines, and probably do some other secret stuff, too. They're getting the ability to employ precision-guided munitions like HAVENAP, the big long-range missile we bought from the Israelis. It's television-guided: A guy sits inside a B-52 and steers the missile to its target, watching a picture of it from a camera in the nose. The majority of pilots who fly B-52s are younger than the planes themselves; years ago, people thought they'd be retired in the 1970s. But the B-1 is a piece of shit and the B-2 isn't ready to go to war—so here we are forty years later and the B-52 is still our main bomber."

Cresting Queen City Summit north of Rachel, we approached the Nye-Lincoln County border, south of which prostitution was illegal. "I'd like to open a whorehouse north of the line," said Farmer. "I'd call it 'Agent X's Blackworld Brothel' and have a three-hundred-foot-tall statue of a woman straddling the highway saying, 'Flyboys welcome.'" Near the site of this proposed venture, we noticed a camouflaged radar dish on a flatbed truck. Beyond it a gray-bearded man was firing Smokey Sam rockets, their smoke trails simulating surface-to-air missiles. Farmer walked into the creosote bush to retrieve one: a lightweight plastic projectile with tail fins, like a little bomb.

"They're simulating an air defense battery," said Farmer. "On that truck is a reprogrammable threat-emitting radar. They can punch up on the computer any kind of radar they want to mimic—Soviet, Chinese, whatever. As airplanes come by, they get painted by the electromagnetic energy; inside the cockpit, the pilot receives a threat warning and does evasive maneuvers, or fires a missile. Or both."

To wit—and without warning—three F-15E Strike Eagles appeared out of the east. In advance of their own noise, they streaked directly over our heads, leaving an earsplitting roar in their wake. "Those are replacing the F-111 as our premier non-stealth strike fighter," Farmer said. "They're really tough and sophisticated, very rugged for the amount of sensors that they have inside. They're probably the best thing we have now for seeing and fighting at night. I can't really think of any better job than what those guys have: Wake up in the morning, strap on an F-15, and go blasting all over the country. It would really suck having to go to war, but up to that point it would be great."

When the crew began packing up, Farmer went over to talk to the Smokey Sam guy. "They're not sending much our way," the gray-bearded man reported, "except for the ones that want to blow our heads off." After he left, Farmer said, "Did you see his badge? It said he worked for Loral. That's a very large defense contractor that does a lot of spooky stuff, mostly with electronics. That badge had a lot of squares nicked out; he probably has access to quite a bit of the range out there. I bet he sees *lots* of stuff."

We continued on through Rachel, stopping at the Quik Pik to check the radiation monitors. In average microRoentgens per hour, area readings for January 1996 were:

Rachel	17.5
Medlins Ranch (Black Mailbox)	17
Tonopah	18.7
Las Vegas	9
Beatty	16.8
Goldfield	15.9
St. George, Utah	8.5

For the sake of comparison, if the figures for Rachel were extrapolated out to a year's worth of exposure, they would total only about half the maximum allowance recommended by the Environmental Protection Agency.

When I told Farmer that I'd seen a DOE report that said Queen City Summit was contaminated with plutonium, he laughed. "I'm not afraid of plutonium," he said. "I find a lot of humor in it, actually—this nasty stuff that they sprinkled everywhere. It's actually quite good on breakfast cereal. When I took a press tour of the Test Site, I asked permission to snowboard Sedan Crater;* they haven't turned me down yet."

* Caused by a 104-kiloton nuclear explosion in 1962.

times they've known I was up there and run stuff anyway. Frankly, I don't think they realize what kind of lenses I'm playing with. Most semiserious amateurs have three hundred millimeters, max, but I shoot a majority of my pictures with a fifteen-hundred f24 with folded optics. It's only this long." He held his hands about nine inches apart. "I also have a twelve - thousand-millimeter that I bought at an auction at Vandenberg Air Force Base for a hundred and fifty dollars. It cost the government twenty-four thousand, but the only use for it is very long-range, narrow-field photography—you need two frames for just one hangar." He'd taken the shots in his wallet collection with a three-thousand-millimeter lens.

Clark said he had a total of between twenty-two hundred and three thousand such images. "I keep the negatives elsewhere—and no, I'm not gonna tell you where. When things get slow, I sit around and look at them under a loupe. I've found all kinds of interesting gadgets—things that pop out of the ground that are concealed near the runways, some of them fifteen feet tall. I've shown them to pilots who say they have no idea what they are."

I asked Clark where he was from and what he did for a living. He told me he'd grown up in Southern California and was self-employed building big-game fishing rods. He'd come to Rachel a year and a half earlier from Lompoc, California, where he'd been a member of an amateur astronomy club and director of operations for a local observatory.

"It was next to the Space Launch Complex at Vandenberg Air Force Base. Almost all the launches there are secret—but a launch is a hell of a show, and since we're paying the bill, I figure we might as well enjoy a little bit of free fireworks. Basically, I don't see the need for secrecy in a lot of things. When I was in the service, we were developing chemical weapons in Utah and attack helicopters in Alabama; I worked for the commanding general of the Continental Army Command in the Pentagon, responsible for all enlisted people in eleven western states. It gave me a perspective most people don't get. I kicked around two- and three-star generals, and had a high-level security clearance. But there isn't much secrecy at the higher levels of the military. It's mostly added on by lower levels of command out of paranoia that they might get their rears in hot water. So at Vanderberg I was watching everything that left the ground and sharing it with the media, since they weren't being very forthcoming at the base."

"Why did you come here?"

"I wanted to get away from state income tax and be closer to my son in were put in prison? And when they came back, they were heroes? I found out they were out there looking for a U.N. camp *so they could find some booze*. And we almost went to war for these knuckleheads! So I told Larry King about it, and Glenn didn't like that either. Glenn has a very strong sense of honor, right and wrong. I don't know what it is, but I think there's something in his past that makes trust a very important part of a friendship. Plus, Glenn isn't antigovernment, but he's *distrustful* of the government, whereas I'm not antigovernment at all. I'd still be in the military if I hadn't gotten cancer.

"Anyway, I let it sit for four or five months and decided maybe I fucked up. I told Glenn I was sorry, which is not something I do very often. So now we're talking again, and I'm glad. I missed him. Glenn has changed a lot since I first met him; he's grown in confidence to the point where he can lead people and motivate action, which is unusual for a quiet guy. I'm a blowhard, but Glenn is succinct. He's a perfect conduit for all this stuff—the best writer of us all, by far. I value his insight. I respect him, and I'm proud of the things he's done."

Further south and east we traveled on 375, passing the Black Mailbox and Groom Lake Road and gazing toward the Groom Mountains in the west, where the sun was about to set on Area 51. We continued over Hancock Summit to U.S. 93, filled up our tanks again in Ash Springs, and then departed the blacktop, heading east on a dirt road toward Delamar Dry Lake, fifteen miles away.

I followed Farmer's dust cloud in the gathering dark. In places where the route got rough, his low-slung transmission filled the air with the smell of burning sage—a Native American cleansing ritual, somewhat modified from the original form. When we reached the dry lake, I expected to go up into the hills, but Farmer drove straight onto the playa; I followed him at a distance, watching for stream drainages that would do serious damage if encountered at high speed.

A rumble arose from my truck tires as they beat their way across the cracked surface of the lake. Occasionally I lost track of Farmer in the growing gloom, but inevitably his cloud would reappear. Soon we both turned our headlights on, despite the fact that we were supposed to be keeping a low profile. Farmer had told me that he sometimes drove in the dark with night-vision goggles, but on this trip he'd left them at home.

When I finally caught up with him, he'd parked his car on the rock shore of an "island" in the lake. A short distance away, I could see where his tracks made doughnuts at the end of his route, with mud thrown up and across the playa from the outer curve of his arc. "I came here in a Cadillac one time and did some maximum speed tests," he told me. "It went 130. A convertible with the top down won't go over 105." Before we left the next morning, he would not only duplicate this feat, but, for the benefit of passing airplane pilots, would also spell out his pseudonym with tire tracks on the lakebed.

We broke out our camping gear. Farmer had a couple of MREs (meals-ready-to-eat), so in the Interceptor spirit, I accepted one. Agent X warned me that, just as with a solar eclipse, "You should never look directly at an MRE"—but in the interests of thorough research, I felt compelled to catalogue the ingredients. Inside the rubber packet were fruit mix, crackers, "beverage base powder," apple jelly, cocoa powder, Taster's Choice, Coffee-mate, sugar, a milk caramel, toilet paper, and a Wet Nap. Surprisingly, the entrée itself—corned beef hash—was edible, though cold. "Corned beef was the best of the old MREs," Farmer informed me. "Some of them were pretty scary—especially tuna casserole and the ham omelette."

After dinner, we hunkered down to the serious business of secret-airplane spotting. "I saw some stealth fighters and Wild Weasels here the other night," Farmer said. "You can recognize F-117s at night from their light pattern—a single red light in the nose. Wild Weasels have a mission called SEAD, or Suppression of Enemy Air Defenses. They're specially equipped F-4G Phantoms—holdovers from the Vietnam War, loaded with electronics for finding enemy surface-to-air missile radar. Some enemy radars are only on for a millisecond because they know Wild Weasels are out there. Once they find you, they come right down the barrel and launch high-speed anti-radiation missiles. Their mission is being taken over now by F-16s, but the last Wild Weasel unit that does it is at Nellis. You see them out here a lot."

Delamar Lake has a high profile among military pilots, who call it Lake Texas because of its shape. "There are stories of people coming out here from Alamo and running into armed Air Force guys telling them not to go any farther," Farmer said. "This used to be a divert site for the X-15. Throughout the history of Black programs, the initial flights that happen at Groom stay within the confines of the Nellis Range, but after they're confi-

dent that the airplane is going to stay in the air, they send them out here to
the east and up toward Utah. Some of the very fast movers go directly out
toward the Pacific Ocean, then come back in over Los Angeles and up this
way. Those are the planes that caused the airquakes the last few years.
Most airplanes heading toward Area 51 come in from the north, make a
big sweep right over this area, and then, following the lights of Alamo and
Ash Springs, drop into Tikaboo Valley and go screaming across to Groom.
When you're traveling seven hundred miles an hour, it only takes a couple
of minutes. One time an A-12 ran out of fuel and crashed to the south of
here. Another time the Air Force lit that whole valley on fire with flares."

Farmer explained that Operation Red Flag consists of "fighters,
bombers, and attack planes coming together from many different nations
and learning to fight each other and drop bombs. France, NATO—I've
even seen Singaporean planes and MiG 29s, probably German—out here.
But Green Flag, which is going on now, is oriented toward electronic warfare. They have a bunch of jamming airplanes: the Air Force EF-111
Raven, the Navy EA-6B Prowler, the RC-135 for classified-mission payloads and electronics intelligence. The Army and Air Force have joint
Stars, which are Boeing 707s—same family as AWACS, or Airborne Warning and Control System—conducting airspace surveillance and bringing in
information from support satellites to control the battle. They have a radar
canoe on the bottom so they can track moving ground targets like tanks
and armored personnel carriers; it sees the geography and lay of the land.
You lay in imagery from roads and cities, and the radar puts in little marks
to show these moving targets—which way they're going and how fast, so
you can zoom in and tell your strike package what they have to hit, relaying
the information to them digitally. So in this one operation, you've got
J-Stars looking at the ground; AWACS looking at the ground, air, and
space; SR-71s with multiple payloads; and unmanned aircraft, all providing
a seamless picture so the commander can sit back and look at the battlespace in real time.

"We're now seeing a lot of these assets that used to be dedicated to
strategic nuclear warfare changed over to command and control and intelligence," Farmer went on. "Until the beginning of the 1990s, there was a
general in an airplane orbiting over the U.S. at all times. The EC-135
Looking Glass used to be the alert aircraft for nuclear forces, but these
sorts of things are becoming our new eyes and ears. Some of it was in-
corporated into Operation Desert Storm. By the turn of the century, our

military will be incomparable; nobody will be able to touch us. Nobody else is as good as us at writing software or digitizing, taking information and displaying it in usable form. And because of our space assets, nobody can match our ability to gather information. Our only shortcoming is human intelligence gathering. The future will hinge on the philosophy of precision force: applying the maximum amount of violence at the exact place where it belongs at the exact time that it's necessary—that's what we're very good at. In the future you'll see a lot less airplanes, soldiers, and ships—conceivably half of what we have now."

I asked Farmer how he'd gotten so interested in this stuff. He told me that his father had once worked for NASA at the Goldstone Deep Space Tracking Station in the California desert. "I thought space landings and X-15s were really cool," he recalled. "I was in the Civil Air Patrol as a kid, so I knew how the military worked and always assumed I'd be in it. I wrote letters to branches of the armed forces, and learned to fly when I was fifteen. I wanted to be an astronaut. But I didn't want to kill anybody, so I ended up joining the Coast Guard. I was on an icebreaker for a couple of years; I was a quartermaster, navigator, rescue swimmer, weapons expert, and photojournalist. Some of the elite helicopter pilots are in the Coast Guard, but I risked my life for fish more than anything else."

For someone whose style was so anarchistic, Farmer seemed surprisingly comfortable with military mores. "I wish I was still in the military," he acknowledged. "Once you know the rules, it's an okay place. It's good to know what kind of clothes you're going to put on in the morning and what you're going to be doing during the day. In the military there's always an opportunity to take risks and do things that very few people get to do—in my case, hanging out of helicopters, being on an icebreaker, and traveling to parts of Alaska. When I worked on joint-forces exercises with Air Force guys, I heard some wild stories about things that actually came to be, like Stealth. That's when I started pumping people about Black projects. I'm still a hawk in a lot of respects; for example, I think there are some technologies we're bypassing that we should be buying now. We need to have a very robust force that's able to read what's going on and counteract things before somebody lobs a nuke into Los Angeles or something. The world's a dangerous place, and as a nation we need to be prepared. And there is a need for secure operating areas like Groom and Tonopah."

Reclining on the lakebed in a folding lawn chair, Farmer looked up at the darkening sky, which was gradually filling with a gauze of stars. "Hey!"

he said. "What's that? Something white with a green tint. That's really weird—zigging and zagging and banking, without any sharp-angled turns."

My naked eye saw nothing at all. "A UFO?" I offered.

"I've seen two of them out here," Farmer divulged. "One was a light that kept bouncing around and then just went away. The other was a colored, floating, glowing orb that popped up behind the jumbled mountains south of Groom Lake. It went straight up, then started jerking around and wobbling up and down—at times making right-angled, or greater than right-angled, turns, then sitting still in a rock-hard hover. It became distorted when it moved—part of it lagged behind the main object, then the trailing edge would catch up. I had a Celestron twelve-hundred-millimeter telescope, and I watched it for an hour and forty-five minutes. It wasn't quite round; it was sort of squashed, and shimmering the whole time as if it were surrounded by some kind of field. It was crimson on top, blue-green on the bottom, and gold in the middle. I have no idea what it was."

I had turned on my headlamp to take notes. Suddenly Farmer blurted, "Got something coming! Drop your light!" Out of nowhere, a dark, diamond-shaped, green-lit specter hurtled overhead going east, filling the basin with a deafening din; on its heels were another craft with a bright blinking strobe, and a third one with no lights at all.

"Wow!" said Farmer. "I've never seen *that* before—a diamond with an all-green light pattern. It was moving *fast*—I'd say six hundred knots, or about seven hundred miles per hour.* That was a strange package; normally you'll have several different types of planes in multiple numbers. It leads me to believe that they were all special mission airplanes—SEAD, recon, or electronic warfare. If I'd had binoculars, I probably could have made out the shape against the light of Venus or the glow of Las Vegas. If they were looking with infrared, they certainly saw *us*. What I really need is a thermal infrared viewer hooked up to a video camera; night vision is good, but infrared is where it's at. And film is good, too, but I think the key to capturing these birds is gonna be digital technology. For Tikaboo Peak, I'd need an eleven-inch mirror telescope or a three-thousand-millimeter lens with a charge couple device attached to the back, downloading into a laptop computer with one-point-three gigabytes. If I had thirty thousand dollars, I could give you a couple of Black airplanes."

No doubt. Still, this all begged the question, since Farmer was so

---

*The speed of sound at sea level and 32 degrees Fahrenheit is 762 miles per hour.

avowedly pro-military, of why he felt driven to detect and expose top-secret technology. Was it sheerly the thrill of the hunt? Did the intrigue simply seduce him into doing something that he actually felt was wrong but couldn't stop himself from doing?

"I never quite put it that way," he said, "but yeah. Ten years ago, I don't think it would have been possible to do this—or the right thing to do, either. Russia was our adversary, and we were constantly staring down the barrel. Coming out and reporting on what was going on at Groom Lake would've been improper. But things are different nowadays; the landscape's a lot more complex. It's not just us versus them. Now there's more reason for the military to justify its existence and spending. I'm not saying *everything* should be revealed, but there are reasons that this stuff shouldn't be so secret—such as the amount of money it costs, and certain environmental concerns. But I still think the push for unmanned vehicles, new sensor technologies, invisibility, increased-performance explosives, and new applications of precision force are all the right thing to do."

"Are any of those things going on at Groom Lake?"

"Some of them, like airborne ballistic lasers and 'advanced concept technology demonstrators' or ACTDs, are probably being worked on there," Farmer said. "Then there are some gee-whiz things, like invisible aircraft. You put an electro-chromic coating on an airplane and a sensor on the top and bottom, telling it whether it should look like the ground from below or the blue sky from above. There's also pretty good anecdotal evidence to indicate that we're working on a 'null field' cloaking device aimed at bending light around an object. I have no idea how it works, but according to the people I've gotten this from, there are no alien overtones to the program."

"Excuse me?"

"I've gotten some indications of alien technology from other people," he said. "Like Jarod, or ex-Air Force types who've seen discs or had access to areas where the stuff was being used. There's no evidence, though—no hole in the ground where you can dig up an alien artifact. No 'Where's the disc?' Information is basically coming in from two streams. One of them is people saying: 'I was abducted! The aliens are here!' The other is God-fearing professionals, doctors or pilots or scientists who don't drink and aren't big believers in the supernatural, but still say, 'Yes, we've seen strange things,' or 'Yes, we've recovered things.'"

"Have you met Jarod?" I asked.

"I met Jarod *first*," he said. "We were speakers at a loonfest in Rachel—the one after the Ultimate UFO Seminar, when things started to sour between Glenn and Little A-Le-Inn. First I met Bill's brother, who was an aircraft mechanic for the Air Logistics Command for a long time. We talked airplanes for a while; then Bill and I sat down and talked for a couple of hours. I was like, 'Either you are one whacked hombre, or else, well, what's up here?' Glenn met him shortly thereafter. I usually see him every trip down here—we have lunch or something like that. It's tough to figure out why he's talking to us, or why his 'supervisors' would allow him to talk; I mean, is he part of some disinformation campaign? Is this the initial part of letting the story out? Or is he crazy? He doesn't seem to be at all. When I talk with him, the cues he gives me are that he's telling the truth. His body language is open and relaxed; his voice is steady; he doesn't blink excessively; he looks me in the eye. So I just keep talking to him and putting things away, cross-referencing them with other things. For all I know, he may be having a great laugh about us chasing after boron or all these nebulous multinational corporations that are supposedly in cahoots with the government and the aliens. But we haven't been able to find any serious flaws in his story thus far. And he isn't playing it for money the way Lazar is, with his videotape and model kit and movie rights and stuff. I think Lazar's story is a bunch of shit; when *he* talks, his voice wavers, he blinks excessively; he may just be uncomfortable on camera, but he has a nervous atmosphere to him that makes me question his sincerity. I mean, come on: You can't lie about your background and have two wives at the same time *and get a Top Secret security clearance!* Lazar seems like a smart guy, but you can be a smart guy and a sociopath at the same time. There are people with borderline personality disorders, schizophrenics, who are able to weave very good stories. It's just a con game that relies on how much you're willing to buy into it. If you were really paranoid and tended to believe in the aliens, Lazar's story would be a pretty good one to latch your teeth into. But there have been disc stories at the Test Site since the sixties. Lazar's saucer design comes from Billy Meier; Zeta Reticuli is mentioned by Betty and Barney Hill; 'S-4' is a real place at TTR. Lazar's story just brings all those things together in one package.

"Still, something that looks like a disc *has* been flown around the Test Site. There are too many stories from too many people who are credible and have no reason to say they've seen these things. I'm probably about two-thirds into Black military technology and one-third into the alien thing—but the alien part is growing. I tried to avoid it in the beginning; I tried to not deal with it. I thought all the people were fucking nuts, but then after I saw some things and talked to people who I thought were credible, it all started to amount to a conclusion that something's going on. I don't know if it's aliens or super-secret weapons we've built, but there *are* discs, there *are* glowing orbs, there *are* wildly maneuverable craft flying around the skies here. And if some of the stories are true, it's very troubling. If you believe Jarod, it means our government sold us out; in fact, they sold out the whole planet. We're nothing more than a resource extraction point for boron—a colonial outpost for a bunch of aliens. That's unsettling; I've actually lost sleep over it. It's affected my friendships, and my relationship with my girlfriend. I'm wrapped up in such a wacky topic that's so far removed from normal people's concerns. Most people might watch a movie about extraterrestrials, or maybe *Star Trek*, but how many people actually live it? In the last five years, I've spent close to a hundred thousand dollars on equipment and trips here. Coming down, alone at first, and crawling around the desert without *Popular Science* or *Sixty Minutes* or *Newsweek* or *Jane's Defence Weekly* behind me, I felt very vulnerable. It was frightening. Now there there are people I can call, who know I'm here, so there's a very low likelihood of anything ever happening to me. But I'm still a little too deep into all this stuff. It's suckered me in; it's changed my life. I have a pseudonym and can't hold down a regular job. But billions of dollars of our wealth are going into this stuff—and if the aliens *are* here, it's the biggest story there is."

It was completely dark now, except for the glowing stars and the gleaming playa. This, I realized, was the Interceptor experience: gazing up at the sky from a lawn chair on a dry lake, waiting for things to appear in the dark while speculating about what was real. It seemed like a very particular activity for a time and place in history—post–Cold War, millennial America—but it wasn't really all that specialized. How different were we from pre-Christian desert nomads sitting beneath the same stars, organizing them into meaningful shapes and investing them with power and influence over our lives? In his conflict between curiosity and patriotism, pragmatism and wonderment, even his contradictory stances as hawk and dove, Agent X was not—despite his best efforts to seem so—unique. On the contrary, he was Everyman: He stood not only for Interceptors but Area 51 insiders; he represented not only the public but the Blackworld spooks; he embodied not only the Pentagon but the paranoid fringe. Lying in his sleeping bag on the surface of Lake Texas, he spoke not only for the nation or even the modern world, but for all humanity down through history—evolutionary "adjustments" and all.

"I don't think people are ready to know the truth," Agent X said before going to sleep. "And I don't think we're going to know the truth any time soon."

ELEVEN

The Extraterrestrial Highway

In spring 1995, the Nevada state legislature began considering a bill to designate Route 375 the "Extraterrestrial Alien Highway." This was the fond wish of Ambassador Merlyn Merlin II of Alpha Draconis, who lobbied for it in the state capitol and, by his own avowal, "put it into the head" of an assemblyman from North Las Vegas, Bob Price. By other accounts, the idea's origin was more terrestrial. The previous year, Glenn Campbell had taken Price's fellow assemblyman, Roy Neighbors of Tonopah, to Freedom Ridge in order to publicize Area 51's failure to carry its weight in county taxes. During the day, Glenn gave Neighbors a copy of the *Viewer's Guide*, whose cover referred to 375 as "America's 'Alien Highway.'" Nothing happened with the taxes, but to Campbell's unpleasant surprise, an Alien Highway bill was subsequently introduced in the state assembly.

On May 19, 1995—without any notice to residents of Rachel other than Joe and Pat Travis—a public hearing on the bill was held in Carson

City, three hundred miles away. As soon as Campbell got wind of it, he faxed a letter of protest. Maintaining that only one Lincoln County business (the Little A-Le-Inn) would benefit from it, he warned that the act would serve to lure scores of gullible travelers into the area, where they would be subject to arrests and fines along the poorly marked border of Area 51. While Campbell believed that "some of the reports that the government has been working with alien hardware deserve serious attention," he charged that the highway designation would not only make light of such claims but would encourage the misidentification of military activity and trivialize the political significance of Area 51. "Many serious environmental, fiscal and worker rights issues remain unresolved at the Groom Lake base," Glenn wrote. "Institutionalizing a 'lighthearted' approach to the area distracts from these issues and makes it much more difficult to have them taken seriously."

Campbell's letter received no attention at the hearing, as (according to the Associated Press) "proponents donned space alien masks, antennae and pointy ears as they made their pitch":

> Backed up by spacy sound effects, Neighbors said on the Assembly floor that reported UFO sightings "are part of the fantasy and excitement of the tourist attraction that is Nevada."
>
> Wearing a Darth Vader mask, Assemblyman Bob Price, D-North Las Vegas, presented a letter supporting the bill from the "intergalactic tourism association."
>
> Saying he couldn't read the letter on account of the earthly pollution's effects on his eyes, "Darth" handed the letter to the "earthling" on his left—a reluctant Assemblyman Wendell Williams, D-Las Vegas.
>
> Up to the challenge, Williams read aloud the note promising that the association would include a stop at "E.T. Highway" as part of its package tour-to-earth offering.
>
> After the floor session, Assembly Co-Speaker Joe Dini, D-Yerington, called Neighbors and Price to the rostrum to present them with gifts from their alien friends, including plaques of recognition and copies of the Klingon Dictionary.

The bill passed the assembly unanimously. It was, however, killed in the state senate, whose transportation chairman refused to give it a hearing because he didn't "have time for frivolity." But Ambassador Merlin remained oddly unbowed. "There's a government secret right now that will take care of the situation," he told the *Las Vegas Review-Journal*. "It will be revealed shortly."

Lo and behold, the following February, the Nevada department of transportation—encouraged by Lieutenant Governor Lonnie Hammargren, chairman of the state tourism commission—took matters into its own hands. After hearing testimony from only two speakers, Ambassador Merlyn and Pat Travis, it went ahead and declared ninety-nine-mile-long Route 375 the Extraterrestrial Highway, vowing to erect signs identifying it as such. The act was quickly approved by the chairman of the board of transportation: Governor Bob Miller.

As it happened, during this same time, Twentieth Century–Fox was preparing its publicity campaign for the blockbuster movie *Independence Day*, a solid third of which was set at the filmmakers' conception of Area 51 (a flying-saucer laboratory under a secret base in a dry lake in the desert). Though the exterior scenes had actually been shot at Bonneville Salt Flats in Utah, Governor Miller saw and seized a public-relations opportunity, flying to L.A. himself and striking a deal with Fox to finance and organize the highway's dedication. Press invitations, which were sent out all over the country, read:

> Nevada Governor Bob Miller and Twentieth Century Fox invite you to witness an event that's the talk of the galaxy: The official dedication of Nevada Highway 375, as "The Extraterrestrial Highway." You'll be joined by the producers and stars of ID4/Independence Day, the soon-to-be-released, epic adventure film that promises to answer the question of "what if . . . ?".
>
> As one of the chosen few, you'll be transported by our VIP shuttle fleet, departing at 10:00AM from the west parking lot of the Las Vegas Convention Center—across Paradise Road—to the town of Rachel. There, you'll experience a "for-your-eyes-only" ceremony that goes where no highway dedication has gone before. Make contact with the unknown. Join us.

The sneak preview was announced on an insert stamped TOP SECRET/EYES ONLY in imitation of the alleged MJ-12 papers (and worded more knowledgeably than the "for-your-eyes-only" reference to the 1981 James Bond movie of the same name). It was to be followed by a reception at Planet Hollywood in Caesar's Palace, where VIPs and members of the press could "mingle with the stars" and "enjoy heavenly food and drink." The next morning, everyone would reconvene in a "giant convoy" of buses, limousines, helicopters, and RVs, the better to endure the two-and-a-half-hour trip to Rachel, where welcoming speeches would be followed by a panel discussion with "some of the nation's leading UFO experts," the installation of the highway signs, and the unveiling of an ID4 monument. The event was set for April 17 and 18, 1996—almost exactly the first anniversary of the closure of Freedom Ridge (not to mention, to conspiracy connoisseurs, the fourth anniversary of the Waco Holocaust).

To Glenn Campbell, who for the past year had been moving away from Rachel and government accountability and toward Las Vegas and UFOs, this state of affairs offered enough inspiration for one last guerrilla protest. He began working overtime on anti-ET Highway propaganda—firing off reports and press releases, publicizing the transportation department's end run around the state legislature, publishing news clips on civil-rights violations along the base border, circulating excerpts from the *Independence Day* script that revealed its exploitation of UFO buffs, demanding to know the governor's travel expenses for cutting his deal with Fox. "Welcome to a Brave New World," he wrote in one of his reports, "where companies fund and organize state events according to their own agenda, where governors endorse commercial products made outside their state, and where the local impacts of these faraway deals are never considered."

As the day of the dedication approached, Glenn formulated an elaborate plan for upsetting the festivities with a "free-speech, performance-art, counter-cultural 'happening' in the Nevada desert." He envisioned an array of signs between Las Vegas and Rachel, bearing a slogan that he called only THE PHRASE, designed to "capture the issues and cause the greatest possible embarrassment to the governor." This motto would be emblazoned on T-shirts worn by a band of "freedom fighters," who would not demean the principle of free speech by heckling official speakers, but instead would unfurl an enormous banner. "Operation Tall Picket," as Glenn called this stratagem, would display THE PHRASE so prominently that it couldn't fail to appear in any news photo or TV coverage of the proceedings.

Most of the Interceptors vowed to attend, so as to oversee this new phase in the public's relationship with Dreamland. Some planned to assist with subversive action along the approach route itself. For example, on the shoulders of 375 and U.S. 93, unauthorized road signs would be erected, guiding the press convoy toward Rachel and the "ID4/ET HWY" ceremony. However, as the train descended Hancock Summit and entered Tikaboo Valley, an identical sign would direct the parade off the blacktop and onto Groom Lake Road. With luck, the entourage would drive all the way to Area 51, where God only knew what would happen when they arrived. This inspired abduction scheme—nicknamed Operation Coyote in homage to old Roadrunner cartoons—was diabolical enough to win the admiration of the Illuminati.

Just before the day of the event, Glenn revealed THE PHRASE. Simultaneously, it announced and asked:

ID4

BUYS

ET GOV

Whose Highway Is It?

The sneak preview of *Independence Day* did not take place in a movie palace. There was no line of limos, no arcing searchlights, no procession of glitterati posing for paparazzi as they made their way along a velvet-roped carpet. After all, this was Las Vegas—which somehow did *not* mean, either, that the event took place on the Strip or even in Glitter Gulch downtown. The venue that Fox procured was the Century Theaters Cinedome 12, a nondescript multiplex in a suburban mall on South Decatur Boulevard, to which "VIPs" were transported in tour buses, and at which representatives of the media were issued yellow press passes bearing the image of a flying saucer.

As I entered, I noticed KLAS-TV reporter George Knapp standing in the aisle. Reportedly Bob Lazar was also in attendance, although I never sighted him. I did, however, note the presence of Governor Miller, a tall man with wavy hair, wearing a dark suit and tie. I asked him whether the state's desires ever conflicted with those of Area 51.

"Eighty-seven percent of Nevada is federal land," Miller answered. "We have to deal with them."

Introducing *Independence Day* was its producer and cowriter, Dean Devlin. A small, dark ex-actor wearing some kind of jumpsuit, Devlin recounted that he and his partner, director Roland Emmerich, had made the deal for "ID4" at "a speed unheard of in Hollywood." Having written the script in four weeks, they'd given it to their agent on a Wednesday, sent it out to studios on Thursday, agreed to terms with Fox on Friday, and entered pre-production on Monday. Explaining that they'd resurrected the fifties theme of menacing aliens because "we felt the cliché had gone to the other extreme since *Close Encounters* and *E.T.*," Devlin quoted Ronald Reagan, Henry Kissinger, and Anthony Hilder (though he declined to credit them) to the effect that, if Earth were faced with a threat from space, all peoples would recognize their common humanity and pull together. He also divulged that the filmmakers had had to make do without military cooperation because the Pentagon requested omission of any reference to Area 51. But, the principled producer declared, "It's impossible to make a movie about UFOs today and not mention it." Besides, he added, "Area 51 is portrayed in the film as a safe haven—secret military bases are the only things that get saved."

During the short question-and-answer period, who should stand up in the audience but Merlyn Merlin II, wearing a yellow floral-print shirt with his customarily Draconian big collar and navy-blue blazer. The ambassador did his earthly duty, lodging a formal request that, in the future, the filmmakers consider making a movie about *friendly* extraterrestrials.

The "sneak preview" was sneaky indeed. It was the equivalent of a mere trailer, showcasing images that would soon be familiar throughout the nation and world: giant spaceships blocking the sun; national landmarks being blown up; fireballs rolling through city streets to engulf hysterical citizens. Altogether, it lasted about eight minutes. For this we'd come to Vegas and taken a bus to a multiplex?

Ambassador Merlyn was not to be dismissed so easily. As the rest of the audience politely dispersed, he made his way to the front of the theater, where he tried to buttonhole Jeff Goldblum, one of the film's attending stars. "I gotta go," Goldblum insisted, but Merlyn managed to press a piece of paper into the actor's hand, urging him to heed its message.

"Message?" Goldblum said. "What kind of message?" He unfolded the paper, which announced that "tourists from Alpha Centauri" would land on Nevada's Extraterrestrial Highway in approximately three years.

The next order of business was the reception at Planet Hollywood, located within "The Shops at Caesar's"—a reproduction of a Roman street replete with cafés, a roaring fountain, and a deep blue sky overhead, although the entire scene was enclosed indoors. The party itself was typical cocktail fare, attended by a crowd of nonnotables trying to attract the few servers who occasionally passed through with meager trays of hors d'oeuvres. Agent X, attired in an all-black Special Forces suit, worked the room for contacts; Ambassador Merlyn stood around in his dorky leather cowboy hat; Bob Price—the assemblyman into whose cortex the Ambassador had implanted the idea of the ET Highway—explained that, like only one other state (Nebraska), the Nevada assembly convenes only every other year. Perhaps as a result, he explained, the state has "a strong chairmanship method of running the legislature," and the transportation committee is allowed to nickname highways by fiat. The designation of U.S. 50 as "The Loneliest Road in America" had proven a boon to Nevada tourism—paving the way, so to speak, for the ET Highway.

The movie stars were literally on another level. They and the governor were holding a press conference downstairs, broadcast back to us "VIPs" on video screens upstairs. Photographs of action idols (who also happened to own Planet Hollywood—Stallone, Schwarzenegger, Willis, et al.) adorned the walls of the restaurant, which was apparently intended to transport the perceived glamour of Tinseltown wherever a franchise was found. Again one was moved to ponder the line between fantasy and reality in these parts, where practically everything seemed to be "virtual," in accord with the audience's apparently endless appetite for hype. Showing his usual colors, at the end of the evening Agent X tried to take home the *Independence Day* placard that had greeted arriving guests; unfortunately, he was foiled, as is also customary, by security guards—this time working for Planet Hollywood instead of Dreamland, though it was getting harder with each passing minute to discern the difference.

At 6:30 the next morning, Glenn Campbell checked in by cell phone from Rachel, where he and his fellow operatives had stayed up all night preparing Tall Picket. "It's going to be a grand debacle!" Glenn exulted, in reference not to his own project but to the highway dedication ceremony. "They're trying to set up a tent right now because it's so windy and overcast. We're making a banner that says, '*E.T. Gov Didn't Count on April Weather.*'" Other in-town protestors planned to distribute an "alternative press kit" to convoy passengers; I, however, drove up to Rachel in advance of the entourage.

When I turned off I-15 onto U.S. 93, I saw the first Interceptor sign for the ID4/ET HWY dedication. There were several more along the route, standing at every intersection, leading north and west. In the direction that the signs pointed, the sky was charcoal gray with distant fingers of rain reaching down to the monumental mountains. Soon it began coming down like a cataract, a bonafide spring storm. Miraculously, though, the sun came out by the time I reached Hancock Summit, where I saw some people photographing yet another unauthorized sign. This one looked downright institutional: Within the traditional yellow diamond denoting an oncoming hazard, a pair of stick figures were suspended in the spreading beam below a flying saucer. The lettering at the bottom said: NEXT 51 MILES.

Descending the pass, I noticed Campbell's Toyota 4Runner parked on the shoulder of Groom Lake Road. At the intersection with 375 was another ID4/ET HWY sign, though it still pointed straight ahead. In respect to (if not for) patrolling authorities, the arrows concealed another set that would be uncovered at the last instant, directing traffic toward Area 51.

Campbell was sitting in his vehicle, accompanied in the front seat by one "Agent Coyote"—the sister, as it turned out, of Lincoln County Commissioner Eve "Mad as Hell" Culverwell. As a recent "live-in assistant" to Campbell in Las Vegas, Coyote had, for those who cared, complicated the question of Glenn's orientation.

"They've set up three tents in Rachel where they're going to conduct the ceremony," Glenn said despondently. "That could sink Tall Picket." He glanced backward out the window toward his ID4/ET placard. "Signs that are really big in the shop don't look so big on the side of the road," he lamented; then, turning to stare through the windshield toward Area 51, he moaned, "All our plans are falling apart."

Rare, resilient Interceptor womanhood reared its supportive head. "You have to have a Silly Putty attitude," Coyote counseled Psychospy. In other words: something sufficiently flexible to stretch, bounce, or reflect the image of any obstacle it encountered.

While waiting for the buses to arrive, Campbell decided to drive down Groom Lake Road. Judging it wiser to play a prank than engineer a crime, he'd altered his scheme of directing the convoy to Area 51; instead he'd installed another sign at the intersection with Mailbox Road, directing traffic diagonally back toward Highway 375. Unfortunately, as he was adjusting it, the first three tour buses came down from Hancock Summit. Apparently ahead of schedule, they roared past Groom Lake Road without even slowing down.

I strolled over to inspect Campbell's sign. The visible arrows still pointed north, the direction in which the buses were disappearing. The ones underneath, pointing west, needed a pair of hands to unveil them. I was the only person in the vicinity; I knew that another bus was due to arrive any minute. But Psychospy was still down the road.

I have no memory of what happened next. All I knew is that several minutes had suddenly ticked by on my watch unaccounted for. Somehow, though, I seem to recall that as I started my truck and departed for Rachel, the arrows on the sign appeared to be pointing west.

Illusion? Reality? Desert delirium? Who knew? After all, this was Dreamland—where "up is down, left is right, black is white, right is wrong, and nothing is as it appears."

In Rachel, the once-empty lots by the A-Le-Inn were jammed with buses and helicopters. Dust was being blown horizontally as car after car pulled into the impromptu parking lot, passing a sign that said SPEED LIMIT: WARP 7. The usual army of UFO vendors was selling souvenirs; Chuck Clark hawked his Area 51 handbook; Pat Travis's daughter Connie offered an array of knickknacks under a sign that said HOME OF THE ALEIN [sic] BURGER. Even Bill Uhouse was present, peddling his alien card deck and T-shirts bearing a dignified rendering of Jarod 1.

As we stood shooting the radioactive breeze, a potbellied Elvis impersonator in a scarlet jumpsuit pulled up in a Cadillac. Another guy was walking around in a Darth Vader mask and shirt that said AREA 51 BOWL-ING TEAM above a picture of an alien in a cowboy hat. This, it turned out, was Assemblyman Bob Price.

Among the representatives from Fox, cell phones were almost as common as clothes. You needed a press or VIP pass to get into the official tents, so Rachel residents and "ordinary" UFO buffs—people who had, in a manner of speaking, prepared the earth for this event—were left twisting in the wind, which was blowing hard enough to sting their eyes. As I stood in the lee of a tent, wishing I'd worn a mask, I saw another tour bus pull up, its sides suspiciously coated with dirt; lo and behold, in its wake came Agent X, bearing the triumphant news that the abduction had gone off as planned. On the drive up from Vegas, he'd infiltrated the convoy in his convertible and, as the parade approached Hancock Summit, fought his way to the front of the line to assume the Virgilian role of "guide." Descending into Tikaboo Valley, he'd then flicked his turn signal well in advance, and slowed to a snail's pace before turning west on Groom Lake Road. Wonder of wonders, the entire entourage—some three dozen vehicles, including several Lincolns and BMWs with California plates— followed him into the desert. At that point Campbell took over, mercifully turning the train north again and leading the clueless flock back toward 375 and Rachel, just as a trio of Nevada state-police cars came roaring up the road.

Inside the tent, the dedication ceremony was getting under way. Rows upon rows of folding chairs were backed by a bank of TV cameras; several *Independence Day* stars—Goldblum, Bill Pullman, Robert Loggia, Brent Spiner—made their way up the center aisle toward seats of honor. A female flack introduced everyone, predicting that the ET Highway would add "another dimension" to Nevada tourism. Unbeknownst to authorities, Agent Coyote, fresh from the convoy abduction, had infiltrated the tent to assume a position behind the podium; when Governor Miller was introduced, she bared her bright yellow T-shirt, which said *ID4 BUYS ET GOV* in big black letters. She was summarily hustled outside by security goons.

"Most people, when they look to the skies, see a friend or foe," said the governor. "Not me—I'm a Nevadan. I see intergalactic tourists." Boasting that his state was the number-one tourist destination in the United States (obviously because of Las Vegas), Miller stressed that "We must never miss a chance to spotlight our tourist product." He was followed by a guy who wore a gray mustache and a multicolored cowboy hat that looked at first glance like camouflage but on closer inspection was made of snakeskin. This was the distinguished lieutenant governor, Lonnie Hammargren, who not only doubled as tourism commissioner but had been a brain surgeon for NASA. Clutching an alien doll, Dr. Hammargren greeted the crowd by saying, "Good afternoon, Earthlings." He went on to provide an 800 phone number for the "ET Experience," which promised prizes to visitors who produced sales receipts from stores along 375.

Pretty soon we all went outside for the unveiling of the signs and monument. The latter—a gift of "Governor Bob Miller, 20th Century Fox, and the Filmmakers and Cast of *Independence Day*"—contained a time capsule to be opened in 2050, "by which time interplanetary visitors shall be regular guests of the planet Earth." The road signs, which would be installed at both ends of Rachel and at the northern and southern ends of the highway, were three feet high by six feet long with pictures of flying saucers and stealth fighters on a green background. By the end of the day, they would be augmented by an array of unauthorized bumper stickers, including Bechtel's globe insignia, an Area 51 parking permit, and the logo of *Snowboarder* magazine. It didn't strain the investigatory mind to guess who might be responsible.

There wasn't much left to do after that, unless you wanted to hang out at the Inn or listen to a sober UFO panel, whose members included George Knapp, Walt Andrus Jr. (international director of the Mutual UFO Network), and Vicki and Don Ecker (editor and research director of *UFO Magazine*). By a ratio of about a hundred to one, the press corps preferred to conduct group interviews with the actors, the most popular of whom seemed to be Brent Spiner, who played Data on *Star Trek: The Next Generation*. Later Spiner would express interest in purchasing one of the ET Gov/ID4 T-shirts, which Campbell was letting go at cost—but when Glenn informed him that the price was five dollars, the actor declared, "It isn't worth that!"

Apparently reenergized by the success of Operation Coyote, Psychospy had resumed his provocations. He was wearing a huge yellow T-shirt over a hooded night-cammo jacket that hung below his knees like a dress. Aiming to forge a photo opportunity, Lord Vader/Assemblyman Price tried to throw an arm around his shoulder, but Campbell shrank from him as if Price were diseased.

"This is our goddamn town and we weren't even invited!" Glenn yelled, exhibiting the manic persona that Stuart Brown compared to a kid whose parents had too many guests over—a not inappropriate analogy for Rachel's present circumstances. Apparently, though, Glenn's point of view on the highway (or maybe the term "our goddamn town") wasn't appreciated by everyone in Rachel. Pat Travis's daughter Connie, for one, was reportedly driven to tears by his agitation. Hence, as Glenn continued to shake his placard and shout his objections, he was suddenly rushed by an assailant and shoved to the ground. The attacker turned out to be Connie's fiancé, Ray West; known around town as "Ray the Hayloader," he was the first person I'd ever talked to in Rachel—the guy playing slots at the A-Le-Inn who told me that he'd crossed the Area 51 border while drunk, but the guards had let him go.

As Ray slunk away and Glenn dusted himself off, another highly symbolic event was unfolding inside the Inn. Before the beaming, red-faced Joe Travis, Steve Medlin—a rancher who had a security clearance to graze his cattle in the Groom Range—was auctioning off the Black Mailbox. Having seen the writing on the wall when his address was changed from "HCR BOX" to "ET HWY," he was opting to cash out and contribute this totem of UFO lore to the personal museum of the highest bidder. Unfortunately, he received only two offers of twenty and forty dollars, but his bacon was saved by a bidder from somewhere beyond the state of mind of Nevada, who had called the previous night to offer a thousand bucks.

Seeking to sever all ties to events of the past few years, Medlin made sure that his new mailbox was painted a brilliant *white*. But like the indefatigable Ambassador Merlyn, the seekers of truth beyond the border were not to be dispersed so easily. Within a few weeks of the receptacle's replacement, some stealthy and stubborn operative slipped in on 375 after dark and repainted the mailbox black.

EPILOGUE

Matters of Ethics
and Principle

In August 1994, attorney Jonathan Turley of the Environmental Crimes Project at George Washington University law school in Washington, D.C., filed a twin suit in federal court against the Environmental Protection Agency and U.S. Department of Defense. The plaintiffs—the widow of one deceased former Area 51 worker and six other anonymous laborers, all of whom claimed that their health had been harmed by open-pit burning of toxic chemicals at Groom Lake—charged that the Pentagon had used secrecy to hide hazardous-waste violations at the base and that the EPA had failed to enforce compliance with the Resource Conservation and Recovery Act there. The government responded to the accusations by invoking the military and state secrets privilege, maintaining that disclosure of any information about the site (even its name, or any chemicals stored there) would cause "exceptionally grave damage" to national security. At first the Air Force continued to refuse to even acknowledge the existence of the base; eventually it would admit the actuality of an "operating location near Groom Lake," but still insisted that some operations in the Nellis Range Complex "remain classified and cannot be discussed."

Turley repeatedly asked U.S. District Judge Philip Pro to limit the government's concealment to things that would truly endanger national security. He said there was precedent for this in other privilege cases—that some courts had even held secret trials, or appointed special judges with high-level security clearances, rather than simply dismiss a controversial case. Justice Department attorneys held, however, that the disclosure of any information at all could create a "mosaic" enabling enemies to deduce sensitive secrets.

Turley responded by filing (under seal) the Groom Lake security manual "DET 3 SP JOB KNOWLEDGE," which, though not marked classified, contained information on many things that the Air Force now claimed were secret—for example, the presence of such "sensitive" substances as paint, jet fuel, car-battery acid, and firefighting equipment. Submitting some three hundred pages of references to Groom Lake or Area 51 that had appeared in government documents (including the Congressional Record), Turley announced that if the government wouldn't confirm the identity of the base, he would subpoena a senior Russian embassy official and former Soviet intelligence officers to do so.

Justice Department lawyers reacted by demanding that Turley turn over "for safekeeping" not only the security manual—which the government now claimed to be classified, although it was available on the Internet (courtesy of Glenn Campbell)—but also his briefs, notes, files, computer records, source names, and media contacts. Turley replied that he would sooner go to jail, declaring that "the suggested authority of the government to rifle through my files to extract objectionable materials is wholly foreign to this legal system." To prevent his stuff from being seized, he and his law students camped out overnight at his George Washington University office. Judge Pro soon issued a court order protecting the confidentiality of the documents, but sealed Turley's office from public entry.

In April 1995, the Environmental Protection Agency, which had earlier admitted that it had never before applied for a permit to investigate Area 51, announced that an inspection of the base had recently taken place. The report—surprise!—was classified.

Justice Department lawyers immediately asked that the lawsuit against the EPA be dismissed. After all, they argued, the facility was now shown to be in compliance with environmental regulations and, moreover, the Air Force was reportedly agreeable to future annual inspections. Turley responded that since the report was secret, nobody could even be sure which facility had been inspected ("A secret public report is something of an oxymoron"), and that, in any case, current and future compliance didn't erase past crimes.

On September 2, 1995, Judge Pro ruled that, owing to the specific demands of the Resource Conservation and Recovery Act, the government must, within one month, either make the EPA report public or seek a presidential exemption. Turley hailed the ruling, saying it showed that "national security [claims] do not trump domestic laws," concluding that the "government can no longer have nameless, faceless bases," and predicting that, "On October 2, citizens will learn they have a new federal facility." Much to his and his clients' disappointment, however, on September 29, President Bill Clinton announced that it was "in the paramount interest of the United States" to keep the contested information secret. "I hereby exempt the Air Force's operating location near Groom Lake, Nevada from any Federal, State, interstate or local provision respecting control and abatement of solid waste or hazardous waste disposal that would require the disclosure of classified information concerning that operating location to any unauthorized person," he wrote.

As Turley observed at the time, this decision was made public on the same day that Clinton announced compensation for past victims of military abuses in radiation experimentation and production. With regard to that admitted injustice, the President said:

> Those who led the government when these decisions were made are no longer here to take responsibility for what they did. They are not here to apologize to the survivors, family members and the communities whose lives were darkened by the shadow of the atom and these choices. There are circumstances where compensation is appropriate as a matter of ethics and principle. I am committed to seeing to it that the United States of America lives up to its responsibility. Our greatness is measured not only in how we so frequently do right, but also how we act when we have done the wrong thing, how we confront our mistakes, make our apologies, and take action.

Decrying the chief executive's "hypocrisy," Turley vowed to fight the exemption in federal court, asking Judge Pro to examine this "unprecedented" attempt to conceal evidence of criminal behavior under the cloak of national security.* However, Pro—who had once ruled that the government *wasn't* liable for injuries to workers exposed to radiation at the Nevada Test Site—found that the President had acted within his authority ("If mere allegations of criminal activity were sufficient to overcome the privilege, the privilege would be eliminated"). Since no evidence was therefore available to the court, he dismissed the plaintiffs' lawsuit.

Turley subsequently filed an appeal with the Ninth U.S. Circuit Court. Before he did, however, the Justice Department announced that it was now investigating the charges of toxic burning—and that, in order to "tie up loose ends," it needed to interview the anonymous workers who had allegedly witnessed illegal activities. Turley objected, claiming that the government really wanted to prosecute his clients for revealing classified information and for committing the environmental crimes that they themselves had tried to expose, but for which effort they'd been rebuffed, and even threatened with reprisals, by the government.

Judge Pro dismissed this fear, okaying the request to interview the workers. He was, however, overruled by the Ninth U.S. Circuit Court, pending its examination of the appeal—which, as of this writing, is still not concluded.

Outside the courtroom, the Interceptors were unearthing yet more disturbing secrets. Glenn Campbell and Tom Mahood discovered that Bill Uhouse (aka Jarod 2) had lied to them about some aspects of his biography. For example, they found that he hadn't been born in Nevada as he claimed, and that during the mid-1960s, when he said he'd spent "a couple of months" in Las Vegas, he'd actually lived there (in a trailer park) for several years. On a trip East, Mahood gave Uhouse the Lazar treatment, failing to find him in any yearbook or alumni directory at Cornell University. Meanwhile, the new kid who Uhouse said had been assigned to him for induction into the secret program showed up at a Las Vegas MUFON

---

*The Supreme Court had once ruled, in a case involving Watergate, that President Richard Nixon couldn't use executive privilege to conceal a crime—but in this case, the government seemed to be arguing that the national security privilege (a form of executive privilege) had more sweeping powers.

meeting; though he did turn out to be Hungarian, he appeared to be merely a young UFO buff who had looked Uhouse up because of the Jarod story. The kid said the idea that he was Jarod's professional protégé was nonsense; he did have a part-time, entry-level job with Lockheed, but he'd gotten it from a bulletin board at the University of Nevada, where he was a student. This in turn seemed to indicate that he wasn't a Stanford professor, which was surprising only in that his name was Zoltan Komar—the moniker of the scientist who had supposedly contacted Uhouse about building a flying disc.

In response to all of the above, Tom Mahood observed that Jarod was "starting to make Lazar look credible."

As for Bob himself, a man named Brian Boyer, from the Brookhaven National Laboratory in upstate New York, contacted Mahood after seeing him talk about Lazar on TV. Boyer said that as a summer student (and amateur photographer) at Los Alamos in 1984–85, he had had his film developed by "a slim goateed guy who had a rocket Honda, wore T-shirts from a Vegas brothel, and had photos of rather uninhibited bikini-clad women visible in the shop." After studying the photographs on Mahood's *Blue Fire* Web site, he confirmed that his photo developer had indeed been Bob Lazar. Meanwhile, Mark Farmer scared up a guy named John Horne who claimed to have known Lazar in Los Alamos. He described Bob as a smart but shady character who was always tinkering with personal projects, had an Uzi carbine at his photo shop, and borrowed money without paying it back. Describing Lazar as "more of a technician than a physicist," he said that Bob was fired from his job at the lab for using government equipment to work on his jet cars, and that he'd left town rather abruptly.

Campbell and Mahood met yet another Las Vegas engineer—a friend of John Lear's, and a Groom Lake worker at the time of Lazar's alleged employment—who said that Bob had actually been hired by the Arcata company to work with Smokey Sam rockets on the Nellis Range. He'd reputedly quit after only two weeks because he considered the job beneath him, but not before becoming familiar with some of the secret procedures around the Test Site, upon which he'd structured his story. This informant was initially so intrigued by Lazar's tale that he got permission to visit Papoose Lake, where he found absolutely nothing.° He also said that he

---

° According to George Knapp, a similar report was made by an elected official who remains nameless.

was the person who'd initially told Lear about "Site Four," in reference to the radar baseline and telemetry installation on the Tonopah Test Range. Afterward, Lear had assigned the name "S-4" to his own map of the Nellis Range, upon which it gradually migrated south to Papoose Lake. Lear later introduced this man to Lazar, at which point he asked Bob some elementary physics and engineering questions, as well as one about "what you see" when you get off the plane at Dreamland. "It's on the right," he hinted, but Lazar was reportedly unable to answer and made an excuse to leave the room. Observing that Lazar had a hobbyist's oscilloscope and chalkboard in his bedroom to match his amateur familiarity with physics, this source concluded that Lazar had made up his saucer story, then used Lear to connect with TV reporter Knapp so as to gain enough credibility to attract Japanese media money.

Another source told Mahood that Lazar had been out poking around the Area 51 border several times before he claimed to have been hired at S-4. Reportedly, Bob had once gone "all the way to the gate," which—if he'd been subjected to the usual ID shakedown by security guards—would have given him good reason (short of employment in a secret saucer program) to hide in the desert when he and his friends later got caught on Groom Lake Road. It also could have informed him that something strange was being tested there on Wednesday nights. The only problem with this particular story was that its source was John Lear.

For a short time in late 1995 and early 1996, Lazar and Huff hosted a talk show on KLAV radio in Las Vegas. Entitled *UFO Line* and airing Fridays from 11:00 P.M. to midnight, it won unexpected praise from both Campbell and Mahood. While the choice of guests was not wide-ranging (over the course of five shows, the hosts brought on George Knapp and John Lear twice each and Lazar's hypnotherapist, Layne Keck, once), Bob and Gene were praised for their humor, irreverence, skepticism, and rollicking go-to-hell style. For Campbell, the peak was achieved with the middle show of the five, in which Lear was challenged to confirm or deny his continuing loyalty to a list of fantastic claims. For the record, he abandoned his allegations that JFK was assassinated by his limousine driver, that Area 51 is covered by a five-square-mile roof, that two billion aliens live in the mountains alongside U.S. Highway 93, and that the Nellis Range has a special jail just for ufologists. He continued to hold, however, that underground tunnels crisscross the Southwest, that extraterrestrials eat human beings, that alien abductees are controlled by electronic implants via remote control, that eighty species of EBEs are visiting Earth, that a race of Reptilians is sequestered in the Nellis Range (and that guards study photos of them so they won't be alarmed if they see any), that the Moon contains not only water but a six-mile-high tower (on its front side), and that, "beyond a shadow of a doubt," there is an extensive underground base at Dulce, New Mexico. Breaking new ground, Lear also revealed that two flying saucers crashed in Nevada in 1995, that the U.S. Navy (as opposed to the Air Force) controls the UFO cover-up, that the latest Groom Range land grab was engineered to decoy attention from more secret facilities, and that the Defense Advanced Research Projects Agency invented the Internet in 1967. Owing to this latter coup, a computer at Sandia Laboratories is capable of tracking "what anybody ever wrote or said or wherever anybody ever went on the Internet with their PC. And not only that, whether your PC is on or not, they can access your hard drive any time they want."

"Now who can argue with that?" Huff asked when Lear was finished, priming the atmosphere for an Internet flame war that broke out between the two shortly thereafter. The conflagration was touched off by Mahood, who had posted some questions to Huff on the alt.conspiracy.area51 newsgroup, including one about why Lear was never mentioned in Huff's *Lazar Synopsis*. Huff responded that not only was Lear "irrelevant" to the story, but was "the biggest asshole/lame brain we had ever met." This prompted Lear to retaliate with the revelation that, when George Knapp first filmed Lazar in profile for his TV show, the taping took place at Lear's house and "you [Huff] were not even in the loop."

"Don't try and jump in here with your lies and bullshit," Huff fired back at Lear, "because I'll lay the truth on the line and let everyone know what a sorry knucklehead you are. You have no idea what was going on because you were being patronized and still are. Bob Lazar thinks you are absolutely crazy, though that does not mean he doesn't like you. Your friendship looks much different through your eyes than it does his. You're like a retarded cousin that you [sic] laugh at, but don't admit is part of the family. You would be the last idiot in the world to know who was in and out of the loop. . . . Bob and I knew each other and had established a friendship before you even knew who he was. I'm one of the few people who doesn't kiss his ass and we have a mutual respect. Considering Bob's public comments, do you think he respects you? The bottom line is that since I destroyed serious ufology by making the tragic error of introducing you to Bob, Bob could never stop abruptly without having to have your head surgically removed from his ass. . . . Bob Lazar and I are friends and business partners and he agrees with me about what happened, not you."

"Bob and you have been very close for the past few years and I have been out of the loop," Lear sorrowfully acknowledged. Still, he maintained that the reason Huff was so hostile to him was "because you [Gene] have no life without Bob Lazar and I do. Bob Lazar is your life and you want to rewrite what happened to him and me and you during those interesting times between the summer of 1988 when you introduced me to Bob and appraised my house in exchange for UFO video tapes and material and the fall of 1991 when my wife Marilee went over to Bob's house with her .45 automatic to shoot his Corvette in retaliation for his dumping dye marker in my pool which was in retaliation for me tieing [sic] a Pepsi can under his Corvette."

When Campbell reported all of this in the *Groom Lake Desert Rat* #33, he accompanied it with a picture of the Three Stooges, in which he portrayed Huff as Moe, Lear as Larry, and Lazar as Curly. This sparked a fresh fusillade from Huff, whose first shot was the public disclosure that Jarod 2 was Bill Uhouse—who had, he said (in apparent reference to a videotaped statement of Uhouse's), decided to "go public" after having his house appraised by Huff and thus learning about Bob Lazar. Huff went on to reveal that Campbell had, during the radio show, sent him and Lazar a warning that a secret caller (Mark Farmer, as it turned out) was planning to attack them on the air, but maintained that he and Lazar attached no importance to anything Campbell said or did, since they considered him nothing more than "the Little A-Le-Inn, Las Vegas division."

At this, Campbell wrote a letter to Lazar, asking him to rein Huff in or "none of us [will be able to] trust anyone else under any circumstances." He received the following reply, entitled "A Message from Bob Lazar," though its return e-mail address was Huff's.

Goober,

Who the fuck do you think you are? I don't control what Gene Huff says or thinks however, I have yet to find something he has said that I disagree with.

Now, stop sending me your stupid bullshit you fucking asshole. Now do you know where Gene gets his language from?

I've forwarded your letter to my attorney, as I do will [*sic*] all letters from psycotic [*sic*] UFO nuts, like you, who threaten me.

Don't bother responding, I don't give a shit what you have to say or plan to do. In addition, any future mail sent to me from you will be discarded.

Shut the fuck up and get a life.

—Bob Lazar

P.S. Eat Me

"Is this Huff impersonating Lazar, Lazar impersonating Huff, or Lazar expressing his true self?" Glenn asked readers of *Rat #34*. "In fact, it makes no difference. . . . They are a conjoined unit: Huff-Lazar or 'Hular' . . . [who] has a way of turning every casual inquiry into a [*sic*] interpersonal World War. . . . To play his game by picking up one of the many gauntlets he throws down is to be sucked into a great black hole of spiraling hatred that drains all human life in its vicinity. . . . We are tired and concede defeat. Let Hular rule the universe!"

Glenn turned out to be tired indeed. In the wake of this latest storm, he soon announced some "shocking news" in a private e-mail to the Interceptors:

Psychospy passed away last night.

I'm doing okay, personally. This is a traumatic event but I think we will all take it in stride.

I just woke up and he was gone. No more of the royal "we," no more desire to comment or keep up on on *everything* that goes on around Area 51.

Since the *Desert Rat* was his creation, the newsletter will have to end with the current issue. I will have to formulate an announce-ment for the readers. All the other work of the Area 51 Research Center will continue without change. . . .

This is a good breaking point, because virtually every story the *Desert Rat* was working on has come to a conclusion—at least for the time being. (1) The lawsuit has failed, (2) My appeal has failed, (3) Freedom Ridge was lost, (4) My detente with Hular has disinte-grated, (5) The Alien Highway has become an official designation and there is no longer any need for additional Area 51 publicity. Although these are only temporary setbacks, I can see no better time to regroup.

In killing off Psychospy and the *Rat*, I am freeing myself of the obligation of producing the newsletter, which was ceasing to be fun anymore. I was becoming an institution, which is not a comfortable place to be, since you have to start pleasing everyone. I would rather return to my terrorist roots. . . .

Replacing the *Rat* will be a much more bland "Groom Lake Update" which will be published only on the web. It will be a monthly accumulation of links to new material. Although it will offer most of the information of the *Rat*, it will have no personality of its own. Any editorial commentary linked to it will come from me in the first person. . . .

This is a life-changing event and I have not yet come to grips with all the implications, but I am confident it is all for the best in the long run.

—Glenn

In some late editions of the *Rat*, Campbell had developed a couple of theories combining the claims of Lazar and Uhouse. The more generous hypothesis held that each man had honestly described actual experiences, but that Lazar's employment (unbeknownst to Bob) merely constituted a kind of low-level tryout, in which he was given irrelevant assignments until he screwed up by breaching security. The more skeptical view posited that con-maverick Lazar invented his story as a goof on the gullible Lear, who had been spinning aliens-at-Area-51 tales for years. After Bob's story was widely circulated (courtesy of TV reporter Knapp), retired Vegas engineer/UFO buff Uhouse undertook to invent something even more elaborate, blending aspects of the Lazar story with historical accents from cover-up folklore and technical details from his own classified engineering experience. In this latter framework, both storytellers got what they most

---

° Interceptor (and *Aviation Week* editor) Michael Dornheim has pointed out—though he admitted that "this observation is imbued with class prejudice"—that a lot of myths get started not by full-fledged scientists but rather by lower-level compartmentalized technicians who aren't "in the loop" but spend lots of time imagining what they'd know if they were.

admitted that "There's some irony there. After all, we want the government to give us its secrets, but we don't want to give them ours."

There were other things about X that troubled Campbell, though. A shameless self-promoter, Farmer was always eager to appear on television—and in that bargain, he seemed willing to stretch the truth by staging reenactments for the camera, going so far as to gesture toward things that weren't even in sight. Then there was his uncontrolled urge for acquisition of kitsch. One time, walking back to the Annex from the San Remo buffet, Mark and Glenn passed through the Tropicana hotel and casino, which happened to be hosting a bioengineering convention. One entrepreneur had set up a sign advertising his business—SPERM WASHING—which so enchanted Farmer that he stole it. "That sort of thing really irritated me," Campbell recalled. "After all, it was the other guy's livelihood." While most Interceptors seemed circumspect about such behavior, it was (as previously observed) important to Glenn to remain above reproach.

Forewarned, I agreed to meet Farmer in the parking lot of the Tonopah supermarket in mid-March, when he was visiting from Alaska for the annual Green Flag exercises in the Nellis Range. The weather for our engagement was glorious—calm and sunny with temperatures in the seventies, hardly sure things for Nevada in March. When Farmer showed up, he was at the wheel of a red convertible, its back seat crammed with camera and survival gear, including a semiautomatic assault rifle. On the glove box he'd taped a yellow sign that said WET in black letters—undoubtedly lifted from some cement sidewalk, but exuding ambiguous connotations away from its customary habitat. The freelance troubleshooter was attired in full-dress three-color* desert cammo: jacket, pants, and broad-brimmed bonnet tied with string beneath his chin to keep it from flying off in the wind. He was also wearing Ray Ban sunglasses, black half-fingered gloves, an olive-green V-necked undershirt, a Fu Manchu moustache, and straight, brown, jaw-length hair.

I was surprised to see that the vehicle was a Mustang. Stuart Brown had told me that Farmer's favorite rent-a-car was the Chrysler LeBaron convertible; the fellow operatives had reportedly made some lively reconnaissance runs in Humvees, Acura NSXs, and other esoteric transport that

---

*Even this was cause for controversy among the Interceptors, some of whom favor six-color, "chocolate-chip"-flecked camouflage.

had arisen from the network of actual tunnels within the Nevada Test Site; and that the mysterious "disc" in the skies above Area 51 could have been an image created by a particle beam. Bidding an official farewell to Area 51, Mahood requested: "Would someone please turn off the lights on the way out?"

A similar, if not very well founded, swan song appeared soon afterward in *Popular Mechanics* (not to be confused with *Popular Science*), whose June 1997 cover announced: "The Air Force has abandoned top-secret testing at its once most secret test site. We know why and we know where they moved it to." As it turned out, the magazine's science and technology editor, Jim Wilson, had driven down Mailbox (not Groom Lake) Road and come to a locked cattle gate accompanied by no guard post. Concluding that the border was no longer being patrolled, Wilson claimed that the base was not only "obsolete," but had been permanently poisoned by 1950s nuclear tests—which, he implied, were really responsible for the illnesses identified in the toxic-waste suit. Wilson went on to announce that "the new Area 51" was actually in Utah, where a vertical-takeoff, Mach 15 aircraft known as the X-33 was being tested at the White Sands Missile Range Utah Launch Complex southeast of Green River and Michael Army Air Field, southwest of Salt Lake City.

These assertions were roundly ridiculed on the Internet, where various observers pointed out that moving the base would cost billions of dollars, that Boeing 737s still shuttled several hundred workers from Las Vegas to Groom Lake every day, and that neither the Utah sites nor the X-33 were secret (nor, in the case of the Green River complex, active). However, riding an apparent ebb tide of interest in Area 51, Wilson tossed a life saver to drifting saucer buffs. Not far from the Utah Launch Complex, he noted, was another place known for UFO sightings: the 480-acre Sherman Ranch, recently purchased by philanthropist Robert Bigelow, who had once funded Bob Lazar (as well as the consortium that allegedly consulted Bill Uhouse about building a flying disc). Bigelow reportedly planned to convert the ranch into a research station for his Institute for Discovery Science, which studies paranormal phenomena, including crop circles and cattle mutilations.

Similar to Lincoln County, the dominant cultural background of this proposed New Dreamland was Mormon, the physical landscape a Cold War–contaminated desert: Michael Air Field was part of the Dugway

Proving Ground, where chemical and biological weapons are tested next door to Wendover Air Force Base, site of final tests for the Hiroshima and Nagasaki bombings. But with a population of a thousand people, Green River bore little resemblance to Rachel—and despite its urban advantages and Spanish Trail origins, Salt Lake City was certainly no Las Vegas. Bars, brothels, and buffets were few and far between.

This mattered little, however, to Glenn Campbell, who in June 1997 broke his most shocking news yet. In a private e-mail entitled "Am I Still an Interceptor?," Glenn revealed that he had been "seduced by the Dark Side": He was, he announced, engaged to be married to his Research Center assistant—not Agent Coyote but Sharon Singer, a devout Christian with four children and three ex-husbands, all of whom continued to reside in or near Rachel, where Sharon herself had been raised.

Meanwhile, Glenn planned to forgo any road or research trip that didn't include his new family of six. The philosophical warrior and roving intellectual terrorist was hence "trapped in Nevada for the next decade at least, committed to a predetermined path in all the ways I said I never would be.

"It is sobering," he admitted in closing, "but I am not afraid."

ACKNOWLEDGMENTS

As has often been observed, the topic of Area 51 is tantamount to a hall of mirrors: reflecting and confusing myriad images, some accurate and many distorted, pertaining not only to military policy but to contemporary psychology. Amid such an atmosphere, I have been fortunate to receive the assistance of several trustworthy and tireless researchers, many of whom are themselves subjects of this book.

First and foremost, obviously, is Glenn Campbell. Similar to many visitors, my initial education on Dreamland was provided by his *Area 51 Viewer's Guide* and later expanded by his *Groom Lake Desert Rat* newsletter, which I have frequently quoted herein. Early on, I found myself in agreement with Glenn's "folklorist" approach to the subject, and internalized his attitude while studying his character. Glenn has since developed his website—www.ufomind.com—into a sprawling resource, not only on Area 51 but on Las Vegas, UFOs, and the sociomilitary landscape of the

American Southwest. Besides sharing his own work, he has aided me in innumerable other ways with advice, lodging, telephone calls, and research materials. It is no exaggeration to say that this book would not exist without him.

Next comes Tom Mahood: professional engineer, physics student, and amateur detective extraordinaire. Besides doing the detailed research described in these pages (and on his website, www.serve.com/mahood/ bluefire.htm), Tom has connected me with many of his own contacts and shared considerable background information with me in confidence. As with Glenn Campbell, Tom's willingness to entertain fantastic ideas, filtered through a lens of refreshingly sarcastic skepticism, has informed much of my own stance. One of my regrets in finishing this book is that I will no longer have an excuse to exchange as much entertaining e-mail with Tom Mahood.

Several other Interceptors have sat still to share their knowledge and insight. The Minister of Words, Stuart Brown (author of the March 1994 *Popular Science* cover story on Area 51) spent a morning with me in Hollywood, providing me with a primer on the parameters of the topic; thereafter, his phone calls and camping monologues kept me in stitches and up-to-date. Aviation historian Peter Merlin sent me copies of his articles on Groom Lake history and nuclear testing; he also contributed a comprehensive Area 51 timeline and brought my attention to the Edgar Allan Poe poem that serves as a Dreamland epigraph. Michael Dornheim of *Aviation Week and Space Technology* provided me with several photographs, as well as a down-to-earth sounding board for flighty ideas. A more recent inductee into the Interceptors, Jim Bakos, was helpful with Web alerts and other astute notices (not to mention inventing and distributing the Ancient Hungarian Decoder Ring). Matt Coolidge of the Center for Land Use Interpretation gave me a file of material (including a videotape) of the Ultimate UFO Seminar; Glenn Campbell's webmaster, Dean Kanipe, strove mightily to send me maps and other electronically encoded material; Chris Rush loaned me magazines and videotapes; Ralph Steiner provided me with audiotapes of his talks and radio programs on UFOs and "the secret government"; Dwight Thibodeaux mailed me huge files on the Black Budget and Area 51; Eric Gullickson, Dave LePell, and Scott Saifer helped me analyze the physics claims of Bob Lazar.

The contributions of a formidable trio of secret-airplane experts— Mark Farmer, John Andrews, and Jim Goodall—are obvious from the fact that they account for entire chapters of *Area 51: The Dreamland Chronicles*.

For helpful actions and advice, I am indebted as always to my editor, Bill Strachan, and my agent, Fred Hill. John Raeside and Rick Kohn gave me useful and enthusiastic feedback as the book progressed. And throughout the project I have been buoyed by my inestimable partner, counselor, companion, supporter, and unswerving ally, Leigh Lightfoot.

Lastly, a nod of gratitude to certain sources who, for reasons I can neither confirm nor deny, must remain anonymous.

SELECTED BIBLIOGRAPHY

Bates, Warren. "Groom Lake Chemicals Can Be Secret." *Las Vegas Review-Journal,* October 3, 1995.

————"Judge Asked to Toss Out Groom Lake Suit." *Las Vegas Review-Journal,* May 24, 1995.

Brown, Stuart. "Searching for the Secrets of Groom Lake." *Popular Science,* March 1994.

Campbell, Glenn. *Area 51 Viewer's Guide.* Area 51 Research Center. Rachel, 1993.

————"The Gospel According to Bob." Transcript of talk by Bob Lazar at the Ultimate UFO Seminar, May 1, 1993.

————"The Groom Lake Land Grab." *Citizen Alert,* Spring 1994.

————"Lazar as a Fictional Character." *MUFON UFO Journal,* February 1994.

————"A Short History of Rachel, Nevada." Paper prepared for the Rachel Senior Center as community service after conviction for obstructing a police officer, January 1996.

Christensen, Jon. "How Military Secrecy Zones Out Nevada." *High Country News,* December 27, 1993.

Garmon, Linda, producer. *Spy in the Sky.* Public television documentary from *The American Experience* series. Corporation for Public Broadcasting, 1996.

Good, Timothy. *Alien Contact: Top-Secret UFO Files Revealed.* New York: William Morrow, 1993.

Hesemann, Michael, producer. *UFOs: Secrets of the Black World*. VHS videotape. 2000 Film Productions, 1995.

Huff, Gene. *The Lazar Synopsis*. Online summary of the Bob Lazar story as posted to the alt.conspiracy.area51 newsgroup, March 12, 1995.

Huff, Gene, and Bob Lazar, producers. *The Lazar Tape and Excerpts from the Government Bible*. VHS videotape. Tri-Dot Publications, 1993.

Jacobs, Margaret. "Secret Air Base Broke Hazardous-Waste Act, Workers' Suit Alleges." *Wall Street Journal*, February 8, 1996.

Kirby, John. "An Interview With Robert Lazar." *MUFON UFO Journal,* October 1993.

Levy, Rachael. "Court Overturns Area 51 Ruling." *Las Vegas Sun,* November 8, 1996.

Lindemann, Michael. *UFOs and the Alien Presence: Six Viewpoints*. Newberg: Wild Flower Press, 1991.

Manning, Mary, and Rachael Levy. "Feds Investigating Burning of Hazardous Waste at Area 51." *Las Vegas Sun,* August 8, 1996.

McGinniss, Paul. *The Black Budget: A Brief Guide to Secret National Security Spending.* Privately published information pamphlet, March 1994.

Merlin, Peter W. "Dreamland—The Air Force's Remote Test Site." *Aerotech News and Review,* April 1, 1994.

———" 'Secret' Base in Nevada Desert Suffered Effects of Nearby Nuclear Testing." *Aerotech News and Review,* October 20, 1995.

———"Test and Decontamination Revisited: Operation Plumbob and Project 57." *Aerotech News and Review,* December 15, 1995.

Paine, Gary. "A Mine, the Military, and a Dry Lake: National Security and the Groom District, Lincoln County, Nevada." *Nevada Historical Society Quarterly,* Spring 1996.

Parrish, Thomas. *The Cold War Encyclopedia.* New York: Henry Holt, 1996.

Peebles, Curtis. *Dark Eagles: A History of Top Secret U.S. Aircraft Programs.* Novato: Presidio Press, 1995.

Rich, Ben R., and Leo Janos. *Skunk Works.* Boston: Little, Brown, 1994.

Rogers, Keith. "Groomed for Secrecy." *Las Vegas Review-Journal,* March 20, 1994.

———"National Security Defense Cut from Groom Lawsuit." *Las Vegas Review-Journal,* November 11, 1994.

Schine, Eric. "Little Gray Men Made My Eyes Turn Red." *Business Week,* June 17, 1991.

Stacy, Dennis. "The Ultimate UFO Seminar." *MUFON UFO Journal,* June 1993.

Sweetman, Bill. "Secret Mach 6 Skyplane." *Popular Science,* March 1993.

Thompson, Keith. *Angels and Aliens.* New York: Fawcett Columbine, 1991.

Walker, Martin. *The Cold War: A History.* New York: Henry Holt, 1994.

Webster, Donovan. "Area 51." *New York Times Magazine,* June 26, 1994.

Weiner, Tim. *Black Check: The Pentagon's Black Budget.* New York: Warner Books, 1990.

————"Spy Agency Admits Accumulating $4 Billion in Secret Money." *New York Times,* May 16, 1996.

————"The Worst-Kept Secret in the Capital." *New York Times,* July 21, 1994.

Weir, Christopher. "Paint It Black." *Metro,* January 9–15, 1997.

Wilson, Cintra. "Cintra Wilson's Fantastic Space Odyssey." *Image* magazine, *San Francisco Examiner,* August 8, 1993.

Wittes, Benjamin. "Suddenly, Your Briefcase Is Classified: Groom Lake Litigation Tests Government's Secrecy Standards." *Legal Times,* June 26, 1995.

Index